CHAIM SOUTINE

CHAIM SOUTINE

GENIUS, OBSESSION, AND A DRAMATIC LIFE IN ART

CELESTE MARCUS

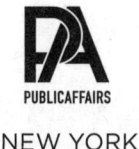

PUBLICAFFAIRS

NEW YORK

PublicAffairs
Hachette Book Group
1290 Avenue of the Americas, New York, NY 10104
www.publicaffairsbooks.com
@Public_Affairs

Printed in the United States of America

First Edition: October 2025

Published by PublicAffairs, an imprint of Hachette Book Group, Inc. The PublicAffairs name and logo is a registered trademark of the Hachette Book Group.

The Hachette Speakers Bureau provides a wide range of authors for speaking events. To find out more, go to hachettespeakersbureau.com or email HachetteSpeakers@hbgusa.com.

PublicAffairs books may be purchased in bulk for business, educational, or promotional use. For more information, please contact your local bookseller or the Hachette Book Group Special Markets Department at special.markets@hbgusa.com.

The publisher is not responsible for websites (or their content) that are not owned by the publisher.

Library of Congress Cataloging-in-Publication Data

Names: Marcus, Celeste, author
Title: Chaim Soutine : genius, obsession, and a dramatic life in art / Celeste Marcus.
Description: First edition. | New York : PublicAffairs, 2025. |
Includes bibliographical references and index.
Identifiers: LCCN 2025008876 | ISBN 9781541703223 hardcover |
ISBN 9781541703247 ebook
Subjects: LCSH: Soutine, Chaim, 1893–1943 | Painters—France—Biography |
LCGFT: Biographies
Classification: LCC ND553.S7 M37 2025 | DDC 759.4 [B]—dc23/eng/20250625
LC record available at https://lccn.loc.gov/2025008876

ISBNs: 9781541703223 (hardcover); 9781541703247 (ebook)

LSC-C

Printing 1, 2025

To Leon Wieseltier
for giving me Soutine

And to Leni Kagan
for sharing him with me

CONTENTS

Chapter 1

Origins

HISTORY GRANTS NO DISPENSATIONS; IT COMES FOR US ALL. People, no matter how exceptional or ordinary, political or disinterested, cannot escape the tumult of their time. This was as true of Chaim Soutine as it is of the rest of us. Soutine spent his golden years at the cultural epicenter of the globe during the busiest period of artistic excitement in the modern era, and he spent them as a giant. Yet he died in poverty, not unlike the poverty into which he was born. His contributions to art and to global human enrichment were singular: No one had ever painted like him before, and no one ever will again. But many painters, poets, and all those with appetites for beauty and excellence have supped at his canvases.

He had the misfortune of being born a Jew in Europe on the cusp of the twentieth century, and a Jew with an unappeasable addiction to the wealth of painting that Europe safeguards. Perhaps this was the reason that he did not leave France even after it was clear his bodily survival depended on it. That would have been like him, though it was also like him not to explain himself, so speculation is an open game.

Soutine consecrated his life entirely to his art, and that monomania yielded an oeuvre worthy of reverence and fascination. His obsessive dedication sealed him from the ordinary rhythms of human life—he had few friends, few lovers, and no family connections maintained with anything like sustained attention. His fanatical devotion to art gave his life meaning, but it could not protect it from the paroxysms of the periods through which he lived and the political upheaval that precipitated his death.

Soutine was born three times. The first was in 1893, as the tenth of what would soon be eleven children fathered by an impoverished mender in Smilovichi, a village some fifty kilometers from Minsk, in today's Belarus.[1] As a child he was underfed (malnutrition crippled him and ultimately contributed to his premature death) and oppressed by the parochialism that is a perpetual feature of life in small, religious villages. Yet in that village, miraculously, Soutine discovered his preternatural interest in art, despite the sepia-toned cultural backwater in which he found himself. He used to scrape a bar of charcoal against a wall or use a stick to trace figures in the mud. These were the early stirrings of a fixation that would drive him all his life.

At twenty years old his second life began as one in a swarm of artists who thronged to Paris in the first half of the twentieth century, freighted with foreign dreams. Soutine lived alongside Chagall, Modigliani, Pascin, and Léger. He frequented the same cafés as Picasso and befriended artists who studied with Matisse. After a decade of bohemian indigence, glamorous in retrospect though at the time he stank of sweat and filth and was tormented by the pangs of an empty belly, Soutine was abruptly scooped from poverty in 1923, when a wealthy American art collector bought fifty or so of his paintings and vaunted him from obscurity into the annals of art history. At last, a respected artist. This is the Soutine who was buried in Montparnasse Cemetery twenty years later, the Soutine whose work hangs on the walls of modern art museums the world over.

These, like all births, were births of circumstance, products of outside forces over which Soutine had little control. But Chaim Soutine remade himself with every brushstroke. His artistic development was an intense saga of autocreation. Two forces course through this man's life: history, which manipulated him the way a palette knife crushes and scrapes the paint on a canvas, and Soutine himself, whose epic struggle for self-mastery, for the discipline and skill to communicate satisfactorily the energy of life itself, is recorded in the riots of paint that seethe on the canvases he left behind. Soutine happened to fumble into the burrows of political and artistic movements and found himself within various communities, but he was a member of no group and he did not cleave to friends. Paint was what occupied him, not ideologies or politics or even culture—paint, its peculiar demands and capacities. Unlike Matisse and Picasso, Soutine did not set about to revolutionize art; he was, to a startling degree, intellectually independent of his context, and so he contributed to the modern revolution without being in the throes of it. Soutine was alone even at the red-hot center.

Because he was a misanthropic, awkward, semisocialized genius, and because, in his own estimation, his work was primary and his personal relations hardly even tertiary, his art and the political and social context in which he made it together account for more or less the whole of the artist's life. For this reason it is exasperating to discover the cataclysmic pronouncements that repeat, in most works on the subject, the notion that Soutine left behind hardly any letters, no diaries, no substantial record of his own thoughts put to paper, and so, with apologies, the man is terribly difficult to know. Left behind no trace of himself? But he is there, right before our eyes. The man was his art, and his paintings bellow from the walls on which they hang. As Hilton Kramer noted, in one of the rare accurate assessments of Soutine, "In a sense, Soutine had no biography outside his art; one might even say that his art was a substitute for a biography."[2] Yes, he left scarcely anything of value except the art to which he consecrated his sickly body and colossal, muscular mind. If he had embalmed his soul and set it behind glass, viewers could hardly achieve greater proximity to the man than they do in the galleries that shelter his work.

In every artist, a cavernous ache to justify one's art, to assure oneself afresh with each new work that one is capable of intelligence and honesty and quickening originality, must rage unabated. Artists are, they ought to be, skinless creatures. Complacency is spiritual suicide, and confidence can set in like rigor mortis, calcifying even brilliance. In front of the canvas (or the microphone, or the keyboard) one is, every time, every minute, on trial. Soutine scholars recognize that the artist was in the grip of a sinister psychic torture, but too often they misdiagnose the pain. They believe his torments were historical. Yet his paintings were not riddled with the anxieties and terrors of the Jew in the twentieth century, as Elie Wiesel once indicated. The Cossacks and then the Nazis stalked him to an early death, but they had no authority inside his head, and there is no evidence of them in his work. There, only his inner demons presided. Owing to his turbulent style, he is often called an expressionist, but Soutine painted what he saw, not what he felt; and what he saw, what he noticed and studied, was energy: not anxiety, not alienation, not abjection, not intensity of feeling, but energy, extreme vitality, as he detected it in the world around him. He studied it, and then strove to seal it in paint. The profundity of that assignment is what tormented him. He scraped himself against his own high standards, and the ensuing lacerations charged his work.

Soutine's fabled torment, his legendary anxiety and pain, is associated with and extrapolated from no paintings more than the ones that he completed in Céret from 1919 to 1921. Pain and anxiety, a heavy spiritual darkness, are what viewers most often remark upon when looking at these twisting works. It is not what Soutine set out to put in them. What an artist means to put in a work, or what he intends the work to mean or to be about, is not necessarily the same thing as what someone else finds there. And neither of these meanings is more true or more valuable, necessarily, than the other. In some cases what viewers find in a painting grants them insight into the artist—perhaps they detect an emotion or an orientation peculiar to the artist, though the artist did not mean to betray that element through their work. But just as often they misinterpret. One can always learn more about the creator through his creations than he meant for viewers to learn. And even when this is not true, the viewer is tempted to believe it—to assign qualities to the artist that the works have not obviously justified.

This projection of emotion onto a painting is an indulgence, and an indulgence too often taken with this particular artist. The viewer must be disciplined and rigorous—she owes it to the artist to be so. One must not extrapolate from one's own associations and assume that the artist felt what she feels. Later in his career Soutine relished painting slabs of meat from the butcher shop. It is often said that this recurring subject betrays his absorbing fascination with death—the art critic David L. Shirey called it a "morbid fascination for flesh."[3] But Soutine's fascination was emphatically with life, with the blood and veins and bones that facilitate living, which is why his still life paintings seem as vital as his portraits and landscapes.

Certainly, the capacity to communicate pain through paint does not confer the capacity to verbalize the meaning of that exercise even to oneself. He could have painted about pain and not have recognized pain as his subject the way one recognizes one's intention cerebrally when articulating an idea. But he didn't. That is not what Soutine was trying to do. And what viewers see in a work can obfuscate other qualities in it that reward scrutiny and demand respect. Partial understanding is one of the occupational hazards of interpretation.

Soutine was not attempting to paint torment or pain or any other inner state. Shirey was exactly wrong when he wrote, "[Soutine's] paintings are not records of visual experience but rather the tormented outpourings of his feeling, what another great expressionist, Kandinsky, called 'inner necessity.' Soutine saw the world as an apocalyptic vision, a place of upheaval, misery and frustration, a delirium of alternating despairs and frantic jubilations.

There was nothing cool or cerebral about Soutine's approach to art." The intensity with which an expression is communicated has nothing necessarily to do with the thoughtfulness with which it was developed. The fact that someone is speaking loudly does not mean that they have not thought about what they are saying. (Soutine's favorite author was Dostoevsky, a writer whose rhetorical power was commensurate with his intellectual precision.)

Mistaking the vehemence of Soutine's painting for an emotional end in itself is repeated often in Soutine literature.

What interested Soutine *was* what he was looking at, not what was inside him. He *was* creating records of visual experience. Viewers look at his works and notice the twistedness, the immense movement that Soutine simulated by painting with great speed and energy, and they conclude that this intensity was meant to communicate something about Soutine when it was in fact meant to communicate something about Céret. This is true even while it is also true that most viewers detect a profound anxiety in the Céret canvases.

Soutine arrived in Paris the summer of 1913, when he was twenty years old, unburdened by any social or communal expectations, sustained only by a consuming faith in his own capacity. It was the same year that the Ballets Russes debuted *Le Sacre du printemps* in Paris. Soutine, blind to the cultural riches he trudged past on his first days in the city, had only fifty rubles in his pockets. The money had been secured for him by the daughter of a certain Dr. Rafelkess, whom Soutine had met in Vilna and who had taken an interest in his success. It is said that he got off the train at the Gare du Nord and muttered the name "Kikoine" at passersby—Michel Kikoine was a close friend with whom he had studied painting in Minsk and Vilna and who had moved to Paris ahead of him and was awaiting his arrival. Or he approached passersby at the station and said, "Passage Dantzig," the address of the artist colony La Ruche in Montparnasse where he hoped to find lodgings. He said so little because he spoke only Russian and Yiddish at the time.[4] The young, destitute, monomaniacal Soutine, wearing the same paint-splattered coat he wore in every season, awkward, unwashed, and poorly fed, for the first time wandered the streets of Paris—a city with centuries of history that both rebuffed and entranced him.

This creative mecca had captivated his imagination long before that fateful summer. Kikoine recounted that while the two were living in a crowded, slovenly Lithuanian boarding house, Soutine fantasized about France: "We lived in the house of a good woman, whose husband was a railway worker, in a room with six beds, 15 kopecks per student. She was waiting for us at every hour of the day and night with a steaming samovar. I can see us again, coming out of school in small groups wading through the mud, splashing with our worn galoches . . . heatedly discussing art, life, and above all the future. Soutine's fertile imagination traveled very far and presently Paris became the center of his preoccupations."[5] But the two men remained together in Vilna for three years, completing studies at the local Academy of Art that would prepare them for the entry exam of the École des Beaux-Arts de Paris, the renowned French academy founded in 1648.

According to Kikoine, "On the 13th of July, 1913, Soutine arrived in Paris, and on the 14th, at four o'clock in the morning, we were both sitting on the pavement in front of the Opera, in line for the free performance given for the national holiday. They played *Hamlet* and Soutine was charmed. He liked everything: the place, the sculptures, the decorations and the songs. He told me that if we didn't make anything of ourselves in a city like Paris, it was because we were really incapable." In truth, it is clear from the records of the police prefecture in Paris that Soutine arrived on or shortly before June 9, 1913, and had been in the city for over a month before Bastille Day of that year.[6] Nonetheless, Kikoine's recollection of the two Russian Jews celebrating their first Fête nationale française at the Paris Opera house is a moving one, even if it was beautified by memory.

On an early summer day in 1913, Soutine slouched toward La Ruche—or "the beehive," so named for its octagonal shape—where he would join one of the most exciting artist colonies in modern history. La Ruche is located in the fifteenth arrondissement of Paris, about an hour and a half's walk from the Gare du Nord train station. If he made the hike on foot, he would have walked down sloping Montmartre with the Basilica Sacré-Coeur (which had been under construction for thirty-eight years and would not be completed for another six) looming high behind him, down the winding hill and, eventually, past the Louvre. Did he understand the significance of that great urban mass when he first saw it? Did his heart pound, as it surely would the many times he entered it? His route would lead him over the Pont du Carrousel, from which he first peered into the Seine. The École des Beaux-Arts, where he would soon commence his studies, was just a block away.

Perhaps by now Soutine would have taken off his stained jacket and slung it over his shoulder as he trudged deeper into the Left

Bank. The rue de Vaugirard would have carried him up a steep hill along rickety blocks all the way to the slaughterhouses and their fields, beside which La Ruche was nestled some thirty minutes from the heart of town. If he followed this path, he would not have seen the Boulevard de Montparnasse his first day in the city—the rue de Vaugirard cuts past it, farther west. Later the barstools and wicker chairs that line that grand thoroughfare would become a kind of home for him, offering constant solace till his death. Soutine moved his studio often—he found routine stultifying—but that strip of cafés and restaurants would be a source, perhaps the only source, of stability for the entirety of his time in Paris. The tables of the café La Rotonde would bear witness to Soutine's transformation from a shy, uncouth novice—inchoately conscious of his own great capacity, trembling with the kinetic energy of this potential—to a successful, established artist, still thin and sickly, but finer, perfumed, and well read, and with a firm grip on the elegant vibrations that vivify his late work. Thirty years and one month after his arrival, he would be buried a short walk away from La Rotonde, in Montparnasse Cemetery, just steps from the site of his own evolution. But that summer day in 1913, no one he passed on the streets could imagine how much those blocks would change and endure in the three decades into which the city was about to be hurled.

The art world into which Soutine was forcing himself was not a place at peace. In that city, salons, the institution upon which most artists' careers depended, were presided over by traditionalists who were anxious to keep bohemians in the streets and out of the galleries. Academic *pompiers* such as William-Adolphe Bouguereau, the distinguished but kitschy painter who was president of the École des Beaux-Arts de Paris, maintained a tyrannical power over the standards of French art, imposing them most publicly by rejecting works that did not conform to the accepted canons of the official Salon of the Académie des Beaux-Arts.

This stranglehold was momentously loosened in 1883. After having been rejected by the Salon three years earlier, the impressionists and postimpressionists organized a Salon des Refusés (the second in twenty years), after which the Société des Artistes Indépendants was founded. Cézanne and Van Gogh were among the participants in the first Salon des Indépendants. (Had their names been whispered amongst the students at the art academies in Minsk and Vilna? Did Soutine know that the tradition into which he was hoping to gain entry was under attack from within? And that he, willing or not, would be enlisted in that battle?) Since the new salon had no jury, it lacked a wider prestige. As an alternative, the competitive Salon d'Automne was held for the first time in 1903, in the newly built Petit Palais, which had been constructed for the World's Fair of 1900. Two years later Matisse, Derain, and their cohort famously exhibited paintings in the hot, violent colors that prompted the art critic Louis Vauxcelles to call them *fauves* or "wild beasts." The year of Soutine's arrival was the same year that the historic Armory Show in the United States first introduced American audiences to the French avant-garde. This enormous exhibition of sixteen hundred paintings infuriated the American public. Students at the Art Institute of Chicago hanged Matisse in effigy and burned copies of what they considered his most offensive paintings.[7]

Van Gogh was cold in a coffin three years before Soutine was born, but his shadow shrouded the city into which legions of scrappy young artists surged at the start of the twentieth century. Soutine himself would spend the first several years of his artistic career working through Van Gogh's legacy, as is evident from the few earliest paintings by his hand to which we still have access, all of which were painted in Paris.[8] Perhaps it was the manifestly profound effect that the dead master had on Soutine that caused him to vociferously insist against this influence later in life, just as he would do with Cézanne. Soutine shirked attachment; his relationship to his work was zealously solitary, and he rebuffed creative companionship. He expressed allegiance only to the great masters who were long dead, so mythologized their memories were practically otherworldly.

This was not true of many of the other artists of the avant-garde with whom Soutine would rub shoulders in Paris. Many of the Jews who flung off their yarmulkes and journeyed out of the past and into the future simply replaced one community for another. Isms abounded. Dadaism, futurism, cubism, surrealism, even expressionism, with which Soutine is often associated (I suspect he would have snarled at the descriptor, as it infringes on his singularity), were new traditions that endeavored to replace old ones. Picasso, Max Jacob, and Apollinaire were not just friends; they were coconspirators. A common kinetic energy flowed through the group and vivified each one's work. They demanded progress from their comrades, onward, onward, into the new world they were building. Similarly, though Marc Chagall did not join a movement or pen a manifesto, and though he associated more comfortably with poets than other painters, he depended on the insights of such figures as Apollinaire and Blaise Cendrars. Their estimation affected his perception of his own work, and their pressure, like a weight on his shoulders, enticed him to break new ground. But Soutine was otherwise constituted. Though he was granted entry at the École des Beaux-Arts in 1913 and studied in the atelier of Fernand Cormon (just as Van Gogh and Toulouse-Lautrec had before him), his true education took place at the Louvre. He devoted himself to Rembrandt, Chardin, and Courbet, who whispered in his ear while he stood before his easel.[9] But a man, even an artist, must eat, and for a Jew in Paris in 1913, the best way to secure nourishment and a safe space to sleep was to shelter with other Jews.

La Ruche, Soutine's first home in Paris, was a near-mythological place. The ambition that burned in the breasts and the brushes of the immigrant artists at La Ruche was not enough to warm them on winter nights. Hunger is what lured them to Paris and hunger is what kept them there—a zealous spiritual hunger that fortified them against the physical hunger which incessantly rumbled in the bellies of these painters, poets, and musicians, many of them Jews, who clawed their way from their respective shtetls to the City of Light. La Ruche was among the many artist complexes in Montparnasse that collectively sheltered the École de Paris, or the "School of Paris," which is what the French art critics christened the swarms of immigrants suddenly overflowing their academies and their galleries in the early decades of the twentieth century.

It is often said that La Ruche was designed by Gustave Eiffel himself. Like many of the legends that cloud the legacy of the School of Paris, this is a half truth. The full tale begins with the World's Fair of 1900, held in Paris from April to October of that year, just over a decade after the international exhibition of 1889, for which Eiffel built his grand tower. (Dumas, Maupassant, Bouguereau, and Meissonier were among the many writers and artists who signed the protest against Eiffel's steel monstrosity, the "ridiculous tower dominating Paris like a gigantic black factory chimney . . . a dishonor to the city.") General Commissioner Alfred Picard, dubbed by the press the most important man in France, was determined that his exhibition in 1900 would exceed in brilliance and magnitude all its predecessors, and it did. Construction began eight years in advance and included the Grand Palais, the Petit Palais, the Métro, the Gare d'Orsay, and the Pont Alexandre. The fairground spanned 543 acres and included pavilions representing forty-seven countries, all battling to demonstrate their technological and cultural preeminence. It was visited by fifty-one million people over the course of six months.

The world's first moving sidewalk, the first passenger trolley-bus line, and an electrotrain ran through the exhibits. The Grande Roue de Paris, a Ferris wheel ninety-six meters high, was the tallest Ferris wheel in the world at its opening. The fair also saw the first escalator, which won first prize at the exposition, and diesel engines, electric cars, dry cell batteries, electric fire engines, a telegraphone, and also the world's first matryoshka dolls. Thus France ushered in the new century by insisting again upon its status as the epicenter of the globe.

Reveling in the celebrations of the fin de siècle, the organizers and the attendees were of course blind to the radical political, social, and cultural convulsions into which the world was about to be thrown. The boys whose blood would soon soak the Continent were mere toddlers. Einstein's theory of general relativity, and its ramifications for the perception and understanding of the world, was fifteen years away. Philosophers and psychologists such as Henri Bergson and William James would soon describe human experience as essentially fractured and confused and improvisatory. Freud was poised to unleash the unconscious on European culture. The transformations that resulted from these upheavals helped to unsettle the stultifying art world as well. This was the context in which the creative tumult at La Ruche was possible.

When the fair was over, the city auctioned off many of the structures that had sprouted up around Paris since 1892. Most of the others were demolished. In a remarkable stroke of magnanimity, however, the renowned (and hugely successful) sculptor Alfred Boucher, a friend of Rodin's and Camille Claudel's mentor, did the city a favor: He bought several items from the municipal auction, including a building-sized octagonal wine rotunda that Eiffel had designed for the exposition, statues of costumed women from the Indochina pavilion, and a grand iron gate from the Palace of Women, all of which were dismantled and then reassembled on the Passage Dantzig in the fifteenth arrondissement. Boucher turned the hodgepodge of structures into La Ruche, which he called the Villa de Medici.

In fact there has never been much about the place reminiscent of the Medici. It consists of bunks, studios, a gallery space, and large rooms into which artists could troop for weekly free life-drawing classes. The eight-sided building does indeed resemble a beehive. Visitors may still climb the same winding wooden steps Soutine once hobbled up and down, all the way to the compact, sunlight-flooded studio in which Chagall worked on the top floor all those years ago. As at its founding, the rent has remained cheap. Boucher never made a fuss when the rent was late. Some of the tenants took unfair advantage—one artist managed to live on credit for twelve years, without producing a single painting or sculpture. A forty-minute walk to the storied cafés La Rotonde and Le Dôme, and an hour by foot from the École des Beaux-Arts, La Ruche was well situated in the burgeoning bohemia of Montparnasse, which soon replaced Montmartre as the hotbed of the avant-garde. (The neighborhood sealed its primary status when Picasso moved from Montmartre to Montparnasse in 1912.) The Beehive opened officially in 1902, and the secretary of state for fine arts (a French position if ever there was one) attended the dedication ceremony, at which an orchestra played "La Marseillaise."

The inside of La Ruche is circular, with a dim skylight so weak it brightens only the top floor, which was therefore the most expensive. (Chagall, among the wealthiest tenants when he first arrived, was able to afford a top-floor space.) All the rest were cast in gloomy shadow unrelieved by the grimy windows that made up a wall of each studio. The stink of unwashed tenants—no contemporary source mentions indoor bathrooms—and the filth were infamous, and they mixed with the pungent scent of oil paints that filled the whole building. Misery was heaviest on the ground floor, where rats, roaches, screeching cats, and mangy dogs took shelter with the poorest tenants, Soutine among them. The mattresses atop the iron beds were infested with bedbugs, the corridors and staircases dusty and stained. All was in a constant state of disorder, so much so that the whole place resembled the backstage of an abandoned theater; dirty busts, statues, vases, moldy fruit, and dead flowers cluttered the hallways, the detritus of innumerable still-life paintings. Every surface was splattered with paint.

In the garden surrounding the building grew lime trees, chestnut trees, lilac bushes, and an enormous cherry tree, all of which have thickened with the years and still keep guard over the building like potbellied gargoyles. From the neighboring slaughterhouses (now long gone, as high-rises have encroached and hulk over the courtyard), where Chagall and others painted, the condemned cows, cattle, and pigs were audible in the dorms.

In other words, if you were a penurious but determined painter, it was home. During the day sculptors and painters who did not live there would use the studio space. They had very little to do with the inhabitants who made up its ecosystem. Next to the main building, down a flight of dank, mud-encrusted steps, stood a double cottage where Boucher kept his own studio and workshop. When he was not wandering the halls and peeking into the studios of the little colony that he had founded, checking on his bees, it was where he worked. Boucher liked to brag that he had influenced Rodin, but his grateful if slightly condescending tenants wondered aloud whether the influence did not run in the opposite direction.

Word of this haven spread quickly among the immigrants with vivid imaginations and empty pockets, and La Ruche expanded considerably in the 1910s. Soutine, Michel Kikoine, Pinchus Krémègne, Fernand Léger, Alexander Archipenko, Henri Laurens, Paul-Albert Girard, and René Thomsen were among the tenants who benefited from Boucher's sanctuary. They were followed by many others of various nationalities, ideals, and dispositions, and Boucher assiduously bought up little huts, shacks, and hovels around the main edifice, into which his colony overflowed. There were nearly 140 workshops by the time he finished expanding. Writers such as the poet Blaise Cendrars (who wrote a poem about the place), Apollinaire, and the art critic Maximilien Gauthier often visited. Rumors circulated that the socialist Adolph Joffe and even Lenin himself dropped by at one time. (It is certain that he and Trotsky frequented Le Dôme, one of the cafés in Montparnasse that would become a haunt for the circle of German artists from La Ruche, during Lenin's brief exile in Paris from 1909 to 1911.)

In the eternal battle between commerce and art, the shopkeepers and the restaurant owners surrounding the hive chose the losing side. Boucher knew that, more often than not, his artists ate and drank on credit. To repay this generous folly he converted a nearby house into a makeshift, dilapidated, and exceedingly romantic theater. Up to three hundred people could squeeze inside for the performances, and the entry fee was optional: Everyone paid what they could. With the help of the city, he organized productions, until he had the brilliant idea to invite undiscovered actors and directors to try their hand at running the show. The gambit was a wild success. Renowned stars of the stage and early film such as Charles Le Bargy, Maurice de Féraudy (the father of Jacques de Féraudy), and Édouard Alexandre de Max had their start there. Marguerite Morena, Jacques Hébertot, and the heartthrob theater actor and movie star Louis Jouvet also appeared at La Ruche. Jouvet (who at the time still spelled his name Jouvey) stuck around for several years. It was at La Ruche that he met Jacques Copeau, the theater director and founder of Théâtre du Vieux-Colombier, where Jouvet would go on to early celebrity.

Jouvet aside, most of the La Ruche denizens were Jews, and the appellation "School of Paris" was meant to distinguish the foreign contaminants from L'École Française, the "School of France," which, according to street gossip as well as literary magazines, the émigrés were polluting. Soutine arrived in Paris when this dynamic was already in full swing, but it only got stronger over his lifetime. In a monograph on the painter André Dunoyer de Segonzac, which appeared in *Le Carnet de la semaine* (a widely read weekly magazine) in 1925, the art critic Louis Vauxcelles (himself a French Jew as well as a textbook arriviste who was petrified that his unsavory Semitic brethren would upset his position in the art establishment) proclaimed that "a barbarian horde has rushed upon Montparnasse, descending [on the art galleries of] rue La Boétie from the cafes of the fourteenth arrondissement. . . . These are people from 'elsewhere' who ignore and at their hearts look down on what Renoir has called the gentleness of the École Française—that is, our race's virtue of tact." (Note that anxious "our.")

The art critic Fritz Vanderpyl was a good deal nastier. In a 1924 article titled "Is There Such a Thing as Jewish Painting?" which appeared in the *Mercure de France*, he gnashed his teeth: "In the absence of any trace of Jewish art in the Louvre, we are nevertheless witnessing a swarming of Jewish painters in the postwar salons. The Lévys are legion, Maxime Lévy, Irene and Flore Lévy, Simon Lévy, Alkan Lévy, Isidore Lévy, Claude Lévy, etc. . . . Not to mention the Lévys who prefer to exhibit under pseudonyms, a move that would be quite in line with the ways of modern Jews, and without mentioning the Weills, the Zadoks, whose names one comes across on every page of the salon catalogues."

A year later the magazine *L'Art vivant* asked significant members of the Parisian art-sphere which ten living artists should be included in the permanent collection of a new museum of French modern art. The prominent Polish Jewish painter Moïse Kisling replied with commendable venom: "Simone Lévy, Leopold Lévy, Rudolph Lévy, Maxime Lévy, Irène Lévy, Flore Lévy, Isidore Lévy, Claude Lévy, Benoit Lévy, et Moïse Kisling." The Jewish painters of Paris had pride.

"You left either famous or dead," Chagall said about La Ruche, into which he moved in the fall of 1911. An overstatement, but barely. Soutine and Chagall overlapped for one year at La Ruche. Other cohabitants included Archipenko, Modigliani, Kikoine, Krémègne, and Lipschitz, as well as many others whose names have been forgotten. Their bohemian romance did not end well, and not only because success eluded so many. In the early 1940s, history found its cruel way to the Beehive, and many of its artists were carted off, by German Nazis and French collaborators, to the notorious deportation center at Drancy in a northeast suburb of Paris, and from there to their extinction in concentration camps in the east, mainly Auschwitz. The Yiddish literature about these people refers to them as "our martyred artists," though in the years Soutine lived and later visited La Ruche, liveliness was certainly among its dominant characteristics. It was an escape—a reprieve, rather—from a hostile world.

Soutine joined many eastern European Jews at La Ruche—they accounted for the majority of its occupants—but the fact that they all fled the same kinds of pogroms does not mean they all came from the same kinds of towns. The term *shtetl* is misleading. Today, the word is often used by Jews to shroud a distant ancestral village in nostalgia. The Yiddish term *shtot* literally means "city," and the diminutive ending in "shtetl" originally marked the place as a small city. "Shtetl" originally referred to any town within the Russian Empire, no matter its size or sophistication, where Jewish citizens lived and contributed significantly to the local economy, the heart of which was the marketplace. The marketplace was the dominant feature of the shtetl, its center, and it is therefore useful to also think of a shtetl as an auxiliary commercial center often just a train stop away from a major city. Shtetls—or more properly *shtetlakh*—differed from other cities and towns because of their Jewishness, history, and peculiar economy. So long as the Russians allowed the shtetls to function in this unique manner, they flourished.

This was permitted for roughly the first fifty years after the Russians began to incorporate more and more of Poland and Lithuania into Russia itself. Russia, as ever, could devour but not digest. It grew increasingly insecure about its cultural hegemony within an empire that had swelled to contain every religion and ethnicity in existence, and myriad cultural identities, none of which dissolved with ease into the Russian welter. The state tightened its reins and gave its blessing to all forms of anti-Semitism, including violent expressions of it. Shtetls were strangled into stagnation and decay, just as other minorities' freedoms were constrained.[10] The archetypal shtetl, Anatevka, created by Sholem Aleichem in his fiction and sentimentalized by *Fiddler on the Roof*, has stamped an image of an impoverished and culturally backward eastern European Jewish life into our collective imagination, but the reality was much richer and more complicated.

The Russian Jewish artists at La Ruche had all been born in Russian towns with Jewish communities, but, for example,

Soutine and Chagall did not come from remotely the same backgrounds. Marc Chagall (born Moishe Shagal), whose paintings, ironically, assisted in the mythification of the shtetl, came from Vitebsk, which was not a village at all but a large multicultural city, the capital of the Vitebsk province. Like Soutine's Smilovichi, Vitebsk is now part of Belarus. Chagall's parents were both born in Lyozno, a town in Mohilev province with 1,660 Jews, who accounted for 67.3 percent of the overall population. (Vitebsk, by contrast, had 34,420 Jews.) Chagall's paternal grandfather moved to Vitebsk with his eldest son, Hatskl, Chagall's father, and worked as a Hebrew teacher (a language he failed to pass on to his grandson—Chagall could not speak or understand even basic Hebrew). A relative of the Shagals back in Lyozno died soon after their arrival, and the eldest remaining daughter, Feyge-Ite, joined the Shagals in Vitebsk and married Hatskl. Feyge-Ite was fifteen years old when Moishe Shagal was born in 1887.

Though Marc would travel to Lyozno to visit family throughout his childhood, he was raised in bustling Vitebsk. He attended *heder*, where the boys were taught Hebrew literacy, Bible, and Jewish practices, until age thirteen, after which his mother was able to bribe her son's way into a Russian school, at which he was expected, for the first time in his life, to speak Russian. That same year he began taking classes at Yuri Pen's School of Art, founded in 1897, and among the first Jewish institutions to train artists. Like many of the Jews of his city, in adolescence Chagall renounced religion and did not engage in Jewish practice or study Jewish texts for the rest of his long life, though, as is clear from his paintings, the tradition became stylistically and symbolically significant to him.[11] Chagall moved to St. Petersburg in 1907 and attended the

St. Petersburg Academy, where he studied with artists like Léon Bakst (who became the celebrated costume designer of the Ballets Russes) and Mstislav Dobuzhinsky. He moved on to Paris in 1910.

Chagall said that the colors in Vitebsk were like those of the shoes of its residents. "Because of this color, we all fled from there."[12] But Vitebsk was technicolor compared to Smilovichi. During Soutine's childhood, 3,498 people lived there, making it only a little larger than Lyozno. It was a small village, then part of the Russian Empire, though it had originally been in the district of Minsk within the Grand Duchy of Lithuania. (The Russians conquered the territory in 1793, one hundred years before Soutine's birth.) Most of its inhabitants were Jews. There were two Orthodox churches, a mosque, and five synagogues. Separate schools for boys and girls had opened in the 1860s, but the Jewish students attended *heder*. The small town also had a postal station, tanneries, two mills, nine bars, two hotels, a bakery, and small wineries and breweries. Fairs were held on Sundays in the square.[13]

Already in the early nineteenth century, the tsar was growing wary of his new Jewish subjects. In 1804 the first statute imposed on all the Jews of Russia required them to adopt surnames. This was an effort to squelch the success of the shtetl by making it easier for the state to track and control its Jewish subjects and to shatter Jewish self-reliance. The change radically altered Jewish legal and administrative status; it was part of the transition of shtetl life from an obscure but tolerated enigma to an entity that could be monitored, classified, and unambiguously identified. Theoretically, after this innovation Jews could forthwith be registered in censuses, issued passports, and recorded in registers. In reality, Jews thwarted their monitors, knowing full well that they could not bear the ensuing taxes that were placed on the community as a whole rather than on individuals. Poor Jews simply could not afford the tax burden—some starved to death from the strain. The surname acquisition process was slow, and over the course of the 1800s Jews selected surnames that generally related to occupations, personal characteristics, or places of residence, though within the community Jews continued to refer to one another using traditional names and nicknames. The name Soutine is the French rendition of Sutin, which was a town in Belarus. All contemporary Sutins are probably descendants of former residents of the region surrounding that location. (Evidence suggests that none of the original Sutins were from Sutin, but instead from the surrounding areas.)[14]

There are records of סוטין, the Hebrew of Soutine's family name, mentioned in Hebrew-language newspapers as residents of Smilovichi. In 1898 the publication *ha-Melitz*, the first Hebrew-language newspaper in Russia, mentioned a Nachum Soutine from Smilovichi who donated money to the Jewish community in the Holy Land in honor of a friend's marriage. The notice reads, "I hereby bless my dear friend Eliyahu Halprin [for his wedding to Hinda Ezherwitz] and donate 50 kopeks to the settlement of the land of Israel on contract 261/10."[15]

The notice reveals a few interesting sociological facts about Soutine's immediate family. First, a close relative who lived nearby had enough money to donate a small amount to the Zionist effort, then in its infancy. Chovevei Tzion, or Lovers of Zion, the organization through which the funds would have been donated, was a network of Russian proto-Zionist organizations that had been founded seventeen years earlier in response to the pogroms rumbling through Russian Jewish communities. Chovevei Tzion was the forerunner of the modern Zionist political movement founded by Theodor Herzl. A member of the Soutine family was a committed supporter of the movement, which means Chaim himself grew up hearing about it. And indeed, in the subsequent few decades, while Soutine was in Paris, some of his siblings fled to the mandate of Palestine. It is also of interest that someone in young Chaim's close circle was a reader of *ha-Melitz* at all. It was a paper of the Haskalah, the Jewish enlightenment, a liberal movement within the Russian Jewish community.

Zalman and Sara Sutin's rickety wooden house, bursting with eleven children, looked out onto the main square of Smilovichi "in which markets used to take place twice or thrice a week. The plot of land that belonged to the Sutins extended toward the Volma River, which would flood their garden in spring. A road to the left of the house led to Minsk, and on the right one of the town's synagogues proudly stood." Faïbich-Schraga Zarfin, an artist six years Soutine's junior who also grew up in Smilovichi, reported that Zalman Sutin, Chaim's father, was "a tailor of a low stature and pleasant appearance, [who] grew up in a very religious family. After the prayers in the synagogue he would go to Zarfin's house together with his friends for a glass of liquor and a piece of cake."[16]

The Soutine mythology regarding his childhood, fattened by gossip over the decades in which he was alive, insists that his early years were miserable, and that this misery tinctured his whole life, dogged him, and darkened the paintings to which he dedicated himself after fleeing Smilovichi. Zarfin paints a radically different picture: "In his childhood, Soutine loved sauntering around the market together with peasants, running around the fields, or spending hours sitting on the riverbank. . . . Already as children, we both drew—he would cover the walls of his house with drawings, and I would draw in my father's account books. Chaim drew portraits, and I drew fire fighters. . . . Soutine liked to copy photographs and made enlarged copies, whose similarity to the original fascinated the village people."

At the age of ten, Soutine left *heder* and began working for his sister Celia's husband, who was a tailor in Minsk, forty kilometers from Smilovichi.[17] Perhaps he lived with his sister's family in the city, though the distance was meager enough that he could have hitched nightly rides home with fellow Smilovichians who worked in the city during the day. After four years in that position, Chaim began an apprenticeship for a photographer in Minsk, and he enrolled in the art school of the painter Jacob Kruger, formally commencing the fine arts education that had informally begun long before.[18]

Decades later Soutine recalled that one of his earliest memories was of studying the patterns cast by a ray of sunshine on the ground. That precocious fascination was the true beginning of his painterly education. A painter must be intensely present, acutely attuned to the infinite and minute qualities that characterize material existence, whipped as it always is by mysterious energies. He must notice that a sun's ray brightens the top of a table but darkens its side, how movement courses through a body, the hues of a flower petal, which dissolve into one another. This presentness, this electric sensitivity, yields knowledge that accumulates over time into an inventory of understandings and techniques with which a painter is able to create a convincing universe on a canvas. Later the peculiar qualities of paint itself must be studied with the same obsessive intensity, since, as Hans Hofmann noted, "Pictorial life is not imitated life, it is, on the contrary, a created reality based on the inherent life within every medium of expression."[19] The tubed substance, the way it spreads, scrapes, and blends, must be mastered so an artist can make it sing. Soutine would become one of the supreme masters of both these dimensions—the world of the canvas and the world around it. He had a startlingly intimate and original relationship with both paint and matter. A profound compulsion drove him to force these two worlds into one another. And the skills required to achieve that end were first acquired in Jacob Kruger's small school.

The scholarship on Soutine often suggests that his father insisted he become a tailor, and that he was brutally punished for pursuing an artistic career. Consider this paragraph written by Maurice Tuchman, a great authority on the painter, in Soutine's catalogue raisonné:

> By the age of thirteen Soutine loved to draw and would sketch on any scrap of paper he could find or on the walls with charcoal. He was ridiculed for this by his family (his father wanted him to become a cobbler or a tailor) and was actually punished physically for his "crime." Two of his older brothers constantly taunted him saying, "A Jew must not paint," and they beat him mercilessly. Their cruelty became almost a ritual. Soutine would break free from his brothers and hide in the woods near the village until hunger forced him home. He would return to find milk and warm black bread, which he dearly loved, laid on the table.

But when he crept into the kitchen he would be beaten again by his waiting brothers.[20]

The source Tuchman gives for this story of the young Soutine's martyrdom for art is Chana Orloff's essay "Mon Ami Soutine," which was published in English in *The Jewish Chronicle* in 1963—twenty years after Soutine's death and about twenty-three years after Orloff's friendship with Soutine was cut off by the Nazi invasion. Orloff was a painter and sculptor who befriended Soutine and lived next door to him in the 1930s. She was apparently repeating stories Soutine himself had told her, though all the Soutine legends, no matter how outlandish or impossible, are attributed by second parties to Soutine himself. Whatever the case may be, her recollections are somewhat inconsistent with Zarfin's, who recalls that Soutine would proudly and regularly visit Smilovichi while he was enrolled in art school in Vilna, and conspicuously walk the streets wearing his school uniform.

Tuchman goes on to claim that Soutine would never have escaped Smilovichi if it had not been for a stroke of dark luck. As the story goes, sometime in 1909 Soutine was caught drawing a portrait of an old Jewish man (which is forbidden according to certain strict readings of Jewish law) and was then badly beaten. His family lodged a complaint, and Soutine was subsequently awarded the money with which he could afford to go study in Minsk. Yet Zarfin and Kikoine both dispute this narrative. Zarfin recalls, "As he was drawing a portrait of the eighty-five-year-old man, the latter's children came running and chased Soutine away, beating him with sticks. Soutine filed a complaint about having been beaten and injured. The lay magistrate, a learned man of German origin, ruled that the wrongdoers should pay a fine of fifteen rubles. Soutine was head over heels with excitement: now he could buy the necessary materials and rent a room, as in our town he was renting a space that he used as a studio."

Zarfin's version of the story makes more sense than Tuchman's. For one thing, Soutine was already working in Minsk when he was ten years old, six years before the alleged incident. Tuchman also says that Kikoine and Soutine departed for Minsk together, with the awarded money, when in fact Kikoine was not from Smilovichi but from Rechytsa, a city about 250 kilometers away. The two met in Minsk. Tuchman conjures an archetypal image of a cruel father intent to force his son into the family business, but, as already explained, Soutine stopped working as an apprentice to a tailor and worked instead for a photographer when he started taking art classes in Minsk.

Soutine's first art teacher, Kruger, was born in 1869 and studied at the Kiev Art School, the Académie Julian in Paris, and then at the Saint Petersburg Academy of Arts. He returned to Minsk in 1900 and began giving classes in 1904. Two years later, Kruger converted three empty rooms in the private two-story home of a confectionary merchant into a small art school. His students were not wealthy, and often he waived the tuition fee. Perhaps Soutine was among the beneficiaries of his generosity—it is difficult to imagine how else young Chaim could have afforded classes. Canvases, brushes, and paints are expensive enough on their own. Even if his parents had been willing to support his education, they would not have had the money to spare. Kruger's style of painting was highly academic. While details about the courses taught in his school are unknown, it is likely that Soutine was given a formal, traditional education for the year and a half that he remained under Kruger's supervision. What is certain is that in those three rooms, Chaim Soutine's artistic career began.

Kikoine's son, Yankel, remembers his father telling him that Soutine had befriended a man named Smilevitch, a dentist, who encouraged him to go study at the Vilna Fine Arts Academy. Heeding the advice, Soutine soon dragged his friend to Vilna, and "a few months later they were registered for classes and hard at work."[21] How he afforded the trip is not clear, though the distance was short enough that Soutine continued to return home to Smilovichi throughout his stay in Vilna.

The school to which Soutine was headed had a complicated history. In 1863, Lithuania and Poland had attempted by military means to break off from the Russian Empire. They failed. In response to that uprising, Russia violently suppressed all traditional expressions of Lithuanian and Polish identity. Cultural institutions were dismantled, and new institutions, designed as agents of Russification, were established. To that end, the Vilna Fine Arts Academy opened its doors in 1866, headed by the artist Ivan Trutnev, an alumnus of the Saint Petersburg Academy of Arts. A district supervisor, Ivan Kornilov, wrote, "Educational institutions must imperceptibly serve for the purpose of moral and, thus, ultimate merging of the Western region with the remaining part of Russia. These are our noble aims and achieving them is the basic duty of the Vilnius Educational District."[22]

The school became legendary for its noted alumni, many of whom, like Soutine, went on to study in Paris, much to the ire of the tsarist officials who had expected to churn out future students and professors of the Saint Petersburg Academy. (Arbit Blatas's memoir about Michel Kikoine is titled *Montparnasse, the Capital of Lithuanian Art*.) Trutnev devoted immense effort to developing a curriculum that would prepare students for entry into the finest academies in Europe. While he remained a loyal patriot of the state, his primary interest was in educating his students, not in feeding them propaganda. He agitated for the Saint Petersburg Academy to send teaching aids, Greek and Roman gypsum heads, and oil paintings from its vast collection, and also textbooks. Soutine benefited from Trutnev's unremitting commitment to securing an exemplary education for his students. Starting in 1871, the Saint Petersburg Academy of Arts held drawing competitions every three years, and then every six years, which drew applicants from across the Russian Empire, and through those competitions the Vilna Fine Arts Academy garnered an empire-wide reputation for excellence. Its students were awarded medals and earned letters of commendation, and its teachers were honored.

It remained open until 1915, when it was forced to shutter due to the war. The academy's entire collection was relocated to Samara, a city located two thousand kilometers west of Vilna at the intersection of the Volga and Samara Rivers. While it remained operative, attendance was open to Jews, women, and the poor. A four-year curriculum was instituted in 1893. Ivan Rybakov, also an alumnus of the Saint Petersburg Academy of Arts, became Trutnev's assistant in 1899; he taught drawing and painting to the male students. After Trutnev's death in 1908, Rybakov was appointed head of the academy, where he remained in management until 1913, when he traveled to France.[23] He and Soutine arrived in that cultural epicenter in the same year. Soutine's journey was funded by the mysterious Dr. Rafelkess, who also sent

Soutine a regular stipend for the first few years of his stay in Paris. The sympathy and magnanimity of this figure severed for good Soutine's connection with Smilovichi. He never returned to the town of his birth.

Zalman Sutin, Chaim's father, had a special coat made in honor of Soutine's impending journey, which he gifted him on Soutine's last stay under his roof. Just a few years later, Soutine's family was either murdered or driven out by pogroms. Soutine kept the coat for quite a while. He is wearing it in all four of his self-portraits, and in the portraits that Modigliani painted of him.[24]

Soutine was enrolled in the atelier of Fernand Cormon at the École des Beaux-Arts on July 17, 1913, about a month after his arrival in Paris.[25] He would have heard about Cormon's studio while still in Vilna. Twenty-eight years earlier, Vincent van Gogh had met Toulouse-Lautrec in that same atelier. Cormon was a painter and a traditionalist, and was more interested in painting than developing artistic theories. Or, as Jules Flandrin furiously wrote, "His head is empty, quite empty! Puts all his effort into knocking up some sort of picture, and that's it! As for ever having given a moment's thought to what art itself might be, he's congenitally incapable of it!"[26] Van Gogh remained in the class until he and Cormon quarreled so violently over artistic differences that the student tried to shoot his teacher. When Matisse arrived at Cormon's door in 1899 and produced a characteristically daring work, Cormon quietly asked his assistant, "Is he over thirty?" (The Beaux-Arts enforced an under-thirty age limit.) "Yes." "Does he know what he's doing?" "Yes." "Then he'll have to go."[27] Soutine arrived fourteen years after Matisse was thrown out.

It is not known how Soutine gained entry to the École des Beaux-Arts, since one had to be accepted into a studio there and could not simply sign up. (This is in contrast with schools like the Russian Academy and the Académie Julian, where students such as Modigliani and Matisse went if they were not accepted at the École des Beaux-Arts—or if, as in Matisse's case, they were removed from it.) It is possible that Soutine simply visited Cormon armed with a portfolio of selected works, and on the basis of that viewing the teacher granted him admission. Soutine had spent the previous three and a half years developing a body of work and would likely have taken the best fruits of that period with him to Paris as a calling card. The French artist Robert Fernier enrolled in Cormon's studio just a month before Soutine did.[28] He describes the studio thusly: "The gray walls were covered, at eye level, with thick palette scrapings which gave them a repulsive appearance. A rickety board held old studies and many more were spread over several rows. . . . A pale light was cast on a forest of easels radiating out from a plateau where a nude model was placed. In a loft, old materials ended their careers. You could make out a cupboard, sinks, and three windows opening onto a shaded and charming courtyard."

Soutine was not the only Russian Jew who matriculated into Cormon's atelier that year. Emmanuel Mané-Katz recalled meeting Soutine in the studio: "In 1913, I entered Cormon's studio, at the École des Beaux-Arts. My Russian shirt and small build won me sympathy and I escaped the usual bullying. I kept quiet in my corner doing my best to pass unnoticed when one day I heard someone singing a Jewish song close to me. I turned around. The singing stopped. I resumed work: the melody resumed.

Exceedingly intrigued, I discovered the explanation for the mystery only at the end of the class. A boy with a tense face and bulging eyes approached me. It was Soutine."[29]

It is possible that Soutine's lifelong dedication to the Louvre was initiated by Cormon. According to Fernier, the renowned professor used to invite groups of students to accompany him to the museum, where he would formally induct them into the French artistic tradition.

> There, in direct communion with the authentic masterpieces of the nineteenth century, he would explain their significance to us, and carry on his lectures in a liberal spirit. He admired Ingres, Courbet, and Manet but his favorite was Delacroix about whom he would often speak. He compared *The Entry of the Crusaders in Constantinople* [Delacroix, 1840], *The Burial at Ornans* [Courbet, 1849–1850], and the *Portrait of M. Bertin* [Ingres, 1832] with *Olympia* [Manet, 1863–1865]: "Paintings which are inspired and executed by different things are linked together by one common trait: genius." What love did he arouse in his students in that room for an art about which they were still ignorant both of its difficulties and of its satisfactions. These visits in his company, filling our hearts with immense trouble, spurred our ambitions.[30]

Soutine spent only a few years under Cormon's tutelage. The earliest existent photo of the artist is a group picture of him and his classmates inside the studio.[31]

Chapter 2

Immigrants in Wartime

Soutine was one year old when the Dreyfus Affair ignited something like a civil war in France. Alfred Dreyfus, a Jewish Alsatian artillery officer, was wrongly convicted of treason for passing military secrets to Germany. The evidence was scant, but Dreyfus became the national object of French bigotry, and citizens scrambled to align themselves with the Dreyfusards and the anti-Dreyfusards—appellations that signified far more than whether or not one believed in the guilt or innocence of the man in question. By the time Soutine arrived in France, the calamity had faded from the forefront of national consciousness, but the wounds were hardly healed.

At that time, Paris was the most liberal city in the most liberal country in Europe. It was the place where immigrants aspired to go to find a new and better life. Soutine was one of the many who went to Paris for precisely that reason. But there were reactionary elements in French society who greatly resented the disruptive surge of foreigners. The liberalism provoked a backlash of rank nationalism that was as violent and ugly then as it is in our own time. Many in the country resented their fellow French citizens' open arms, and they made their displeasure known.

Xenophobia usually gains potency in wartime. The assassination of Franz Ferdinand, Archduke of Austria, was committed in Sarajevo on June 28, 1914—just a year after Soutine's arrival in Paris—initiating a torrent of bloodshed that would drown an era of human history. The next month, Germany declared war on Russia and then on France. At the start of the war, pressure was high in France to defend the country, even among bohemian artists and writers. Charles Péguy, the celebrated essayist and editor, was among the first of thousands who would die on behalf of France. He was killed in battle in September 1914. Foreigners were suspected of disloyalty and were vigilantly surveilled. It was in their interest to serve on behalf of their adoptive homeland. On July 29, "The appeal to foreigners living in France" was launched by leading expat intellectuals. They plastered posters all over Paris and printed calls to arms in major newspapers and magazines.[1] Among the literary figures to lead this initiative was the Swiss poet and novelist Blaise Cendrars, who left behind a wife, Félicie, and infant at home in Forges-par-Barbizon to go fight. Felicie, who would later become a dear friend of Soutine's, wrote in terror of the suspicion and hatred she provoked in her neighbors who mistook her for a German and a spy:

One day, the rage of the villagers was unleashed on me and my baby. "Death to spies!" In their patriotism they threw stones through my windows. Best friends suddenly became enemies. The grocer refused to service me, the laundry woman would not wash the baby's blankets, the creamery would not sell me milk. All were turned against me and shouted that I was the cause of the nation's distress. Two armed police officers came and declared "by order of the mayor you are under arrest, pending your deportation to a concentration camp." One of the officers stayed to keep watch over the baby, the other escorted me to the mayor. Peasants gathered, raised their fists and shouted at me. . . . My landlord warned me that he could no longer keep me as a tenant, since he was beset by peasants who accused him of giving asylum to a spy. The doctor no longer dares come to care for the baby.[2]

The surge of anti-immigrant sentiment metastasized over the subsequent years of misery. Initially, though, a significant subset of the foreigners who had first encountered and come to expect a liberal order in France expressed ardent solidarity for the country. On August 3, the Society of Jewish Immigrants issued the following proclamation:

Brothers! France, the country of liberty, equality, and fraternity, France, liberator of humanity, France which, first among all nations, recognized us, and gave us, Jews, the rights of men and citizens; France where we found, we and our families, for many years a refuge and a shelter, France is in danger! . . . We, Jewish immigrants, what shall we do? Shall we, while all of France rises as one man to defend his country, cross our arms? No, for if we are not yet French by right, we are heart and soul, and it is our sacred obligation to place ourselves entirely at the disposal of this great and noble nation, and to participate in her defense. Brothers! This is the means by which we will pay our tribute of gratitude to the country where we found moral emancipation and material well-being. Jewish immigrants, do your duty, and long live France![3]

Many, though not all, heeded the cry. The bands of immigrant artists that had developed an ecosystem within Montparnasse over the preceding decades were scattered. Cendrars was sent to the front in 1914 and served until he lost his right arm in battle a year later and was discharged. (One of his memoirs of the war years is titled *The Severed Hand*.) The Polish Jewish artist Moïse Kisling returned from a visit to Belgium to enlist in the Foreign Legion. He served until he was badly wounded in 1916, after which he was awarded French citizenship.[4] While serving as an infantryman in the French army in 1916, Guillaume Apollinaire, who had been born in Rome, suffered a serious shrapnel wound to the head from which he would never fully recover.[5] A number of other foreign transplants, such as Modigliani, Manuel Ortiz de Zárate, Diego Rivera, and Emmanuel Mané-Katz, tried to volunteer but were rejected due to poor health. Others, like Picasso (a pacifist) and Brancusi, preferred to stay neutral. The Japanese artist Tsuguharu Foujita, unable to make a living in Paris during the war, left for London. Jules Pascin did the same and departed from London to the United States in 1914, where he remained for much of the war.[6] Marc Chagall had gone to visit family in Vitebsk just before war broke out and was stranded there for some years. For the stragglers who remained in Paris, scraping together enough money to quiet their growling bellies proved increasingly onerous.

The whole country was enlisted in the struggle against the Germans. On August 4, President Raymond Poincaré exhorted the French people to do their part to defend their nation: "In the war that is now beginning, France will have Right on her side, whose eternal moral power peoples can no more disregard with impunity than individuals can. France will be heroically defended by all her sons; nothing can break their *Union sacrée* in the face of the enemy; today they are all united as brothers in indignation against the aggressor, and at the same time united in patriotic faith."[7]

Union sacrée rose to a semireligious imperative. There was honor in the sacrifices that French citizens back home were forced to make, and the sacrifices were plentiful: According to some scholars, the cost of living in wartime Paris rose by 200 percent. Others put the number as high as 400 percent.[8] Civilians began to refer to *la vie chère* as a shorthand for their contribution to the war effort. Necessities, food especially, became scarce and expensive, and the hunt for basic goods was conceived as a counterpart to the battle being waged by soldiers on the front. Poverty bred resentment—contempt for the landowners, butchers, and merchants who became the face of rising prices; xenophobia toward foreigners partaking in the little allotted to French citizens; and protracted outrage toward the government for its inefficiency and indecision regarding price regulations and provisions—which lasted till peace was restored.

The first year of the war was a deep shock. One million Parisians fled the city in 1914. Many remembered the siege of 1870–

1871, during which German soldiers besieged the capital from September 19 to January 28. The siege coincided with a particularly bitter winter, and toward the end of the crisis between three thousand and four thousand people were dying per week from cold and starvation. Many were alive who still remembered that dark time, and those who could not remember had been told horror stories about that macabre chapter in the city's history. Partly due to the specter of those months, Parisians hoarded food, which caused prices to skyrocket. Potatoes in particular became exorbitantly expensive—a development that affected the poorest in the city disproportionately.

Terror over rising prices stoked xenophobia. On August 2, 1914, a number of cafés and groceries assumed to be owned by Germans and Austrians were attacked and pillaged. Rioters ransacked the Café Viennois and the Pschor brasserie. The hardest hit were the Appenrodt restaurant chain and the Maggi dairies, the latter of which was owned by a Swiss family that had been targeted by the far-right monarchist movement Action Française and accused of aiding the Germans. Three hundred people rushed the branch on rue Richer, which they trashed and gutted. One boy grabbed a handful of eggs, juggled them, and yelled, "Down with Germany! Who wants some Prussian eggs!" before throwing them against a window while singing "The Marseillaise." Other stores with German-sounding names fell victim to the same violence. Four or five hundred men stormed Klein's leather goods on Boulevard des Italiens, vandalizing and robbing it. A crowd stormed a bar called Chope du Châtelet because a German had hid inside it. Mobs also attacked stores whose owners they believed had hiked prices to capitalize on the terror. A police officer noted, "More or less grave scenes have broken out this evening at diverse locations in Paris where shopkeepers raised prices excessively on basic consumer goods. Certain stores have been the object of serious incidents; thieves have even taken advantage of the circumstances to steal considerable quantities of goods and cash."[9]

It is difficult to ascertain exactly how Soutine lived for the duration of the war, though it is safe to assume he spent much of it in Paris. Some sources report that he and Kikoine volunteered, digging trenches for the "army of workers," a paramilitary group of foreigners utilized by the French government. By September 2, German troops had reached Senlis, a commune in northern France less than fifty kilometers from the heart of Paris. When the French government fled southward to Bordeaux that same night, half a million Parisians followed. A month later the Germans were dealt their first defeat at the Battle of the Marne, the conflict that saved the French capital from destruction.[10] Soutine, it seems, was among the workers digging trenches within the city in case the Germans ever got close enough to turn Paris into a war zone. Physically weak and lacking in courage, he could do no more than this to aid France's war effort. Kikoine told Pierre Courthion, author of one of the most important monographs on Soutine, that one day, while he and Soutine were painting in a city near Paris, "Soutine heard the thunder of cannon fire and [frightened,] he left for his Paris home. He was not very brave. However, he did not hesitate to volunteer for the 'army of workers.' It was a question of digging trenches to measure dimensions, etc. But this activity was only intermittent."[11]

At the start of the war, Soutine moved into a studio at Cité Falguière, a cul-de-sac located a short distance from La Ruche. His new home was close enough to the Beehive that he could still visit his friends every day. This was useful, since the artists who remained in the city grew intensely mutually dependent during the war. The art market slowed to a glacial pace, salons were postponed, art collectors' wallets squeezed shut, and those who had received an allowance from relatives were suddenly on their own. The artists' stipends provided by the French government dwindled rapidly. Yet creative solutions abounded. The Russian painter Marie Vassilieff, who had won a scholarship from the tsarina to study in Paris, was responsible for one of them.

Vassilieff was a revered figure in Montparnasse. Born in 1884, she came to Paris in 1907, at which time, as she would have told you herself, she was unbearably beautiful. Legend has it that days after her arrival, Henri Rousseau spotted her on a park bench and fell immediately in love. He proposed marriage, she declined—bad breath, she explained. In 1908, when Matisse found an abandoned convent to use for a studio, he was stalked by a crowd of implacable groupies, most of whom were foreigners, including Vassilieff. For two years the young master gave them grudging instruction. (This became known as Matisse Academy.) From 1910 on, Vassilieff exhibited her brightly colored cubist paintings regularly at the Salon d'Automne and the Salon des Indépendants. Vassilief cofounded and served as director of the Académie Russe, where many of the artists of Montparnasse would go for free life-drawing classes. After she resigned owing to tensions with coworkers, she founded the Vassilieff Academy on Avenue du Maine. During the war she transformed her academy into a canteen where hungry artists could always find something to eat. A Swedish painter remembered that "literary events, music shows, and legendary parties distracted the indigent artists from their bleak circumstances. These bashes, which buzzed with the chatter of many languages, would last until the early morning, since the police considered Vassilieff's canteen a private club and so did not impose a curfew. Such glittering celebrities as Matisse, Picasso, Modigliani, Soutine, Zadkine, Cendrars, Léger, the Swedish sculptor Ninnan Santesson, the Russian Marevna, and the Chilean Manuel Ortiz de Zárate were all regulars."[12]

When the war was finally over, and rationing ended and unemployment ebbed, the French capital shimmied back to its place at the apex of global culture and sophistication. Woodrow Wilson became the first American president to visit Paris when he came for a six-month stay to assist in negotiating a new map of Europe.[13] Ernest Hemingway, James Joyce, Josephine Baker, Ho Chi Minh, Léopold Senghor, and many other luminaries and eventual luminaries surged into the city. In Montparnasse especially, the revival was dazzling. The streets teemed and the wine flowed. Food was easier to come by. When Lucy, Aïcha, and Kiki—the famous artists' models of Montparnasse—stripped in studios and nightclubs across the city, they were fleshy and carefree. The great cafés had come back to life.

Yet even when the bombs stopped, the memory of horror tinctured the merriment and the swaying hips in and around La Ruche. The School of Paris was essentially melancholy. These artists from elsewhere had intimate knowledge of hardship. They remembered it from their childhoods, and at La Ruche the hard times persisted for almost all of them. At their most lighthearted they were never silly, even the ones who dabbled in surrealism. The Soviet novelist and journalist Ilya Ehrenburg recalled, "We stayed at La Rotonde because we were attracted by each other. The scandals were not what appealed to us, and we were not even inspired by new and bold aesthetic theories. Quite simply . . . the feeling of our common distress united us."[14] He was speaking specifically of the Jewish artists who had come to Paris to escape the pogroms ravaging the villages from which their families sent them anguished letters. Yiddish writers such as Sholem Asch, Oyzer Varshavksi, and Joseph Milbauer used to drop by La Rotonde, perhaps on their way from or to the Triangle, a Yiddish bookshop and publishing house just a short walk away.

A mathematician named Kiveliovitch ran the Triangle Press and Bookstore at 6 rue Stanislas. In a former life he had been a student of the legendary French mathematician Jacques Hadamard. To attract the La Ruche crowd, the Triangle published a series of booklets about famous Jewish artists, short monographs with black and white reproductions. Jacques Loutchansky, Adolf Féder, Leopold Gottlieb, Moïse Kisling, Pinchus Krémègne, Jacques Lipschitz, Marc Chagall, and Abraham Mintchine came regularly to leaf through the stacks in the single narrow room. Some of the artists of the Beehive and its surroundings became subjects for the monographs, which are now bibliophilic rarities.

One day the Marxist-Zionist activist Y. Nayman sprinted into the store and breathlessly announced that the previous Sunday he had seen the Jewish sculptor Marek Szwarc kneeling in prayer at the Sacré-Coeur in Montmartre. A scandal! Szwarc had fallen off the path, which came as a surprise to his coreligionists. Jewishness, for most of the Jews in Montparnasse, was mainly an identity imposed upon them by anti-Semitic prejudice, but Szwarc's Jewishness had been fuller. He practiced Judaism and was an active member of the small observant cohort at La Ruche. For a few years in the early 1910s, he, Henri Epstein, Moissey Kogan, and other yarmulke-clad residents of the hive founded and ran *Makhmadim*, a publication dedicated to defining Jewish art that was funded by the influential Russian art critic Vladimir Stassov. (The title means "delicacies" or "precious things" in Yiddish and Hebrew.) The series had no text and featured only reproductions of drawings by Jewish artists. The issues were thematically devoted to occasions on the Jewish calendar, such as the Sabbath and the holidays. This was an attempt to give some substance to the appellation "Jewish School," so often used by the critics of the period. The series is now even rarer than the Triangle's publications.

The squalor of the war years was undeniable but not always unpleasant. The Russian artist Chana Orloff, with whom Soutine would form a close friendship in later years, recalled the era fondly: "During the war [of 1914–1918] it was marvelous. It is shameful to say so. The place where I worked to earn my livelihood was closed. I was doing fashion sketches when the French government organized federal aid for artists. We received twenty-six centimes a day as well as meals in cantines. It was an ideal life. I could work on my sculpture night and day without trying to earn anything."[15] It is likely that whatever state benefits were granted to Orloff were also doled into Soutine's open palms, since the two were both Russian nationals and so would have been equally eligible. The funds would have been keenly welcome, since the stipend that Dr. Rafelkess had been forwarding to Soutine from Vilna halted abruptly when the Germans invaded Lithuania in July of 1915.[16]

In 1915, the sculptor Jacques Lipschitz did Soutine the enormous favor of introducing him to Amedeo Modigliani, thus initiating what was arguably the most important relationship of Soutine's personal and professional life.[17] From then until just before Modigliani's death in 1918, the two were inseparable. Modigliani's devotion conferred numerous benefits, including a front row seat to his dramatic and glamorous antics—glamorous, that is, before his inevitable nightly devolution into a drunken slovenliness. Vassilieff, like everyone else, adored Modigliani, and he tested this adoration regularly by wreaking havoc while grotesquely drunk. Marevna, who wrote a lively but not always reliable memoir of life at La Ruche, recalls one evening at the canteen when Modi (which is what everyone called him) stripped naked while reciting Dante—in Italian, he was from Livorno—to the frantic delight of giggling American girls.

It is certain that the war years were sweetened for Soutine by the sudden and overwhelming influence of his friendship with Modigliani. In *Cors de Chasse*, his memoir of his time in Paris, the artist Gabriel Fournier described the budding brotherhood: "Soutine grew in Modigliani's shadow. [Modigliani] lavished attention on Soutine that was almost paternal. Their mutual affection was touching, to the point that, when left alone, Soutine seemed almost like a lost child in search of his friend."[18] They were, at least in appearance, opposites, and onlookers constantly raised their eyebrows at the pair—one cultivated, suave, and devastatingly handsome, the other sickly and painfully lacking in social graces with barely passable French. Acquaintances who knew Soutine in those early years invariably recall his deplorable hygiene; William Fifield, the author of Modigliani's first biography, claimed that

Soutine suffered from "filthophilia."[19] Modigliani, in contrast, radiated a kind of princeliness, even when he could hardly afford to feed himself: "Modigliani, at his most destitute, never looked poor. His suit would be clean, his shirt, which he had washed the night before, rumpled but otherwise presentable, his shoes cleaned, and no one knew how he managed, but every morning, bright and early, he was shaved and ready for work. Modigliani the outgoing, vivacious intellectual and this diamond in the rough took one look at each other and became friends. Soutine said, 'He gave me confidence in myself.'"[20]

Something else distinguished the two men from one another: By the time of their meeting, Modigliani, although not yet famous or sought after (this status was conferred upon him only after his early death), was, within the confines of the Montparnasse bubble, acknowledged as a great artist and revered by the small, increasingly significant School of Paris. Even while destitute, his charisma inspired loyalty, and in those years loyalty was worth a lot. With these powers, he gifted Soutine his start. Modigliani was the first and only one of Soutine's peers to advocate for him, to proclaim his genius, and to shepherd him from obscurity toward a glowing career. Soutine's debt to his friend was singular.

It is possible that he never forgave Modigliani for this magnanimous act of charity. From all we can ascertain about Soutine's character, he was zealous about his own creative autonomy and independence, and he found debts of any kind infuriating and stultifying. The novelist and journalist Emil Szittya, who knew Soutine and Modigliani and analyzed their strange bond, had a sinister impression of Soutine's conception of his friend:

They drank and they went hungry together. Modigliani had sympathy for all those from Slavic countries and he loved to paint them. He declared one day to Soutine: "I love you because you are a pain in the ass." Soutine was jealous of Modigliani, even for his capacity to drink. . . . Soutine enviously examined the paintings of his successful friend. . . . Although he was the first of the Montparnasse group to take Soutine seriously and to defend him, after the death of the Italian, [Soutine] spoke of him only with hatred. He maintained that Modigliani had wanted to destroy him, and had led him to drink for this purpose.[21]

Modigliani was born in Tuscany and raised in Livorno by Sephardic Jewish parents who spoke French as well as Italian and some Hebrew. Sephardic Jews, or Spanish Portuguese Jews from the Iberian Peninsula, are markedly different in their customs from their Ashkenazi, or eastern European, brethren. Prayer, kashrut, the observance of essential holidays—all vary significantly between the two groups. This distinction was even more pronounced at the beginning of the twentieth century in Paris, which had just been flooded by a mass of Ashkenazi Jews fleeing a fresh spate of pogroms in Russia. Fifield notes that Modigliani did not *look* Jewish, by which he means that he did not look Ashkenazi.[22] Fifield's characterization is representative: It is impossible to ignore the specifically anti-Ashkenazi anti-Semitism that colored the adoration of the Sephardic Modigliani and undergirded the shameless contrasts drawn between him and Soutine by both their contemporary onlookers and the biographers who recorded the juxtaposition.

Modigliani was intensely proud of his Jewish heritage, just as his mother had taught him to be. She, Eugenie Garsin-Modigliani, had written *L'histoire de notre famille*, an account of her and her husband's lineages going back to the late 1700s and through to Modigliani's birth in 1884.[23] His mother insisted that she could trace her lineage directly to the great philosopher Baruch Spinoza's family—Portuguese Jews who lived as Marranos, or crypto-Jews, in Portugal and France until they relocated to Amsterdam, in the tolerant Dutch Republic, in the early seventeenth century. They were indeed related to a woman named Regina Spinoza, who spoke the Sephardic Jewish dialect Ladino, so perhaps this origin story was true. Jeanne Modigliani, Amedeo's daughter, who became a historian of Italian Jewish history, insists that her family was also related to Uriel da Costa, the tragic seventeenth-century apostate, and Moses Mendelssohn, the paragon of religion in modern German Jewry.[24] Regardless of whether these claims are true (it seems fantastic that figures as significant and distinct as da Costa, who was born Christian, and Mendelssohn could have been related to each other), it is evident that the family placed itself in the upper echelons of a Sephardic enlightenment tradition. Perhaps Soutine's Jewishness somewhat inspired Modigliani's dedication. In any case, he clearly esteemed Soutine, considered him a genius, and was intent on utilizing his own charms and social capital to secure support for him. If gratitude for charity was a virtue of which Soutine was incapable, Modigliani gave him grounds for discomfort.

Modigliani moved to Paris in 1906 and a few years later fell in with the growing School of Paris that held court at La Ruche. He was invariably destitute and suffered terribly from the tuberculosis that eventually killed him. The disease, which then had no cure, made earning a living even more impossible than it would have been for an immigrant artist. However, in 1913 lightning struck: The British sculptor Jacob Epstein introduced Modi to the Welsh painter Augustus John, who, taken by Modigliani's sculptures, bought two of them. This acquisition funded a trip home to Italy to visit his family, which is why Modigliani did not meet Soutine until the following year, after his return to France.

Modigliani had been living in Paris for nine years before he finally found a dealer. Guillaume Chéron had a gallery on the rue la Boétie. Chéron had worked first as a bookmaker and then as a wine merchant in the South of France. He became interested in the art market after marrying the daughter of the well-known dealer André Devambez, at which time he moved to the capital. He was not a romantic man, pledged to the stewardship of great art, but, to borrow a joke from Robert Hughes, instead believed that the only thing for a painting to do is hang on a wall and become more expensive. His interest in young, desperate artists was primarily mercenary. He printed the following analysis in a financial brochure: "The painting has become a veritable value of speculation that, taken at its emission, that is to say at the beginning of a young talent full of promise, represents an operation of the first order. There is not an instance where a collection patiently and intelligently formed, then dispersed ten or fifteen years later, has not realized a plus-value representing five to ten times its purchase price. What other financial investment can say as much?"[25]

Chéron employed a school of artists, each of whom he paid fifteen francs a day in exchange for which they were expected to produce, daily, a full-size picture. This mind-numbing form of labor was nonetheless better than nothing, and Modigliani ensured that his new agent took on Soutine as soon as he could. Fifield chillingly described the factory-*cum*-studio where Chéron's artists were made to work:

> The merchant locked [Modigliani] in the cellar at his place on rue la Boétie with his servant girl, who would serve as model, and a bottle of marc, absinthe just now having been suppressed. Kicks on the door; and he would be let up, it being understood the picture was finished. One day, as a collage, [Modigliani] glued a phrase of a folk song around a picture in a halo; and Chéron replaced it with lines of Baudelaire, which Modigliani ought to have thought an improvement. "No!" he said, when he saw it, "Sheephead!" "If I am a sheephead I won't handle you." "Lick my ass," Modigliani said.[26]

A later biographer of Modigliani, Meryle Secrest, has pointed out that, while it is true the studio was located in the basement, the same space contained a dining room in which Chéron and his guests would have lunch each day, so myths of incarcerations in dank dungeon-like studios are exaggerations. (Still, there are few less accommodating places to set up an easel than a room with no windows, no matter how well appointed it is.) Whether the conditions were as dramatic as some historians have claimed, and whether the rupture was as nasty as Fifield describes it, Modigliani's time under Chéron's care was limited to a year or two.

There were echelons in the Parisian art world, and the School of Paris was on the bottom rung. One could be a rising star among the artists at La Ruche and be totally unheard of among a higher order of gallerists, and certainly among the dealers who serviced the wealthiest families in the city. Fame in the immigrant community did not mean fame in the establishment. Picasso, like many of the residents at La Ruche, was not a French native, but his influence and renown were so powerful that he cannot be grouped with others of similar backgrounds. It is a testament to Modigliani's success that Picasso knew him and respected him. And with Picasso's respect came the loyalty of the members of his group, among them the poet Max Jacob. Jacob, born to a Jewish family in Quimper, wrestled all his life with both his faith and his sexuality—he was a homosexual who vacillated wildly between an enthusiastically debauched life of the senses and total commitment to a severe Catholicism to which he eventually converted. Picasso, who was the love of his life, acted as godfather at the conversion ceremony. Jacob was an intensely social person, very well connected and respected among the artists and dealers in Paris, and when he heard that Modigliani had left Chéron's stable, he took it upon himself to connect the agentless artist with Paul Guillaume.

Guillaume was a fascinating and significant figure in his day, and he is remembered still as one of the most influential French art dealers of the twentieth century. His enormous collection, which includes the second-largest public collection of Soutine paintings in the world, is preserved in its entirety at the Musée de l'Orangerie, just a ten-minute walk along the Seine from the Louvre. There is no more significant collection of Soutines in the world, in terms of both breadth and symbolism. Though the Barnes collection in Philadelphia is almost as large, Guillaume's Soutine collection spans the entirety of Soutine's oeuvre, from 1919 to

1934, whereas Barnes never bought a Soutine after 1925. Because of Guillaume's early and devoted collecting, and because the collection is preserved in the heart of Paris in the same stretch of the city as the Louvre, the entire room dedicated to Soutine in the Orangerie establishes Soutine's permanent place in the pantheon of Parisian art. The curators placed all the Soutines on view at any given time in the same room. Thus, Paris always contains a mini retrospective of Soutine's work. Few artists in the world have such an honor, and it is Soutine's lot solely because of Paul Guillaume. Soutine himself could not possibly have hoped for more. It was through Modigliani that Guillaume first formed an attachment to Soutine that would last for the rest of Soutine's life.

For all these reasons, it is important to understand who Guillaume was and how he became that person. Purely by virtue of Guillaume's exquisite taste and capacity to promote the work that fascinated him, he rose rapidly from obscurity to a dealer with an international clientele. It was precisely his interest in the works by Soutine, Picasso, Matisse, Modigliani, and others in their cohort that fueled his rise to international prominence and renown. He saw before any other dealer the investment opportunity in the iconoclasms being perpetrated by these immigrant painters.

First-class art dealers like Nathan Wildenstein, Ernest and René Gimpel, and Jacques Seligmann, who catered to the wealthiest French families and dealt primarily in eighteenth-century French fine art, were not interested in the foreign riffraff agitating several rungs below them on the social ladder. Ambroise Vollard, the famous and fearsome dealer who represented Cézanne and Renoir, had shuttered his gallery for the duration of the war. He spent those years in Spain and Switzerland lecturing on behalf of the French Information Service.[27] Still, his artists were not ready to take a chance on an agent as inexperienced as Guillaume—not yet. At the same time, established avant-garde artists, like Matisse and Picasso, already had representation. But artists who, like Modigliani, inspired enthusiasm and confidence even though they had not yet achieved any kind of market success were prime candidates for Guillaume's stewardship. It is a testament to Modigliani's social success that before the year was over, Max Jacob had facilitated his introduction to Guillaume. Jacob admired Modigliani. After his early death, the poet described him warmly: "He could be a charming companion, laugh like a child, and be lyrical in translating Dante, making one love and understand him. He was courteous. That was his real nature, but nevertheless he was just as often crazily irritable, sensitive, and annoyed for some reason he didn't know himself."[28]

Jacob's plan required some tact. Guillaume was a proud man, and Jacob, cunning as ever, was aware that he could not simply instruct him to take on a client. Guillaume needed to make the choice himself. At least, he needed to think that he had. Accounts differ on the specifics of the scheme, but it is certain that something like the following was arranged: Jacob scheduled a meeting with Guillaume at Le Dôme and told Modigliani to arrive at the appointed spot ahead of time with a portfolio of his drawings ostentatiously displayed on the table. Guillaume spotted the work, was intrigued, and sat himself down by Modigliani's side, just as Jacob predicted he would. A partnership soon blossomed.[29]

Guillaume was born in Paris on November 28, 1891, to parents who had left the region of Haute-Saône in northeastern France to marry and raise a family in the capital. They were among the first generation of young French people who left their hometowns to seek fortune in the City of Light. His father was a *garçon de recettes*, or uniformed bank messenger, a position sufficiently comfortable that his bride had no need to work. However, in 1904, when Paul was thirteen years old, his father died at the age of forty-five. This tragedy shunted Paul swiftly out of childhood into the role of breadwinner for his mother and two sisters. He detested the world in which he was then trapped and began looking for a path toward a more glamorous milieu. Even at that tender age, he was conscious of the drama unfolding in the art world. The same year his father died, the Salon d'Automne exhibited a retrospective of Cézanne and Renoir. The following year, an entourage of daring painters led by a young Matisse submitted paintings in hot, bright colors to the Salon d'Automne. And Guillaume recalled the moment that Louis Vauxcelles wrote, of a Renaissance statue that happened to be placed in the same room as these radical works, "Mais c'est Donatello parmi les Fauves." *But it is Donatello among the wild beasts.* The birth of Fauvism changed Guillaume's life.

After his father's passing, Paul Guillaume and his small family lived in the ninth arrondissement, which cradles Montmartre. His artistic education began in the neighborhood cafés, which were frequented by the artists, critics, and poets who held court at the Bateau-Lavoir, a dilapidated shack that was subdivided into twenty studios. The name literally means "washhouse boat," and it was thus christened by Max Jacob because the noise it made while swaying in the wind was reminiscent of the creaking wash-boats buffeted to and fro on the Seine. Picasso, Apollinaire, André Salmon, Max Jacob, Maurice Raynal, André Derain, and Maurice de Vlaminck would discuss the trajectory of modern art and the dramas wracking the art world while the young Guillaume listened quietly in a corner.

As a teenager Guillaume began work in an upscale garage on Avenue de la Grande Armée, which is where he first rubbed shoulders with the upper class. This position facilitated his entry into the sphere into which he planned to matriculate, and it occasioned his first encounter with African art—an introduction that would be almost as significant for the world of modern art as it was for Guillaume himself. One day a shipment of rubber from Gabon happened to contain a glass case displaying an African sculpture that had been included in the cargo. This happenstance ignited an obsession that would sustain Guillaume for the rest of his career. Armed with this precious work, he was able to strike up a relationship with Apollinaire, who put him in contact with the sculptor Joseph Brummer. Brummer owned a boutique of ancient art on Boulevard Raspail. Thus, Guillaume's first sale was made.

Over time Guillaume began to make direct contact with correspondents in Africa who called on him at his personal address laden with wooden sculptures from Nigeria and the Congo. He became obsessed with the study of African art and used his modest salary to fund travel to the museums of other countries with renowned collections to buttress his understanding of the field and its history. As his knowledge swelled, so did his network, and he was eventually able to accrue enough connections and cash to wean himself off the job at the garage and support a career entirely within the art market. In 1912, under the pseudonym Guy Romain, he founded La Société des Mélanophiles (Society of

Melanophiles) in order to institutionalize his efforts to raise awareness about African art in France. The aims of the society were as
follows: "Some artists have come together to study the wild soul in
these pacific works; their goal is to acquire an in-depth knowledge
of negro art: the negro art society will strive to collect important
documentation. It will collect, in addition to fetishes and sculpted
wood, all sorts of historical curiosities. Finally, it will organize
trips to the colonies and create a small museum that will interest
artists and scholars."[30]

His hard work and consistent appreciation for excellence won
him the sustained, emphatic support of Apollinaire, who championed Guillaume in the press. He assured his readers that Paul
Guillaume was "a name that all who wish to be aware of the
annals and curiosities of the African Peoples known to us as sav-
ages must know."[31] The society organized trips to Africa and was
active until 1919. Though the organization itself did not last long,
its effects took root: African art was in vogue thanks in large part
to Guillaume's obsessive machinations. Gallerists wanted to show
it, collectors wanted to buy it, and artists turned to it for inspiration and direction.

Guillaume became the most important dealer of African art
in Paris. At the same time he joined a tradition of dealers who
expanded the content and deepened the integrity of their vocation.
Like Ambroise Vollard before him, Guillaume considered it part
of his mission to identify, nurture, and fund fresh talent.[32] The
art market was his to manipulate and deepen as much as it was an
arena in which to make a profit. He contributed to the culture.

His first gallery, Galerie Paul Guillaume, at 6 rue de
Miromesnil, was modest. It opened its doors in February 1914,

an inopportune year to attempt a grand venture. The opening was not a memorable party, though a few well-known artists like Giorgio de Chirico and Francis Picabia put in appearances. The very first exhibition held at the gallery featured two Russian artists, Nathalie Gontcharova and Michel Larionov, who had both participated in the exhibition *L'Union des artistes russes*, which Diaghilev had organized in Saint Petersburg.[33] The influential critic Waldemar George later rhapsodized about the event, "Paul Guillaume, who was not yet a master of elegance though his star soared in the firmament of trade in African paintings and sculpture, bid welcome to his guests. His paradoxical spirit was a bit off putting, but his audacity and erudition fascinated all the collectors. He chatted with Paul Poiret, that dictator of taste who, in just a matter of years, had revised the values and standards of decorative art and haute couture. . . . The gallery was the focal point of world painting."[34]

Still, making inroads was slow work. Eventually Picasso lost his old dealer, Daniel-Henry Kahnweiler, after the latter was forced to leave the country during the war due to his German citizenship. Thus, Picasso was in need of new representation. Members of his gang were on the lookout for a suitable replacement, and André Level wrote to Apollinaire in 1917, "[Léonce] Rosenberg [Guillaume's chief competitor, the other notable up-and-coming gallerist] as well as Paul Guillaume strike me as having a future, the one as much as the other. I like the decisiveness and faith of the former. I know the latter less well but have already had occasion to appreciate his taste, which is discerning and not without assurance, as my purchases from him bear out."[35]

Picasso eventually selected Léonce Rosenberg, and Guillaume had to look elsewhere for his first star artist. It did not take him long. After the war he managed to persuade André Derain to abandon Kahnweiler, which was his first major breakthrough, and the relationship proved a success for both agent and artist. Under Guillaume's guidance, Derain's star skyrocketed. Significantly for our story, Guillaume also courted and won the confidence of the wealthy art collector Alfred Barnes, who would in time become among the most important people in Soutine's life, though they met only once.

Paul Guillaume's meteoric rise can be attributed at least in part to his impeccable presentation, often remarked upon, always exquisite. It was a virtue he did not share with Modigliani or Soutine. The story goes that one day he arrived at Modigliani's apartment, found the artist still asleep, and shook him awake. Bleary-eyed and visibly hungover, Modi explained that he had spent the previous night drinking until the wee hours, and asked the agent to wait while he washed and dressed. Guillaume watched in horror as the artist used a handless mug in lieu of a chamber pot, took that same vessel out into the hall, where the sink was located, emptied its contents, filled it with fresh water, and, in front of the aghast Guillaume, rinsed his mouth with the contents.

The partnership between Modi and Guillaume was mutually profitable, though it did not last long, or at least it soon changed shape. Modigliani found a new agent, Léopold Zborowski, within two years. By 1917 he had moved out of the studio in which Guillaume had installed him in the Bateau-Lavoir and had set up shop in a two-bedroom walk-up in the heart of Montparnasse. Still, Guillaume continued to carry Modigliani's work in his gallery, and after the artist's death he was proud to proclaim in print that it was he who had made Modigliani a household name in Paris.

Guillaume never did take Soutine on as a client. He complained that Soutine shirked "all the vain hygienic practices favored by our century. . . . It is an article of faith to him that ablution is a heresy." Many accounts confirm this testimony, especially accounts from Soutine's early years. Soutine used Chéron's headquarters as his official address through 1917.[36] However, Guillaume certainly heard about Soutine through Modigliani, and he carried Soutine's paintings in his gallery. That association would prove transformative for Soutine.

Professionally, then, Soutine was deeply indebted to Modigliani. But there was a dark price for those benefits. Modigliani's excesses were a rite of passage for a certain kind of Parisian bohemian, and if one wanted to bask in his aura, one had to be prepared to drink for it. The pair's early, desperate years of friendship were drenched in alcohol, a vice that Soutine, with his stomach ulcers and weak health, could not afford to indulge. Later he would blame Modigliani for his period of drunken debauchery.

All the politics and the socializing and the overwhelming wealth of cultural riches were, for Soutine, merely context for his work. Modigliani met Soutine when Soutine was hardly at the cusp of developing his own relationship with painting, but what he saw was enough to convince him of his friend's worth. Soutine was grateful for the friendship and for the community that came with it, but Modigliani's drunken revelries were also distractions for him. He had come to Paris to paint, and painting was his way of life. For him, exhilarations on dance floors and barstools were nothing compared to his rushes in the studio.

As would become clearer, painting was not a social activity for Soutine. His painter friends went to La Rotonde as much to discuss painting as to drink and eat. Making art was a dialogical exercise for them. This was profoundly untrue for Soutine. He was not interested in what the other painters were doing, what they were thinking about, what they were looking at and attempting to convey. Even Modigliani's interest in Soutine was an interest Soutine could not understand because he was not curious about his peers.

Soutine's paintings are always, from the first straight through to the last, attempts to communicate a vibrancy that he saw in front of him. They are articulations of energy. He painted only from life, never from memory, never from a photograph, never even directly from the Old Master paintings he so revered, as so many artists have and do. A full understanding of Soutine's interests renders this pattern totally logical: It would have been nonsensical for him to paint any other way, since the very essence of his work, the lifelong project, was to convey through paint the vitality of the world he lived in, the charges that ran through it and energized it. This also explains why there are hardly any drawings in his hand that remain, and why so many of his acquaintances recall that he never drew but put brush to canvas straight on without peremptory sketches. It is useful to think of Soutine's paintings as pantheistic. Something sacred energizes every rendered object and sensation. And every object, every stretch of air, is uncannily and often disturbingly alive in Soutine's paintings. This all-overness is conveyed with different degrees of urgency and tact over the course of his oeuvre, but it is synonymous with his name. The great art historian Élie Faure noticed these energies and their semireligious quality: "I will be accused of lacking spirituality if I write that the matter in painting is all the painting, consequently all the spirit. . . . I know that if this fire burns at the hearth of the matter, as vile as it is, it will radiate to the limits of spiritual space as the spark of god. Soutine is one of the rare religious painters the world has known because Soutine's material is one of the most carnal that painting has expressed."[37]

This strange, even paradoxical duality—the extreme tactility of his paintings, and the spirituality communicated through that materiality—is unique to Soutine. He freezes flux and churning through paint, through a plastic, static substance. He saw energy in all things, animate or not. Never in any period of his career does this fantastic vitalism abate, though the aspects of vitality that he chose to focus on, or the techniques that he used to facilitate that communication, did change significantly over time. He had many influences, most of them from the French classical tradition, though he held no painter in higher regard than Rembrandt.

The earliest of Soutine's paintings that we have are from 1915.[38] These works constitute the first period of note, though most accounts of Soutine scholars consider his Céret period (1918–1920) his earliest of significance. This is understandable given that it was the Céret works which first earned him international recognition and acclaim. Still, he had already cultivated a distinct style before Céret, from which the Céret period marked a violent departure, and so these earlier canvases must be considered on their own terms, wholly distinct from later periods.

His three primary influences during those first years in Paris were Cézanne, Van Gogh, and Pierre Bonnard. Cézanne's and Van Gogh's influences are obvious—one sees them in the chosen subjects, in the handling of paint and the rendering of shapes, and also in the choice of colors. There is no greater example of painted energies than Cézanne's hatched and charged brushstrokes, and no more iconic example of painted agitation than Van Gogh's. Clearly these precedents informed Soutine's approach. Bonnard's influence is no less essential, though a little more difficult to identify. He is the only contemporary painter whose traces are visible in Soutine's work for a sustained period, and those traces are most obvious in the still lifes of flowers done during the early years. The use of color, its vibrancy, clarity, and the remarkably creative and unexpected juxtapositions, are all informed by Bonnard's palette. The application of the colors, too, the "surface quality of the brush-strokes," bear Bonnard's influence.[39]

Soutine's later paintings are astonishingly cohesive, by which I mean that each one looks like a single organism. All the objects and spaces are smoothly fitted into one another, reminiscent of knotted veins, or of the bones in a skeleton. And while all the elements are distinctly delineated, they seem to be made of the same material and charged by the same energies. Every stretch of canvas is lavished with equal attention. In the earliest paintings, the cohesion is much more attenuated. He has not yet developed the "all-over" quality that invigorates his later works. In *Still Life with Lemons* (1916), a painting that awkwardly translates Cézanne's formalism, the lemons, the bottle, and the table on which they sit are all rendered in a way that resembles how those objects would have looked placed on a table in front of the artist. Whereas later, what interests Soutine most is how the objects in the painting relate to one another and how they create a pulsing harmony within the picture plane, on this canvas he is obviously concerned with verisimilitude.

Consider the pair of paintings of a flight of red stairs in Cagnes-sur-Mer that Soutine painted five years apart (the earlier of which is now in an anonymous private collection and the second is in the Museum of Modern Art in Moscow). In the early painting, completed in 1918 during Soutine's first trip to the South of France, he took pains to reproduce the shapes and colors as they would have appeared to him. This realism is reminiscent of Utrillo. In the second painting, Soutine has distorted all the objects and intensified all the colors. It is more vibrant, freer, and the harmony is charged with an intensity lacking in the earlier version. The verticality of the red steps is more emphatic and directional. It would be a mistake to interpret this development as symptomatic of a waning interest in representation. It is not that rendering likeness became less important to him—Soutine was *always* trying to communicate the energies in front of him. But later he achieved a greater freedom to articulate less obvious aspects of reality—relations and not just objects—and he was able to do so with greater felicity.

In the early years, though, Soutine was choosing realistic colors. The liberties he took were related to composition and paint application.

CHAPTER 3

Fleeing Southward

SOUTINE AND THE OTHER ARTISTS WHO REMAINED IN Paris during the Great War grappled with the pace of technological change that had swiftly reshaped so much of human life, as the mechanisms of war itself made grotesquely plain. Like the factory workers who went on strike as the cost of living skyrocketed, artists had to develop new capacities for working in wartime. They, too, had to produce, just like the brickmakers and the bakers did. Ravel completed *Le Tombeau de Couperin* in Paris in 1917, not far from where Proust, sickly and holed up in his home, labored to finish the second volume of *In Search of Lost Time*. That same year, Diaghilev persuaded Cocteau, Picasso, Massine, and Satie to together create *Parade* for the Ballets Russes, which was stranded in Paris during the war. Life went mercilessly on, faster and louder, perhaps, than it had before.

For Soutine, like the others from remote backwaters of eastern Europe, the encounter with the brutishness of contemporary technology was acutely disconcerting. He had been thrown into a major metropolis during a period of rapid transition: Modernity was breathing down everybody's necks, and it was especially jarring for the twenty-four-year-old from Smilovichi who not four years earlier had never even been in a city with an art museum or a subway system. His life now bore no resemblance to anything he had imagined human life could be, and industrialization was changing the shape of almost everything and the lived experience of almost everyone. And there were other differences too: Soutine was now part of a collective that talked about these changes with sophistication and avidity—his friends were not only artists but intellectuals. This new cohort considered themselves implicated by modernity because they believed themselves to be tasked with understanding it and speeding it up and deepening it. They weren't just affected by the pace of change; they were contributing to it. Their easels and their writing tables were the laboratories of modern art and modern thought.

In his memoir, the celebrated Soviet writer Ilya Ehrenburg transcribed a conversation that took place in 1917 among several members of Soutine's community. Soutine himself was absent (was he visiting Kikoine and his wife outside Paris? Or working late to meet his daily painting quota set by the exacting Chéron?), though Modigliani brings him up over the course of the conversation, as he was wont to do. Ehrenburg, Modigliani, and the model Margot were sipping drinks together at La Rotonde that evening. When the Mexican artist Diego Rivera ducked in, they motioned for him to join them. Rivera was meeting a group—the

Russian poet Max Voloshin, the Russian writer and revolutionary Boris Savinkov, the Polish Socialist Edward Lipinski, and the
artist Fernand Léger. The whole lot had to push together several
of the café's square, rickety tables and pull up a number of worn
wooden chairs in order for everyone to fit comfortably. The next
several hours were whiled away making conversation and downing
several bottles of alcohol. They stayed till closing time, after which
Modigliani invited the crowd back to his place for more of the
same merriment. The troop collected their hats and coats from the
hooks nailed to the great pillars holding up the place, and followed
Modi to his cramped, paint-stained apartment, where the following conversation took place:

Léger: The war will soon be over. The soldiers don't want to go
on fighting. The Germans, too, will realize that it's senseless.
Germans always think more slowly, but they are bound to
realize it. It will be necessary to rebuild the devastated areas
and countries. I think the politicians will be driven out:
They are bankrupt. Engineers, technicians, perhaps workers,
too, will replace them. Of course Renoir is a good artist, but
it is difficult to believe that he is living in our day. Tanks and
Renoir? Where should the inspiration come from? Science,
technology, labor. Sport, too.

Voloshin: I don't believe that's enough for people. Can Europe
be transformed into America? The war has ploughed up not
only Picardy but the very heart of man. Hobbes called the
State "the Leviathan." Men can become automatic tigers;
they've had experience of it and they've acquired the taste.

I prefer Léger's canvases to machines. Being the slave of inanimate creatures doesn't appeal to me.

Modigliani: You're all a lot of bloody innocents. Do you think anyone's going to say to you: "My dear fellows, take your choice"? The only people who make a choice today are the ones with self-inflicted wounds, and they get shot for it. When the war is over everyone will be put in prison. Nostradamus was right, everyone will have to put on convicts' uniforms. At the very most, the academics will be entitled to wear checkered trousers instead of striped ones.

Léger: No. People have changed. They are waking up.

Lipinski: That's true. Of course, capitalism cannot create anything any more, it can only destroy. But consciousness is growing. Perhaps we're on the eve of decision. No one knows where it will start: In Paris, in the trenches, or in Petersburg.

Savinkov: "Consciousness" is a myth. In Germany there were a lot of socialists, but when they heard "*eins, zwei*" they started marching pretty fast. The worst is still ahead.

Lipinski: No, the worst is behind us. The Socialists can—

Modigliani: Do you know what the Socialists are like? Bald-headed parrots. I said so to my brother. Please don't take offense: The Socialists are better than the rest all the same. But you don't understand anything. Thomas a Minister!

What's the difference between Mussolini and Cadorna? Rubbish! Soutine has painted a marvelous portrait. There's a Rembrandt, believe it or not. But he'll be put behind bars like everyone else. Listen (this was to Léger), you want to organize the world. But the world can't be measured with a rule. There are people—

Léger: There were good painters in the past, too. We need a new approach. Art will survive if it finds the language of the modern world.

Rivera: No one in Paris needs art. Paris is dying. Art is dying. Zapata's peasants never saw a machine in their lives, but they are a hundred times more modern than Poincaré [the president of France]. I am sure that if we were to show them our art, they would understand it. Who built the Gothic cathedrals and the Aztec temples? Everybody. And for everybody. Ilya, you're a pessimist because you're too civilized. Art needs to swallow a mouthful of barbarity. Negro sculpture saved Picasso. Soon you'll all go to the Congo or to Peru. A school of savagery is what is wanted.

Ehrenburg: There's enough savagery where we are. I don't care for exoticism. Who'll go to the Congo? The Zetlins, perhaps Max [Voloshin], to write another cycle of sonnets. I detest machines. What's wanted is goodness. When I see posters advertising Cadum soap, I know that the baby surrounded by soap bubbles is pure and good. How terrible that Hindenburg and Poincaré were babies too.

Rivera: You're a European, and that is your misfortune. Europe is at its last gasp. The Americans will come, the Asians and the Africans . . .

Savinkov: The Americans will soon declare war and land. What Asians do you mean? The Japanese?

Rivera: For all I know.[1]

This was the sort of conversation that filled the rooms in which Soutine painted, drank, and, when he could get his hands on food, ate. These men and women made up the milieu in which he became a Parisian.

His friend Rivera was right, at least in part: The Americans did indeed join the war in December of that year, but peace was still a long way off. On March 12, 1918, nine squadrons of German airplanes dropped bombs over the city of Paris and its surrounding suburbs. Soutine would have felt the ground tremble if he was locked away in Chéron's cellar. Outside, 34 people were killed by the bombs themselves and 79 were injured. In the mad crush to board the subways, an additional 66 people were suffocated to death, most of them women and children. The official report of the raid reads, "According to the first news, nearly sixty enemy airplanes succeeded in crossing our lines. Thanks to the curtain fire which our artillery maintained throughout the raid with great intensity, a certain number of the machines failed to reach their objectives. Nevertheless numerous bombs were dropped on Paris and its suburbs. Several buildings were demolished and took fire."[2]

The gruesome coupling of technological advancement with human brutality reached a new zenith during World War I, and Soutine was there to witness it (though he never considered it his responsibility as an artist to document the war). As part of those macabre innovations, between 1917 and 1918 a German arms manufacturer developed a new kind of cannon, similar to Big Bertha and often confused with it, called "The Paris Gun," so named because it had been designed specifically to shell Paris from 120 kilometers away—a distance then unheard of and unimaginable. This weapon was fired on the city for several months beginning on March 23, 1918 (just two days before Claude Debussy died in Paris of a long illness). The first round made landfall at 7:18 a.m., and over the next several hours twenty more were fired at fifteen-minute intervals. One of the bombs hit the northern facade of the church of Saint-Gervais, about four kilometers from Chéron's studio, on the same side of the Seine. The bomb killed 91 parishioners, 52 women among them, and injured 68. Between March 23 and August 9, 183 projectiles were launched on the city. Deaths totaled 256, and 620 people were injured.[3]

During these same months a particularly lethal strain of influenza was brought over to Europe from America. US soldiers had contracted it in a training camp in Kansas in March and carried it across the ocean. By autumn it had infected most of France. This flu claimed thirty thousand lives in Paris. By the time the epidemic had run its course, a third of the global population had been infected with it, and worldwide thirty million people had died (among them a promising young artist in Vienna named Egon Schiele).[4] Given the close quarters in which Soutine lived and worked, and the fact that he could afford neither soap nor water for washing at regular intervals, it is a small miracle that he was not among the dead.

To escape the blood, bombing, and pestilence, thousands of Parisians queued at the railway stations hoping to secure safe passage out of the city. Ticket sales were frozen at the Gare Montparnasse due to excessive demand. Modigliani's agent, Léopold Zborowski, was among those planning to vacate Paris. Modigliani had presented Soutine to Zborowski in 1916 and begged him to represent Soutine, which Zborowski grudgingly agreed to do. He and his wife, Anna, did not like Soutine and resented that the two painters were a package deal, but Zborowski saw that Modigliani could not be acquired unless Soutine came with him. This, apparently, went as far as bringing Soutine along with them when the group fled Paris. Once more Soutine was indebted to Modigliani for introducing him to a man who would change his life: Zborowski would oversee Soutine's affairs until the agent's death two decades later. So, in 1918, Zborowski rounded up his wife, Anna, Modigliani and his lover, Jeanne Hébuterne, Jeanne's mother, and Soutine, and took them all on a trip to the Côte d'Azur. This timely change of scene was funded by a wealthy man named Jonas Netter, who had recently developed what would blossom into a sustained, expensive interest in Modigliani and then in Soutine as well.

Netter, a Jew from Alsace, was a quiet, modest man who didn't like to attract attention. He played music prodigiously and could have had a career as a pianist, though his shy demeanor predisposed him to private office life.[5] Netter represented successful French manufacturing firms in the export-import business, and he did it well enough to accrue a fortune large enough to sate his thirst for excellent modern art. His son Gérard recalled that his father began collecting paintings after happening upon Zborowski's offices: "When my father saw two Utrillos and a Modigliani hanging in [Zborowski's] salon he bought them immediately. It was a *coup de foudre*. He kept going back and ended up buying up the whole of the School of Paris."

But Jonas Netter's relations with Zborowski were rather tormented. The agent, certain that Netter's obsessive interest in the painters he supported would not waver, constantly went back on their verbal agreements. And Zborowski was making a safe bet: Netter's dedication to the arts only intensified. His love for Modigliani in particular reached wild proportions. Netter bought his first Modigliani canvas in 1915 and went on to buy another fifty-one over the next several years. In the end his collection accounted for about 15 percent of Modigliani's total production—a massive amount for any one collector. Zborowski could count on Netter to pay large sums in order to keep Modi and his friends safe away from Paris and supplied with paint and brushes.

Modigliani wasn't the only artist to whom Netter was devoted. He adored Soutine, too, and this fact was sometimes discomfiting to Zborowski, who disliked Soutine immensely. Netter and Zborowski had a deal: Netter would provide Zborowski with regular funding, and periodically Netter would recommend a painter whom he expected Zborowski to take on in exchange for continued support. Soutine was Netter's cause. He had been among the very first to acquire one of Soutine's paintings, and he believed in him. But despite Modigliani's protestations, Zborowski's dislike for Soutine was intractable—and exacerbated by Anna Zborowski's complementary aversion to the Smilovichian, whom she found grotesque. It was thanks to Netter's insistence that Soutine was included in the trip, though once they all disembarked in Nice, it appears that Zborowski more or less left Soutine to fend for himself.

Despite the hordes straining to buy tickets at railway stations across Paris (or perhaps because of them), leaving the city at that time was considered an act of cowardice, even or especially for immigrants who had found freedom and sanctuary within its precincts. Gratitude, some thought, was warranted, and gratitude comes with strings. During a war one has a duty to defend one's adopted home. Anyway, shouldn't Soutine have loved the city? It seems sensible to deduce from his biography that he felt a deep loyalty to Paris, since he always returned to it despite fairly regular excursions away (this trip to the Côte d'Azur was the first of several sojourns out of the city and its suburbs since he had arrived there five years earlier). Paris was his refuge, and others, like Blaise Cendrars, who were similarly indebted to the rare, revolutionary cosmopolitanism of the French capital, pledged themselves to Paris as to a second mother. Not Soutine. He was a monomaniac, his religion was art, and the family to which he pledged fealty was the artistic tradition he had encountered in Paris, not Paris itself. He was loyal to the Louvre. It was his *patrie*.

Others noticed this apparent lack of loyalty and commented on it. Cendrars bitterly condemned Zborowski for engineering the retreat: "That damned Zborowski was not afraid to commit this crime for the sake of profit, but was afraid of a few shells dropped by Big Bertha on Paris and had only one desire: to get the hell out of there. Since Modigliani did not want to leave Paris at any price, Zborowski had the cunning to take his painter to a doctor's who declared that Modigliani would have no more than three months to live if he continued drinking as he had been. It's possible the doctor was right. Modigliani stopped protesting and allowed himself to be driven Southward by Zborowski and his entourage."[6]

Modigliani had tuberculosis, a condition that was not improved by his debilitating alcoholism. His friend, the sculptor Ossip Zadkine, was released from the army in 1917 and recalls sitting with Modigliani shortly thereafter: "He was thin and emaciated and could no longer take much alcohol—one glass was enough to make him drunk. But he continued to sit with friends at the table and draw. Occasionally he sang in a hoarse voice; he could hardly get his breath."[7] His health was deteriorating rapidly, a fact that unnerved his friends almost as much as it did his pregnant girlfriend. In those years the sea air was thought to be the best cure for tuberculosis, and it was probably this consideration that inspired Zborowski to relocate his gang to the South of France, with the intention of keeping Modigliani there through the winter of the following year.

Soutine's first big excursion out of Paris lasted several months. Preparations for departure likely took at least a month, so the trip probably began in late April or early June. The artist Foujita and his wife, Fernande Barrey—a model who had sat for Modigliani and Soutine—had also left Paris for the Côte d'Azur during the same period.[8] All of them descended on Nice, where Jeanne Hébuterne and her mother rented an apartment on rue Messéna and Modigliani settled down the block at the Hotel Tarelli at 5 rue de France. Soutine found lodgings close by. Zborowski soon left them all for Paris but would fly down to visit and to pick up paintings to sell.

The entire journey southward, culminating in his arrival in Nice, was transformative for Soutine. He had, of course, made long journeys before—but never to anywhere remotely like the Côte d'Azur. The splendor of the South of France is arresting even for nonartists who lack a cultivated appreciation for beauty. On the ride down Soutine was mesmerized by the hills and houses, which Cézanne had prepared him to appreciate. He stared at the rolling fields and the gentle geometries of the farmhouses and noted with relish the choices the old man had made while converting this landscape into his own, unprecedented vernacular. When at last they arrived in Nice, Soutine was confronted with an intensity of natural beauty the likes of which he had never seen before. The impact of this encounter cannot be overstated; it was deeply affecting for Soutine, an artist for whom the act of painting was no more or less than the activity of straining to express the stirring energies of the outside world on canvas. This journey was as significant for Soutine as industrialization was for the cubists. The raw power of the colors was equaled by the majesty of the mountains that towered over the seaside. This confrontation, this vast sublimity, changed Soutine forever.

Soutine and his comrades soon found other artists, friends from Paris, who had fled to the South for safety just as they had. One of them was the painter Léopold Survage, who had moved there the previous year. Survage found Soutine utterly unsociable and recalled that he "prowled around all day. In the evening, exhausted, he went to sleep at the home of Félicie Cendrars."[9] Félicie Cendrars was a Polish Jew who had met her husband, the poet Blaise, at the University of Bern in 1908. She and Soutine became very close during his stay in the South, in no small part because she spoke Russian and so could communicate with him freely. It would be many years before Soutine's French was good enough to be of any use in conversation. Félicie's presence and amiability were lucky things for him since he needed friends desperately—he was very low on cash, and friendliness was often the only thing that stood between him and an empty stomach. Modigliani was committed to Soutine, of course, but on this trip Modigliani had his own money troubles, and anyway he was distracted by constant bitter arguments with his girlfriend's priggish mother.

Indeed, prowling around all day, as Survage put it, may have been most of what Soutine could afford to do. It is not clear what money he had to live on or to buy painting materials with. The following year he would begin an official business partnership with Zborowski, through which he would be assured a stipend each month, but in 1918 he was still more or less fending for himself.

The entire gang soon uprooted and moved fifteen kilometers southwest to Cagnes-sur-Mer, which had the advantage of being cheaper while still within traveling distance of the friends installed in Nice. There, the Zborowskis, Foujita, and Fernande Barrey rented space from a man named Pere Curel, a trumpet player. Soutine, for his part, rented a small room from a poor family on the edge of town. Despite the low price of living in the town, Soutine spent much of his time there hungry. Fernande Barrey recalled:

We had not seen Soutine for two days, so Foujita and I went to see what was going on with him. We arrived in front of the house situated on the side of Cagnes, and called to him from outside. His head appeared in the opening of a sky-light. "I can't come down!" he cried to us, "Zborowski has not returned. He went to Nice to try to sell a painting. . . . I'm very hungry." His lunch depended on [Zborowski's] success. We told him to come down and took him to Pere Curel's where we were renting a floor with the Zborowskis. I gave him two slices of lamb. Only two because he would have eaten all of it and there would have been nothing left for us. The next day he came back kindly, to thank me, he brought me an oil painting and a small owl. "Choose," he said to me. I chose the owl, I was young! Not quite in my hand, the owl flew away and Soutine took leave laughing.[10]

Barrey and Foujita were not the only ones who noticed that Soutine could not afford to eat. The little girl whose family rented Soutine his room recalled, many years later, his time there: "Just imagine [he stayed in] a room barely half the size of my kitchen. Just below him, we had the pig. Of course, we kept [his room] clean, but Mr. Soutine was so poor that he couldn't eat every day. My mother often told me to bring him a plate of soup or pasta when she made it. [It was on such an occasion] that one day he told me he wanted to paint my portrait."[11] The painting of the girl has since been lost.

While in such straits, Soutine turned to the man whom many of the artists in Montparnasse relied on when they desperately needed quick cash: the police commissioner Léon Zamaron. It was known that when no one else would buy a painting, the commissioner could be depended on to put down money for one or two.

Zamaron, born in 1872, was perhaps the most poetic police commissioner the world has ever known. He arrived in Paris from Landaville when he was eighteen years old. He was beautiful, cultivated, and, from the first, wholly unpolitical. (When the Dreyfus trial began four years after his arrival in the capital and tore apart families and friends, he did not pick a side.) When he was twenty-six years old, while working as a policeman, he met Hélène Durst-Wild, the young daughter of the wealthy Durst-Wild family, which owned a brick factory and a hat factory. They fell instantly in love and married two years later. He served in many capacities within the police department before being named police commissioner in 1906, a post he held for the subsequent thirty-eight years. He developed a taste for avant-garde paintings and a fondness for the painters producing them. As commissioner, he was responsible for keeping track of and generally handling foreigners in the city, which meant he was well positioned to meet the artists he admired and render essential services. During his tenure, his office in police prefecture 211 was nicknamed Musée Zamaron because its walls were crowded with paintings by the likes of Chagall, Soutine, Modigliani, and Henri Epstein (whom he believed was the most talented of all). He had no theory of art, belonged to no school, and championed none of the causes of the artists to whom he was so devoted. He had on his walls paintings by renowned and unknown hands alike. The thousands of canvases that he bought were selected solely on the basis of his admiration for them.[12]

To his beloved painters Zamaron provided official as well as pecuniary support. Every year he helped the organizers of the Salon d'Automne procure the necessary licenses to set up their stalls, and he took the opportunity to visit the grounds while the galleries were being set up, communing with the paintings before crowds separated him from them. One day the art critic Louis Vauxcelles, whose taste and manner Zamaron considered rather stuffy, barged into his office and begged for help disentangling his son-in-law from legal troubles. Zamaron seized the moment to demand that Vauxcelles use his social and cultural currency to pressure the Salon d'Automne committee to accept the paintings of the School of Paris. He knew for a fact that Marie Vassilieff's paintings, which he considered excellent, had been rejected that year. Vauxcelles ignored his plea. Still, the artists of La Ruche had much reason to be grateful to Zamaron. Their scandalized neighbors regularly lodged charges against them for disorderly conduct, and when they were subsequently carted into Zamaron's office on the rue Delambre, they could count on him to have the charges dropped. Despite the breadth and quality of his collection and the power he wielded in the bohemian art world, his legend largely died with him. He left behind no collection, no interviews, and no record of his contribution to this period of cultural history. His children knew nothing of his role in the art world and inherited nothing from him but heavy debts.[13]

Soutine wrote three letters to Zamaron from Cagnes in 1918. Of the first, only a portion remains.[14] It reads:

18 June 1918

Dear Mr. Zamaron,

I ask forgiveness for not having thanked you earlier for your order. I write French very badly and in this way I always have to resort to the kindness of a friend to do so. I am here in a marvelous country where I can paint pretty canvases for you at my ease. I have finished some of them and soon I will send them to you. I bought a few canvases and tubes of paint in Nice, I paid a lot of money and this month my 150 f. is somewhat tight.

The second reads:

Cagnes 23 July 1918

Dear sir, please excuse me if I [didn't answer] you sooner because it is very difficult for me not being able to write. Thank you very much for the 200 f you sent me now I am starting to work a lot more than before. I don't have much more to say to you, dear sir, receive my best regards.

C Soutine.

Here is my address: C Soutin [sic] rue du Vallonet N 10 Cagnes A maritimes[15]

And the third reads:

Levens, Sept. 29, 1918

Dear Mr. Zamaron, I am ready to leave for Paris. There is only one obstacle, I lack fifty francs for the road. Would you, dear sir, have the kindness to send me this sum by telegraph, so that I can set out on the 5th of October at the latest. I've been doing pretty well this past month, and I hope you'll like my paintings. Please accept, sir, my most sincere greetings and my thanks in advance.

C Soutine

P.S. my current addresses: in Levens near Nice (A.M.) at Mme. Cendrars

Based on these letters, Soutine was chiefly dependent on Zamaron in these months for support. And the support was meager: 150 francs in the summer of 1917 would have been equivalent to about $26 then and about $620 today. Privates in the American armed forces made $30 a month, and they had no living expenses. The cost of a few months' worth of canvases and high-quality paints could easily run to much more than $620 today, and these were absolute necessities for Soutine. How he fed himself remains a mystery.

Lack of sustenance would have been acutely felt in Cagnes-sur-Mer. The vertiginousness of the place is dizzying. The trek on foot from the beach and its surrounding shops up to Haut-de-Cagnes, where Soutine lived and painted, leaves even the fit and well fed winded. The narrow streets are so steep one feels on the way up as if one could lean forward and kiss the concrete, and on the way down as if one would make better progress using the street as a slide. On those stretches that run along the edge of the mountain, pedestrians teeter high above the yawning, wild greens of the valley below. The beauty of the place is not calm, it is not sleepy. It provokes vigilance, which is precisely what a starving artist often fails to muster.

Soutine's stay in the South of France likely lasted from the end of March to the beginning of October—about six months total. For the duration he was extremely hard up. He produced about twelve landscapes and seven still lifes. If he did paint a single portrait, as the young girl's testimony indicates, none are known to us. The dearth of portraits can be attributed to the fact that he could not afford to pay for a model. In Paris there were free group sessions in various art schools where one could get a model without having to pay, as well as many painters and painters' friends who were accustomed to posing for one another—but not so in

Cagnes. Many of Soutine's early portraits are of other artists or figures in the art world. Beginning in 1920, he started several series of men in uniforms—including altar boys, bell boys (see inset page 7, *top*), valets, waiters, and chefs, because they charged little or no money. No such options were available to him in Cagnes.

Only five Soutine landscapes that precede his trip to Cagnes have been authenticated. It is inconceivable that the paintings we have are the only ones he made. Surely he painted many in the years between his first art class in Minsk and his earliest known landscape, which his catalogue raisonné dates to 1915–1916.[16] It is not surprising, though, that so few paintings from his earliest years remain. If he could not sell them, he would have had to leave them behind—he had no space to store unsold works, and he likely hemorrhaged paintings each time he moved, packing up and bringing along only those he liked best. Once Zborowski became his agent, Soutine would give completed paintings to him so that Zborowski could try to sell them. When potential buyers were interested in looking at Soutine's works, they would have approached Zborowski and asked to see the relevant works in his collection rather than approaching Soutine directly. The authenticators of Soutine's works are confident that he completed many paintings once he became an established painter that have still not been discovered—but there is hope that they will be found. The ones that predate 1918, though, are the least likely to be salvaged.

The paucity of early paintings makes it difficult to detect how the atmosphere in Cagnes affected Soutine's work, since one cannot compare the Cagnes landscapes to the ones immediately preceding them. It is clear from later periods that location affected Soutine very strongly, which is one of the reasons he moved as often as he did. The quality of the light, the natural palette, and the available geometries in the landscapes in which he found himself altered his sense of possibility while he painted, the way that the tone or quality of a friend's mind might alter your mood via pure proximity. Of course, where he was to some degree determined what he painted, since he only painted from life and so had to paint what he saw around him. But it did more than this. It also changed the tempo of his paintings: the energy with which he painted and the energy he was attempting to convey. The mood of his environment was as much a tool in his efforts as his tubes of paint were.

The first landscape that the catalogue raisonné explicitly identifies as one painted on this trip is *Landscape of the South of France*. (Soutine did not title any of his paintings. Sometimes the titles that are used in the catalogue raisonné were inherited from the owners of the paintings, and sometimes the editors developed their own titles to communicate something about the subject of the work.) Two paintings precede *Landscape of the South of France* in the catalogue; they were clearly painted outside Paris. If they were not done in the South then Soutine painted them in the suburbs around the city, on visits to Kikoine and his wife.[17]

It is fruitful, however, to compare the Cagnes landscapes of 1918 to the ones Soutine painted five years later, when he returned to the seaside city for a long stay. This comparison reveals the marked impact of the intervening years. The early paintings are of the same city (in the case of the red staircase, mentioned in Chapter 2, two paintings are of precisely the same place in the city), but they appear to be rendered by a very different hand. The 1918 paintings are oddly dulled by any standard, though manifestly so when contrasted with Soutine's later series. It seems that in 1918 Soutine added white to convey light rather than making each color a brighter version of itself. White, somewhat ironically, muddies colors. It does not clean them. (Clement Greenberg characterized the early paintings as "a trifle muddy, perhaps, because the pigment has been wrestled with so hard.")[18] If one wants to make a green lighter, one should add yellow. If one wants to mute it, one should add white. The difference between these two techniques is the difference between a pulsating painting and a dulled one. In the 1918 canvases Soutine has not yet developed his touch for coloration. He has also not yet developed his idiosyncratic sense of motion. These landscapes sit still in a way that his later works do not.

Soutine's paintings from this period are sometimes described—when they are described at all, and often they are overlooked entirely on the assumption that his first significant period would not begin till the following year—as uncharacteristically classical, by which it is meant that they are more literal than Soutine is expected to be.[19] The best known Soutine landscapes, the ones with which he is most commonly associated, were rendered in Céret between 1919 and 1922. They are, with overwhelming regularity, dark, intensely angular, claustrophobic, devoid of oxygen. There is hardly any sky in the Céret series, whereas the later Cagnes landscapes are airy and bright, and the motion within them is circular, as if a wind were sweeping the colors around and up. It is tempting to consider the 1918 Cagnes landscapes as a sort of midpoint between the two later series, since they are neither dark nor bright, angular nor circular, airless nor airy, but it is more accurate to think of this as a period before which Soutine has learned to throw himself into his work the way he later does. There is an almost ferocious energy that is let loose first in Céret, and which he has not yet tapped in 1918. In that year he was still developing basic competence. Once that energy is freed, Soutine spends the rest of his life attempting to temper and manipulate its force with the competence, the masterly understanding of paint, that he had honed. After Céret, so much of what Soutine is painting is life force. But in 1918, each landscape looks more like the thing he was looking at than his subsequent landscapes do. Almost all depict country roads—rendered in yellows or whites—bordered by trees and pale yellowish-white bridges and buildings topped with terra-cotta roofs. The base color in almost all the landscapes, the color that serves as a vernacular for the work, is white.

This is not true of the still lifes painted in the same period. Most of the still lifes that Soutine painted in Cagnes are of flowers. His first rendering of this subject was completed the previous year, but he carried the theme with him to the South of France. The flower series is the first of his still lifes in which he has intentionally placed objects in relation to one another for the purpose of painting them—as opposed to, say, painting a table set for mealtime, or some other similarly unarranged composition. Through the practice of painting, an artist develops a sense of what ought to be included in the work and what ought to be left out of it. The colors, shapes, and composition of a painting must be selected, and the more opportunity a painter has to experiment with the question of omission and inclusion, the more adept he becomes at editing what he sees. (This is also true of painters who do not paint from life, though the challenge is obviously of a different kind for them.) In his early works, the backgrounds of Soutine's portraits and still lifes are simply the environment in which his subject was situated, but over the course of the flower series one can see that he grows confident in inventing and enhancing these spaces.

Consider two still lifes that Soutine completed within at most a year of one another to understand the significance of these choices. The first, of a vase of sunflowers (see inset page 1, *bottom*), is now in the collection of the Barnes Foundation. In it, the yellow in the table and the greenery behind the sunflowers blunts the yellow in the flowers. The white in the sand-colored ground in the lower right of the canvas distracts the viewer from the focal point of the study. A dark frame, particularly where the sand color is placed, would have grounded the painting pleasingly, as the background does in any example from the red gladioli series Soutine painted around the same time. The gladioli themselves could not have been positioned in darkness as Soutine chose to paint them because then the flowers would not have been so bright. The richness of the red petals is accentuated by the dark field in which they appear, and the abstract coloration within this darkness—the streaks of blackish brown, and the glimmers of red—dramatize the flowers rather than distracting from them. Greenberg observes, rightly, of this series that "the quiet, burning clarity of its color reveals an extraordinary gift for paint."[20] This is when Soutine's genius for color emerges.

The flower still lifes mark the beginning of his fascination with this subject, which would transition into his great series of red gladioli, completed in 1919. In the earlier paintings, the same brown pitcher is depicted several times over serving as a vase for an overflowing bouquet. In all likelihood, they were wildflowers picked from nearby fields, for which he would not have had to pay.

The colors in the paintings are hot and vivid. Rich and luscious reds, yellows, and pinks cluster in beds of deep greens. Billowing streaks of mysterious black make up the backgrounds of some of these still lifes, though even the lighter palettes are not muted by white as the landscapes are. In one instance Soutine painted a background largely white but kept the flowers' reds and greens pure and vivid, somehow maintaining the purity of the colors in these works, which he was unable to render in the landscapes from the same trip.

The discrepancy is puzzling. It may have to do with essential differences between the two types of paintings. Among the primary differences between a still life and a landscape is that the composition of the still life is designed by the artist before the actual work of painting commences. Soutine presumably placed the flowers in the jug, the jug on the table, and the table in or out of the available light source. The structure was predetermined by Soutine. A landscape leaves far less in the hands of the painter. There is always much more in a landscape than the artist can responsibly render, and the light outside is totally diffused across all objects, rather than localized on a particular subject.

The brightness of a seaside town like Cagnes is particularly difficult to depict, and in 1918 Soutine would have had no experience painting anything like it, since he would have only ever painted in Minsk, Vilna, Paris, and its suburbs. The brightness was unsettling—it always is for new painters, since it blinds as much as it reveals, and there is no experience like attempting to paint the intensity of the sun. His friend Jacques Lipschitz once remarked that Soutine "was one of the rare examples in our day of a painter who could make his pigments breathe light. It is something which cannot be learned or acquired. It is a gift of God. There was a quality in his painting that one has not seen for generations—this power to translate life into paint—paint into life."[21] Lipschitz was right to admire Soutine's facility with light, but it was not a gift of God. Soutine taught it to himself, and that effort took him years.

In his lucid, insightful text in the catalogue for the Soutine retrospective held at the Tate in 1963, David Sylvester observes that the surfaces of these flower paintings bear the influence of "Bonnard's post impressionist manner of brush-stroking."[22] The comparison with Bonnard is apt—the brushstrokes in the relevant painting, *Still Life with Chair*, are pearl-like, thicker, and gentler than pointillist daubs, and indeed strikingly Bonnardesque—and it has broader implications.[23] Though Soutine moves away from this style of paint application, his ambition and overarching project are similar to Bonnard's. Both artists were interested in communicating a dimension of vitality, of being, that does not lend itself naturally to visualization. Andrew Forge observed that, when standing before a Soutine painting, "you have the feeling that Soutine is inventing painting while you look."[24] He meant that what Soutine aimed to do through painting was fundamentally different from any other artist's perceived project. His objective and orientation, his sense of what was possible to achieve, was not borrowed or learned from anyone else. It was specific to him. The same was true of Bonnard.

Bonnard's colors are not the colors we see in life—they are warmer, and richer—but they amplify elements of living that we would otherwise overlook. Bonnard considered these elements as essential as the integrities of the shapes and the oxygen that create or agitate moods in his spaces. His colors are not literal—indeed, his assignment of colors to objects is ravishingly perverse—but they teach us about the relations between the colors we see in life, and they teach us how to notice nuances that we would otherwise not know how to see. Soutine's paintings achieve a similar effect, but through different means. He studies the contribution that inner intensity makes to outer experience. Exaggeration can serve truth more effectively than verisimilitude. That axiom is essential to an understanding of Soutine's work.

If Soutine did return to Paris in October 1918, he would have arrived a month before the armistice was signed in Compiègne. Finally the fighting stopped. It would take another six months for the peace negotiations to conclude—the Treaty of Versaille was not signed until June 28, 1919—but Europe awoke that November from a years-long, blood-soaked nightmare. Léger stirringly described the sudden relief: "Man, exasperated, tense, alienated for the past four years, finally raises his head, opens his eyes, looks around, relaxes and recaptures his taste for life: his frenzy to dance, to spend money, to be able to walk upright, to scream, to yell. . . . An explosion of life-forces fills the world."[25]

Soutine, so sensitive to his surroundings, could hardly have failed to notice the currents of human electricity again coursing through France after years of deadening quiet. The year 1919 would be one of reawakenings and renewals, and Soutine would begin the period of painting for which he is best known. The fruit of that project would ignite his career—and he would spend the rest of his life tormented by it, and driven to destroy every vestige of the work that earned him his name.

Chapter 4

Céret Revolution

The fall of 1918 was an unsettled time across Europe. Sitting still in the city was not the pleasure it had once been, and Soutine returned to Paris itching to depart. His hunger for travel had been whetted, stimulating the peripateticism that would last the rest of his life, though he was forced to wait a few months before setting off again. Soutine arrived in the capital in October or November and remained through February or March of the following year. This time, Zborowski paid for Soutine's second journey to the South, and it was to be a very different trip. He went to Céret, a small town in southwestern France nestled in the foothills of the Pyrenees on the banks of the Tech River. The place had become a destination for artists since Picasso's storied time there, which transpired just a few years earlier.

Picasso's favorite of his Catalan friends, the sculptor Manolo, had settled in Céret in the early 1900s with his and Picasso's patron

Frank Burty Haviland. (Some of Haviland's paintings are on display in the small modern art museum in Céret today.) It was, they told Picasso, as close to Spain as one could get without crossing the border: Residents held bullfights and Sardana dances, and they spoke Catalan. Plus, importantly, it was cheap. The two men had been beseeching Picasso to join them there for two years before they finally managed to persuade him in the summer of 1911. Picasso's sojourn marked the beginning of Céret's status as one of the headquarters of the avant-garde. It was an auspicious time for his visit: He and Georges Braque had for the previous few years been working toward a fresh phase in their careers—one that would alter art history forever. Shortly after Picasso's arrival in Céret, Braque (along with Juan Gris) followed him, and there the two men labored toward the development of cubism, earning Céret the appellation "The Mecca of the Cubists." Braque and Picasso had been working side by side since 1908, so intensely bound up in one another's work they achieved a kind of fusion. Braque said of that time, "Picasso is Spanish and I'm French: we know all the differences that entails, but during those years the differences didn't count."[1]

It remains mysterious why Soutine chose to go to Céret since he was not an active member of the country's artistic culture in the way that Gris and Picasso and Chagall—who also went there—were. Soutine preferred solitude. Pierre Courthion suggests that a fellow lodger at the Cité Falguière, Pierre Brune, spoke glowingly of the town and encouraged Soutine to visit. Perhaps Brune told Soutine that Cèret, like Cagnes, is a city stacked on the vertiginous feet of a mountain with a geometric topography Soutine would find provocative. Kikoine wrote that Zborowski sent Soutine on the trip "with promises that he would provide him with paints and food, but nothing at all came of this and in a black misery Soutine painted with despair."[2]

Most of the paintings Soutine completed during this period were landscapes and portraits. Landscapes predominated. It was an extremely productive period. He worked obsessively. Zborowski's account of his encounter with Soutine in Céret is illustrative:

Do you know how he does his paintings? He goes off into the country and lives like a tramp in a sort of pigsty. He gets up at three in the morning, and walks twenty kilometers loaded down with his paints and canvas to find a site that pleases him, and at night returns to sleep, forgetting entirely to eat a thing. . . . Sir! I paid him a monthly stipend for two years, without his giving me anything in return. When I finally went to [Céret] to make inquiries, I found three hundred paintings piled one on top of the other in his attaché, the windows of which he had not opened once in two years "so that the canvases don't get damaged." When I went to go find something for him to eat he set fire to them, giving as his excuse that he wasn't satisfied with them. However, I managed to save a few, but only after a knock-down fight with him.[3]

In order to produce three hundred paintings in two years, Soutine would have completed about one painting every two to three days. That is a frenzy of output the likes of which he would never repeat. The canvases that survived his violence attest to the energy with which he must have painted.

Each of Soutine's paintings, especially from Céret, is like a single organism. Every shape and stroke is bound up in and wrapped around the others in a kind of heaving unity. In the Céret paintings this boundedness is tight—the forms are knotted together. There is a common rhythm that undergirds the entire work; energy charges every inch of every canvas in equal proportion, just as blood flows to every part of the body and a single pulse regulates every limb. There are no trivial passages. The works are structured on angular scaffoldings: Thick lines and corners cut through the canvases, and these lines are often painted on the same tilt, as if the painting itself had been completed on an angle. (David Sylvester attributes this style of painting to Van Gogh's influence on Soutine: "Soutine's embarkation into the world of violent sensation at Céret was precipitated by certain late landscapes of Van Gogh—hence the emphasis upon linear and repetitive movements and hints of deep, off-centre perspective.")[4] The compositions all look like they are compressed and pushed toward one edge of the painting.

In the first half of the Céret period, Soutine was working himself into this rhythm, learning how to channel his immense energy into his work, and learning also how to feel comfortable departing from the canons of realism. Citizens of the twenty-first century cannot possibly imagine the titanic creative independence that abstraction demanded of artists in the early 1900s. Any departure from naturalistic representation was an act of revolution. And for Soutine, an artist who had only ever admired the great masters, abstraction was tantamount to heresy. Everything he had been taught, and most of what he had had the opportunity to admire in school and in the museums where he worshiped, was figurative. And yet Céret was the crucible in which he forced himself away from the traditions he loved and from the only voices that had ever really been admitted into the interior of his mind while he painted.

The Céret paintings are the first canvases in which he gives himself over to the activity of painting, an activity that was physically arduous. He had to develop a method, since the pace of the painting itself, which must have been very fast and must have required literal muscle, was unlike anything he would have been taught, and utterly unlike anything his fellow painters were attempting in those years. Certainly the maelstrom that was the cubist movement in those years helped Soutine detach himself from realism. But in the Céret paintings he moves through and past cubism too. One can track his trajectory out from under cubism through the early Céret works. The harsh verticality of Céret loops and shimmies away, his geometries become gentler, and his distortions of space shift further from the ones Picasso and Braque taught artists of the period to strive for through cubism.

Soutine quickly moved into his own motion, developing his own tone. Painting as no one else has painted requires a great deal of conviction. In Soutine's case, conviction was deepened by crippling isolation. He discovered while in Céret that his closest friend and greatest champion had died: Modiglani was thirty-six years old when a neighbor found him delirious in his bed in Paris, clutching his distraught wife, Jeanne Hébuterne. The artist was taken to a nearby hospital, where he contracted meningitis and died on January 24, 1920. Two days later Jeanne killed herself by jumping from a fifth-floor window. She was eight months pregnant. Their three-year-old daughter was left to be raised by Jeanne's parents. Jacques Lipschitz, the man who introduced Soutine and Modigliani, recalled what transpired at the hospital when Jeanne went there to visit her husband's corpse: "Jeanne Hebuterne had come [to the hospital morgue], thrown herself upon Modigliani and covered his face with kisses. She fought furiously with officials who tried to pull her away because they knew how dangerous it was for her—especially pregnant as she was—to touch the open sores that covered his face. It was only a few hours later that she returned to her father's house and threw herself from its rooftop. Her family forbade that she be buried beside her husband."[5]

Unlike Soutine, who would not hear about Modigliani's death till long after the fact, Lipschitz attended the funeral: "The day of the funeral everyone went to say goodbye to Modigliani. There was not a single soul left in Montparnasse—anyway you could well believe it. On foot we trekked in an endless procession all the way across Paris to Père Lachaise and it seemed as if there were clouds of flowers."[6]

Soutine mourned Modigliani in solitude. There is no record of his grief or of friends in Céret who witnessed it or consoled him. If it had any effect on his work, it was only to thrust him more deeply into himself and into the Céretan energy in which he had already begun to work.

This energy reached its apex in 1921. *Hill at Céret* and *Red Roofs, Céret*, both painted that year, are archetypal examples of Soutine's Céret landscape apotheosis. (See inset pages 2 and 3, *bottom*.) After the execution of these two paintings, Soutine's canvases steady into greater legibility, the forms uncouple from one another, and the spaces become less claustrophobic. Soutine spent the rest of his career teaching himself to temper and manage the energy unleashed during the first half of the Céret period. In the subsequent twenty years, he endeavored to harness the energies unleashed at Céret without either diluting them or allowing them to overwhelm and take complete possession of him.

The portraits and still lifes from this period are similarly convulsed, and likewise in these canvases the backgrounds seem as alive as the people they contain, as if all elements of the painting were bound up with and dependent on one another—as if they all shared a single life force. They seem sometimes like the innards of a living creature, pulsing as one. The backgrounds twist and swirl in motion with the faces and bodies, especially in the earlier Céret portraits. A subset within the portraits from this period is the praying man series, which Soutine was commissioned to paint by the Swiss painter Emile Lejeune (whose portrait Soutine also painted in 1922–1923).[7] The series uses the same man, a certain "Monsieur Racine," in the same pose, with hands clasped together as if in prayer. As in the landscapes, the fore- and backgrounds vibrate together into a single heaving plane. The colors are as vital as the brush is swift. And, as in the landscapes, Soutine distorts the bodies of the figures to charge the canvases with rhythmic complexity.

In all the paintings from this period, Soutine is developing his felicity for color. There are no solid patches in these paintings, and there never will be again in his work. Every color contains other colors. A brown jacket hums with green, red, yellow, blue, and white. Light greens and blues swim within the fleshy cheeks of a child's face. Soutine did not move his brush back and forth over a single stretch to achieve uniform color. He moved the brush quickly *once* over one space so each stroke is still visible.

This is among the reasons that the energy reads so forcefully in his work—one can still see the attack of the brush, it is never camouflaged by repetition. He didn't dull the color by repeating his stroke. If one runs the brush back and forth, color solidifies. If there are already other colors on that portion of the canvases, they mix to muddiness. If one wants to add a pure color to a canvas that already has wet paint on it, the only way to do so is to move the brush (or any other applicator) over the surface once. Soutine would stand in front of the canvas with as many as forty brushes, dipping each in paint *once*, applying it to the canvas, and then throwing the brush on the floor and reaching rapidly for another one.[8] If he wanted a thicker stretch of a single color, he would use a bigger brush, or he would scrape the color onto the canvas using a palette knife, or the back end of a brush, or sometimes his fingers. (He once dislocated his thumb that way.) Over time he perfected this style of coloration, allowing for many different colors tightly wound around one another without dilution or corruption. In the Céret paintings, though, the colors are not yet as pure as they would be later. These paintings are airless. He was still developing this capacity.

Obscurity offers a purifying safety. It is a hermetic defense against misunderstanding. Like every individual who has been paid the clumsy compliment of fame, Soutine's legend is limited in a way that always misrepresents him. Legend does that: It eschews subtlety and nuance and rarely considers development. The stages of an artist's life are forgotten. Whatever society deems salient is what gets remembered. Soutine is thus remembered best for the Céret period—a period during which he broke the dam that imprisoned his creative spirit and the pent-up waters went wild with fresh freedom. He wrestled this ferocity into a new delicacy over the next two decades. The wealth and celebrity he accrued in those years he obsessively enlisted in his attempt to find and destroy every possible vestige of the Céret paintings. He came to hate them. But it was too late: Those paintings remain the most famous of all his works. A single person was responsible for this injustice, and he is the same man to whom Soutine owes his career. His name was Albert Barnes.

CHAPTER 5

Celebrity

By THE END OF 1923 SOUTINE WAS KNOWN ON BOTH SIDES of the Atlantic as a formidable painter. He had an allowance from Zborowski of twenty-five francs a day and a personal chauffeur paid for by the dealer. Young painters would sit at La Rotonde ostentatiously reading *The Brothers Karamazov* and *Crime and Punishment*—Soutine's favorite novels—hoping to catch his eye. In 1924 the film director Jean Epstein asked Soutine to make a brief celebrity appearance in his bizarre film *Les lion des Mogols*. About an hour into the movie, a smiling and indisputably dashing Soutine dances gleefully alongside none other than Kiki de Montparnasse—"The Queen of Montparnasse"—one of the glitteriest and sexiest figures of les Anneés folles.

The Soutine who returned from Céret in late 1922 would hardly have recognized the dashing dancer in Epstein's film. No one, least of all Soutine himself, could have foreseen such an enormous transformation. Zborowski certainly didn't. He drove all the way down to the forested village in the Pyrenees where Soutine was ensconced and crammed his car's trunk full of the canvases that he managed to salvage from Soutine's immolations, and then grimly wound his way back up to Paris, thoroughly expecting to earn back exactly none of the money he had spent on Soutine in Céret. The painter was considered unsellable at the time. Pinchus Krémègne recalled standing in Zborowski's house in the country shortly before Albert Barnes acquired the works. "There in the room, [Zborowski] brought seventy unframed Soutine paintings. He started casting the canvases onto the ground one after the other. He looked at them and said to me 'What can I do with all this!'"[1]

Barnes would change all of that. He made his massive Soutine acquisition while still in the early stages of assembling what remains one of the most impressive collections of modern art in the world. He was not unusual among wealthy art collectors for being eccentric, acerbic, and exacting, but he was markedly and impressively capable of recognizing and nurturing promising young painters, and of esteeming them as on par with the Old Masters. Unlike his friends Leo and Gertrude Stein, Barnes hung his avant-garde purchases next to great works from the thirteenth century, as well as canvases by Chardin and Renoir. Barnes's impact was calculated. He was rigorously philosophical, and he had his own theory of art and art history, which he codified in a long treatise titled *The Art in Painting* (1925). That theory informed the way he organized his paintings and how he taught art history at the school he established in his mansion in Merion, Pennsylvania.

Albert Coombs Barnes was born in 1872 to a poor family in a rough part of Philadelphia known today as Fishtown. His father was a butcher who lost his right arm and his livelihood during the Civil War at the Battle of Cold Harbor. He collected a disability pension of eight dollars a month and scraped by working odd jobs. Barnes's mother was a passionate Methodist who took her son to camp meetings and revivals run by the African American Methodist community in Philadelphia, instilling in the young boy an early, formative affinity for the principles of what would later become the civil rights movement. Albert attended the competitive public Central High School, where he met and formed a lasting friendship with William Glackens, who became a significant American painter and advised Barnes in his early collecting gambits. Barnes graduated from the University of Pennsylvania Medical School in 1889, paying his way by tutoring, boxing, and playing semiprofessional baseball.[2] After graduating he worked as a resident physician at the Pennsylvania State Hospital for the Insane. His time there marked him. Decades later it allowed Barnes to roll his eyes at the accusations of lunacy leveled by critics at the avant-garde artists he came to champion.

Barnes never practiced medicine again. Instead, he spent his meager savings on a flight to Germany, where he studied chemistry for several years. He put the study to good use, and after a number of successful business ventures, founded his own company in 1908. That same year he patented the recipe for Argyrol. You may have heard of Argyrol if you've ever visited the Barnes Foundation and read about the founder's fortune. If not, you may be forgiven for not knowing that the substance is an antiseptic that has various medicinal virtues. It was a lucrative discovery. Lucky for Barnes, for Soutine, and for us.

By 1911, just two years before Soutine's arrival in Paris, Barnes had accumulated enough capital to instruct his aesthetic coconspirator William Glackens to go to France with $20,000 and return with as many masterpieces as that money would buy. It bought twenty paintings. (Today's equivalent, roughly $6.5 million, would be barely enough to buy one of the paintings that now grace the walls of the Barnes Foundation.) Initially, they hung on the walls of Barnes's factory and were used in the lectures he held about art history for his employees. Those twenty paintings formed the beginnings of a historic collection, of which Barnes was, in his lifetime, notoriously possessive. He set up his collection in Lower Merion, a suburb of Philadelphia, and kept his treasures under lock and key. Only Albert Einstein, John Dewey, and the actress Katharine Cornell were allowed to visit whenever they liked. Everyone else had to apply for permission, and many were rejected. (Among them was the great art historian and critic Meyer Schapiro, who was turned away repeatedly.)

The exact circumstances under which Barnes first saw Soutine's paintings are obscured by the many, contradictory accounts left by those involved. Barnes himself recounted contradictory versions of the story. Paul Guillaume, Léopold Zborowski, and Jacques Lipschitz all claimed credit for introducing Barnes to Soutine's work. (Of course the fact that they clamored for credit is a testament to the importance of Barnes' acquisition.) In one account Barnes said that Zborowski showed him Soutine's paintings in 1921. In another he said, "The first time I ever saw a Soutine was in 1922 in a small bistro in Montparnasse and I bought it. Paul Guillaume [who by then was serving as Barnes's primary agent in Paris] was with me and he knew that Zborowski had a lot of Soutine's paintings." Zborowski remembered things slightly differently. He reported that Barnes saw Soutines for the first time while visiting his home on the hunt for paintings by Modigliani and Kisling.[3] Guillaume, for his part, recalled that Barnes caught sight of Soutine's *The Pastry Chef* while at his gallery and fell immediately in love.

Whatever the case may be, Barnes did buy that canvas from Guillaume in 1922 for 3,000 francs. In December of that year or January of the next, the American millionaire spent just over 37,600 francs total on Soutine canvases. He bought primarily from Zborowski, who had the most to offer. The "unsellable" Soutine made his agent a lump sum of 20,400 francs in that transaction. Guillaume sold Barnes another fifteen paintings in addition to *The Pastry Chef*, and Barnes bought a final canvas from the dealer Georges Aubry. He returned to Lower Merion in 1923 freighted with fifty-four Soutines. He would acquire only another five in his lifetime, but that first purchase changed Soutine's life.

For the next six years, the prices of Soutine's paintings for sale at auction multiplied eightfold. Some have speculated that Barnes invested so heavily in Soutine from the start because he hoped to make money selling the works later. Soutine was the first painter whose work Barnes bought in such enormous quantity who was not already an important figure in the Parisian art world. Matisse and Picasso, whose paintings also feature prominently in Barnes's collection, were by then household names in France. If Barnes intended not only to collect Soutine's work but also to launch his career, he was successful. Barnes wrote to Guillaume in 1923, "It is fairly certain that the dealers here [in America] who have connections in Paris will start to buy Soutines. I hope the prices do not go too high before you get all the good ones to be bought. In my mind there is no doubt that he will rank higher than any painter since Van Gogh and I believe a fortune can be made by selling those paintings at several times the price I paid."[4] Indeed, four years later the Parisian dealer René Gimpel, who moved in posher circles than that of Montparnasse bohemia, wrote in his diary, "His is a star that's rising in the firmament of French painting. . . . His paintings, which couldn't find a buyer a year ago, today sell for tens of thousands of francs and increase in price every day."[5] Of the fifty-nine Soutines Barnes purchased during his lifetime, he sold thirty-eight and kept sixteen on permanent display in his galleries. But he also esteemed Soutine as a painter regardless of the money-making opportunity he offered.

Soutine had his first solo exhibition in Paris at the Gallery Bing in 1927, and three more solo shows before the end of 1929. In the year of the Bing exhibition, the art critic Waldemar George (born Jerzy Waldemar Jarociński) devoted a monograph to Soutine. Two years later the famed art historian Élie Faure, whose canonical history of art Jean-Paul Belmondo can be seen reading in the opening scene of the film *Pierrot le fou*, published another monograph on the painter. Already in 1926 Faure had written to the American critic Walter Pach, "There's no star to see in view, except perhaps Soutine . . . whose importance increases every day."[6] By any standard, Soutine had "made it."

And by any standard, this was an odd way of making it. In the Parisian avant-garde, one became successful not through financial success but by achieving a level of respect within circles of fellow artists. If market success came at all it came only after an artist had become a force of influence among his peers.

Three decades before Soutine arrived in France, Manet, Paris's ur-rebel, was the king of his band of experimental friends long before he achieved the modest financial success that gave him and his family financial security. During the second half of the 1860s, on Thursdays and Sundays, a crowd that often included artists and writers such as Zola, Duranty, Renoir, Mallarmé, and Degas would gather at the Café Guerbois and circle round Manet while he held court. Manet, like Soutine, was deeply indebted to the Old Masters, and the Guerbois group would go with him to the Louvre, where he lectured before canvases of Watteau and Ingres.[7] When he suffered a setback or struggled with creative fatigue, he depended on his friends to buoy his spirits. (Is there a less Soutinian impulse?) Hours spent at the café were essential for the others as well. Monet said of those evenings, "Nothing could be more interesting than these *causeries* with their perpetual clash of opinions. They kept our wits sharpened, they encouraged us with stores of enthusiasm that for weeks and weeks kept us up until the final shaping of the idea was accomplished. From them we emerged tempered more highly, with firmer will, with our thoughts clearer and more distinct."[8]

Ironically, despite the fact that Manet was the father of the avant-garde, his standard for success remained the official Salon of the Académie des Beaux-Arts, which was a synecdoche for establishment approval. He never stopped submitting to the Salon despite being repeatedly rejected, and he was subsequently censured by the press and society when he resorted to showing in alternative venues. He was rewarded for this compulsive loyalty in the final four years of his life, when every painting he submitted to the Salon was accepted. (He died young, at fifty-one, eleven days after his foot was amputated due to the gangrene contracted from syphilis.) By that time the art world was influenced by the political shift leftward that affected the entire country, and Salon standards became likewise more progressive.[9] But even then, the public for whose approval Manet had been laboring for decades was not the public with which he had ever been associated. He earned his success gradually. There was no lightning bolt—no Barnesian miracle—for Manet.

In the first decade of the twentieth century, Matisse and Picasso succeeded Manet as champions of the new. Matisse's star rose first, long before Soutine's arrival on the scene. (Soutine himself revered Matisse. So much so that, one day while he was walking on the street in Paris and caught sight of Matisse, he was so starstruck that he ran away rather than risk approaching the great master. Soutine never learned that the respect was mutual: Matisse himself owned two of Soutine's paintings.)[10] Matisse was older than Picasso, and Picasso did not move to Paris from Catalonia until 1900. Matisse had begun his artistic career at the start of the previous decade. He had been born into a wealthy family, but in 1902 his wife's father was arrested in connection with a financial scandal, and Matisse was left to support her extended family—a total of seven additional mouths to feed. He had at that point not achieved any material success as a painter and was suddenly under considerable financial pressure to make something of himself. (Soutine's habitual solitariness was in this sense a saving grace.) By the time Matisse had painted the painting that would so captivate the American expat art critic and collector Leo Stein, he was in bad need of cash.

In his financial hardship he was like Soutine, but unlike Soutine Matisse was revered by fellow painters. Before Barnes's great acquisition even those who admired Soutine's work and considered him a great painter did not expect him to become a household name. It was a great shock when the collector from Philadelphia transformed him into exactly that. All of Montparnasse rumbled with the news. Over the course of an afternoon Soutine went from being a destitute, luckless emigrant from a tiny village in a world far away to a prized jewel in one of the greatest modern art collections in the entire world. Barnes's reverence put Soutine's canvases in the company of paintings by artists such as Cezanne, Renoir, Picasso, and Matisse. Today the Barnes collection contains more Cezanne paintings than the entire city of Paris. Altogether the collection is estimated at between $20 billion and $30 billion. Had Soutine still been praying on that December day in Paris, even he could not have had the imaginative capacity to ask for such luck. But Soutine was not constitutionally predisposed toward gratitude. After the great windfall, he hardly ever mentioned Barnes's name.

Barnes did not need Soutine to be grateful; he needed him to be impactful. It was he, more than Soutine himself, who put Soutine literally on the same walls as Matisse and Picasso. Barnes believed that Matisse was the greatest painter of his day, but he bought more Soutines than he did Matisses (fifty-nine to fifty-four), and he took a greater risk with Soutine. By the time Barnes started collecting in 1912, both Picasso and Matisse were renowned. But Barnes set out to make Soutine's name. Unlike the artist whose paintings he had just acquired in such quantity, the American collector did want to influence the modern art world on both sides of the ocean, and he wanted to use Soutine—and indeed every artist in his collection—to do so. Barnes developed a theory of art, and he used his collection to illustrate and teach that theory at the academy he ran.

Like Soutine, Barnes believed that a deep community linked the great traditions of art throughout history. His treatise *The Art in Painting* was a book-length effort to "trace in the history of painting the essential continuity of the great traditions and to show that the best of the modern painters use the same means, to the same general ends, as did the great Florentines, Venetians, Dutchmen and Spaniards." (In Soutine's paintings Barnes detected an affinity with Tintoretto, for example, which is why visitors to the Barnes Foundation in Philadelphia today can see Soutine hanging alongside Tintoretto and draw the same conclusion.) He believed that his theory offered an objective standard by which one could measure the quality of any painting, and that, through study, anyone could develop the power to distinguish bad art from good. He was, after all, a scientist first and always wanted to "offer a type of analysis which should lead to the elimination of the prevailing habit of judging paintings by either academic rules or emotional irrelevancy."[11] Soutine was another ingredient in his laboratory.

Barnes officially began preparations for the establishment of the Barnes Foundation in the fall of 1922, a few months before the trip that would transform Soutine's life. On that occasion he had not yet decided exactly where or how accessible he wanted his foundation to be. Stirrings of ambitious, iconoclastic artists at the Pennsylvania Academy of Fine Art (PAFA) persuaded Barnes that the institution might be open to collaborating with him on his great project. He tested that theory in 1923. Just before he left Paris, Paul Guillaume held a show of all the paintings that Barnes had purchased. It was a great success, as Barnes himself wrote to friends back home in Philadelphia. Upon his return they insisted that he repeat the triumph homeside.[12]

Their protestations yielded the first and last public exhibition of Barnes's collection in his lifetime. The show was held at PAFA from April 9 to May 11. It did not go as planned. Despite the exciting lurches toward the avant-garde that Barnes had noticed, the Philadelphia public did not appreciate the works he put before them. The response of the critics was vicious. One declared, "It is as if the room were infested with some infectious scourge," and wondered "why the Academy should sponsor this sort of trash." All the paintings were collectively reviled, but the commenters hated Soutine most of all. He was disproportionately represented in the show, which may explain why he, more than Derain, Picasso, or even Matisse, bore the brunt of the philistinism. In the *Public Ledger*, the art critic Edith Powell described Soutine as "insane" and asked readers, "Are we willing to give careful attention to what . . . seems to us diseased and degenerate? Is it a good thing to visit morgues, insane asylums, and jails?" *The Philadelphia Inquirer* jeered that Soutine's Céret paintings were nothing but a "series of seemingly incomprehensible masses of paint, known as landscapes." Barnes, furious, penned letters to the critics directly, expressing his displeasure. To Powell he wrote that she would "never be a real art critic until she had relations with the ice man" and went on to explain in explicit detail exactly what he meant by that.[13]

Soutine never heard about the outrage he had elicited across the pond. He never had occasion to learn whether his ego was as easily bruised as Manet's or Matisse's. Barnes took offense on his behalf. The experience soured the collector on the Philadelphia art world establishment, to put it mildly. His dreams of partnering with the Philadelphia Museum of Art withered into dust, and he spent the subsequent years ensuring that the social elite that had rebuffed him would have an impossible time getting in to see his collection. There are humorous accounts of Barnes refusing entry to art world colossi such as Erwin Panofsky, the Princeton art historian who finally snuck in disguised as a chauffeur, and T. S. Eliot, whom Barnes rejected with a note that read simply "Nuts" (he had his dog, Fidèle, sign the message).[14] Barnes's decision to privatize the collection and turn away requests to visit had the effect of suffocating the recognition of Soutine that Barnes's purchase should have amplified, and of course it similarly affected all the unheard-of artists whose work Barnes would go on to acquire in Paris.

Unfortunately for Dr. Barnes, his wounded pride kept him from achieving all his goals. Educating the public struck him as less appealing after being scorned by it. He had told Forbes Watson, editor of *The Arts* and the man to whom Barnes gave permission to make the first public announcement of his foundation, "Primarily the hope is that every person, whatever station in life, will be allowed to get his own reactions to whatever the Foundation has to offer. That means that academism, conformity to worn-out conditions, counterfeits in art, living and thinking, can have no place in the intended scope of the Foundation."[15] His success was partial: He did manage to keep out the academy, but he kept out the rest of the public too. It is unfortunately the case that "every person, whatever station" for the most part hears about works of art worth seeing from those guilty of "academism." The establishment broadcasts to the vulgar, often to the chagrin of both.

Forbes rewarded Barnes for his special access by championing the foundation: "Many of the paintings are of a sort that are not generally taken for granted by the large public. . . . The fact that many people are likely to be nonplussed, on their first introduction to this collection, only shows how much we need such a museum as the proposed one at Merion. And it is not at all a bad scheme to have this just a little off the beaten track. It gives people a chance to show a little energy in their desire to enjoy art."[16] But the kind of people predisposed to "show a little energy in their desire to enjoy art" were precisely the kind that Barnes turned away.

Somewhat ironically, the massive acquisition of Soutines by an American millionaire was more acutely felt in Paris than in Philadelphia. Barnes did Soutine the favor of immediately selling several of his freshly bought canvases to galleries in Paris, with the intention of igniting interest in the artist in the City of Light. As mentioned, some have conjectured that he did this in order to increase the value of a Soutine painting and thus the value of his collection. He certainly was proud of the fact that he spotted artists before their stars rose, but Barnes's maniacal possessiveness of his paintings was so manifest—he spent so much effort and money to keep them in his collection long after their prices skyrocketed—that it is impossible to believe he saw them primarily as money-making opportunities. Yet his influence did earn money for other people. Zborowski's circumstances, for instance, were permanently altered. After the whirlwind of Barnes's trip and purchases, the dealer could at last live a life of luxury. He and his wife frequented fancy restaurants and nightclubs in couture clothes and fur coats. By 1927 he was able to open a gallery on the corner of rue Visconti and rue de Seine in an old butcher's shop.[17]

Soutine's life was far and away the most altered. He greeted his notoriety eagerly and without grace. Fame meant he could afford a new social circle, and he acquired one immediately. Many of his old Jewish acquaintances came to resent him for the neglect with which he treated them for the rest of his life. Caring for each other was part of their ethos, and abandoning one's friends when good fortune struck was a breach of their social contract. Soutine's antipathy to longtime friends began at the same time that he developed a deep aversion to the Céret paintings. He did not like to be reminded of his former lives.

Money changed his personal presentation too, though this took a little while. Starting in 1924 he began spending ludicrous sums on silk ties, English suits, and manicures. (He was always vain about his hands, which were very beautiful—long, elegant, and pale.) But all these changes were superficial. In his temperament and manner, in his essence, Soutine remained much what he had been before, despite the grooming and affectations. Art was still his constant concern, his primary interest and occupation. He would never again have to produce a painting a day to earn enough to eat. After 1923, until the shadow of war once again fell over Paris a decade and a half later, Soutine did not have to worry about going hungry. The Barnes purchase did not make him a wealthy man overnight, but it did give him financial security. From then on he worked obsessively due not to economic necessity but to inner necessity. His monomania was unaltered by Barnes's purchase.

CHAPTER 6

Soutine and the Masters

WHAT MADE SOUTINE PRODUCE PAINTINGS THAT HE hated? From the first, he detested the Céret pictures. What motivates an artist to create works that anger him so bitterly he tries his best to set them all on fire or shred them to ribbons? It is a peculiar curse for an artist to make only what displeases him. But painting is not a rational exercise. It is clear from the drama of Soutine's canvases that he created them in a state of excitation. Not madness, not torment, but the strange, almost spiritual state that sometimes seizes artists—and always differently for each—when they are in the throes of creation. What emerges from beneath the brush is always at least in part a surprise. Even when one begins with intention, intention reacts chemically with circumstance and the ensuing result cannot be foreseen. Creation is not meditated in a way that can be explained coherently afterward. When the fog of inspiration lifts, one doesn't return to one's senses so much as discover new ones. A different realm of the mind was activated and then vacated, and in its afterlife we find ourselves altered. After the Céret period, Soutine never returned to that space inside himself, even when he did return physically to Céret.

The compositional dynamism of Soutine's paintings—not just how the structures within them are arranged but also how those structures share and radiate energy—is its own odyssey. Tracking the flow of vitality within his canvases is one method of tracing his artistic development. As I have suggested, Soutine was among those artists who realize at some stage in their careers that their true subject, no matter the literal objects rendered on the canvases, is energy (and if they do not realize this in language, they at least give themselves over to the task in practice). If they began their careers as figurative painters, the transition from trying to capture the shape and color of, say, a tree to using the shape and color of the tree to capture its movement is visible in their oeuvre. For Soutine, this transition reached a pitch in Céret. The energy in these paintings is overwhelming, shooting, asphyxiating. It seems to crush and twist the canvases. And this energy seems to be essential to the place itself rather than to the particular subjects of any given canvas. There is a Céretian charge, an overpowering vibration, that dominates the works.

Yet over the course of 1922 and into 1923, Soutine extricated himself from the spirit of Céret, and its grip never reasserted itself in quite the same way. He had begun a new period. Zborowski sent Soutine back to Cagnes shortly after Barnes's departure. He was only there a short while. One of the earliest landscapes he painted on that trip testifies to the incubation of a new phase in Soutine's relationship with energy, and a new phase in his relationship with the sky. Soutine and the sky is a fascinating romance. It begins badly: He abuses dark or light in the first several years of his career. The sky is almost invariably muddy or whipped. It is not refreshing, it does not offer an empyrean. The sky can do this in a landscape painting. It can be used to quiet the scene or to localize the energy in it. Think of the calm of a Renoir or Hopper sky, and compare it to the tumult in any Van Gogh landscape. In Soutine's later years, and particularly in the final decade of his life, he treats the sky with great respect. It is given due space and accorded its own texture. This took time. These later, miraculous paintings are foreshadowed in the early Cagnes landscapes such as *Landscape with Figures*, which he painted in 1922.

This canvas is one of his earliest steps toward a new kind of landscape, one with more oxygen and a gentler rhythm. The curve that swells from the lower right corner to the upper left would be repeated and multiplied in one of his most exciting series, the crazy houses of Cagnes (see inset page 4, *top*)—a series that was, due to unfortunate circumstances, actually completed outside the city. Soutine was forced to leave Cagnes earlier than he had intended. One day a grocer with whom Soutine had a running tab spotted Soutine painting and asked if he could see the canvas. Soutine, ever unwilling to share any unfinished paintings with spectators, refused vociferously. The grocer mistook Soutine's eccentricity for brazen rudeness, and promptly picked up Soutine's easel and paints and threw them into the nearby ravine. A grocer with whom one has a running tab is an imprudent enemy to make. Soutine decamped shortly thereafter to La Gaude, a town ten kilometers away.

There, Soutine gave himself over to the embryonic style foreshadowed at the end of 1922. The harsh geometrics of Céret are replaced by a whimsical loopiness. The points of focus in each painting, and sometimes there are more than one, are clearly rendered in a foreground against a softer background. When there are multiple subjects they swirl in rhythm with one another—as if swaying to the same music—but still distinguishable. Houses are painted on crazily looming hills with the sky as a distinct background, offering refuge from the energy of the hills and houses.[1]

On this trip, as in Cagnes in 1918, Soutine asked the children of the people from whom he rented a room to pose for him. Decades later, the little girl who had served as a model for him remembered that he forced her and a friend to stay put for long sessions while he worked: "He forgot to let us rest!" The odd artist positioned her and her fellow model on top of a small table in his sparse, cramped room.

Compared to the financial straits he had endured just a few months earlier, Soutine did not suffer from money troubles. But he had not yet accrued the wealth that would allow him to buy fancy clothes. The model remembered that she and her mother washed the single pair of pants and shirt he owned each night because it was the only set he had. "He wasn't rich. He ate with the family, I served him at the table. He didn't speak very much." This was not, she hastened to add, because he could not speak French. "He spoke French well, we could understand him very easily," she said. There just wasn't much opportunity to talk to him. He would wake up early every morning and spend the day outside looking for the right view and then painting it until he was forced home by the setting sun. The children in the village would run after him and try to catch a glimpse of his canvases, but his habitual secrecy kept him from obliging them. He repeatedly chased them away. But he was not a rough person. Despite his awkwardness she remembered him as being "very sweet."[2]

Zborowski had apparently not given Soutine enough cash for rent. The artist decided to pay for his keep at the young girl's home by giving her mother paintings, which she was too polite to refuse though she thought they were terrible. When Zborowski discovered that Soutine had left several of his works in La Gaude with an inn-keeper who couldn't possibly know their worth, he was apoplectic. He wrote to Raymond Gaudet, an artist he knew in Cagnes, asking him to rescue the abandoned works and bring them to Paris. Gaudet borrowed a car from Claude Renoir, the great artist's son, packed up the canvases, and drove them to Zborowski's apartment.

Soutine left La Gaude and returned to Paris in triumph. Perhaps they did not yet know his name down south, but they remembered it in Montparnasse. The Russian painter Grégoire Michonze, who arrived in Paris at the end of 1923, said, "I remember the light gray corduroy suit he wore and the gleaming spots of color on his pants. He was already famous at the time. His life in Montparnasse was much talked about. Everyone knew he drank countless café crème to calm his stomachaches."[3]

But Soutine stayed in Paris for only a short while before leaving again for Cagnes. He was a peripatetic painter: He needed to move, to refresh his senses, find a new landscape, expose himself to a fresh kind of light. As was clear in Céret, a novel landscape didn't necessarily make him happy, but it did provoke him. He wrote a miserable letter to Zborowski soon after arriving in Cagnes, begging him for the means to leave the town:

Dear Zborowski,

I have received the money-order. I thank you. I am sorry not to have written you sooner about my work.

It is the first time in my life that I have not been able to do anything.

I am in a bad state of mind and I am demoralized, and that influences me.

I have only seven canvases. I am sorry. I wanted to leave Cagnes, this landscape that I cannot endure. I even went for a few days to Cap Martin where I thought of settling down. It displeased me. I had to rub out the canvases I started. I am in Cagnes against my will, where, instead of landscapes, I shall be forced to do some miserable still lifes. You will understand in what a state of indecision I am. Can't you suggest some place for me? Because, several times I have had the intention of returning to Paris.

Your,
Soutine[4]

It was an empty threat—he did paint landscapes. And they are among his strongest, examples of a rare and especially delightful admixture: whimsy and genius. Céret is despairing; Cagnes is delightful.

Over the subsequent two years Soutine completed three of the most important series of his oeuvre: the rayfish series, inspired by Chardin's *The Ray* (for an early example, see inset page 4, *bottom*); the hanging-fowl series; and the great skinned-carcass series, inspired by Rembrandt's *Slaughtered Ox*, at whose bloodied feet he would have prayed where it and *The Ray* hang in the Louvre.

The first and last of these were "quotations" from the Old Masters he revered most. It is an astonishing fact that Soutine was moved to paint these subjects. Imagine the kinship he must have felt with Chardin and with Rembrandt, to see these two master-pieces and decide to repeat them. This kinship, this certainty that he and Chardin and Rembrandt are participating in the same tra-dition, is as arresting as the ensuing paintings themselves. It brings to mind Diderot's insight, relayed gently to a painter in 1765:

> A taste for the extraordinary is typical of mediocrity. When one despairs of making something that's beautiful, natural, and simple, one attempts something that's bizarre. Trust me, go back to jasmine, jonquils, tuberoses, and grapes, and beware of heeding my advice too late. This Rembrandt was a painter of unique gifts, this Rembrandt sacrifices everything to the magic of light and shadow; leave him alone, for he was possessed of the rarest master, and nothing less will make us indulge the darkness, smokiness, harshness, and other such faults entailed by his approach. And then this Rembrandt was a great draftsman, such a touch he had! Such expression, such characterization! Do you have all that? Do you think you ever will?[5]

Soutine did not believe he was attempting something bizarre. He was provoked by Rembrandt's darkness for the same reason that he kindled to Chardin's delicacy: their incommensurability with anything he had seen. This jarring singularity is on the short list of qualities Rembrandt and Chardin share, and it was this that drew Soutine to them both.

There are students who want to be like their teachers, and so they adopt their tone, their philosophical orientation, their style. The artists in Montparnasse who became cubists after watching Picasso were like this. Soutine was their opposite. Soutine converted the master's tone into his own vernacular. He practiced a sort of pictorial translation, except that a translator's job is to maintain the spirit of the original, and Soutine set himself the task of resuscitating Rembrandt and Chardin and Courbet with their forms but his soul. Because of his exacting eccentricities, to execute the paintings, he had not only to see the Chardin and the Rembrandt and be moved by them, but also to vacate the holy space in the Louvre, leave the museum, go to a butcher's shop or an abattoir, buy the carcasses of fowl, rays, oxen, and calves, string them up in his studio or his apartment on rue du Saint-Gothard, and set to work. All the while possessed by what he had seen in the museum. So many steps intervened between the solemnity of the gallery and the execution of his own interpretation. What spiritual stamina!

The differences between the ray, poultry, and beef series, which were done sequentially beginning with the Chardin "translation," show well the compositional transition Soutine's work underwent in the mid 1920s. He was moving toward still lifes in which one figure dominates the whole painting, occupying a single, settled space. In the ray paintings the fish looms over the composition, but other objects are in view in the foreground—a pitcher, tomatoes—sometimes on the table over which the ray is suspended, sometimes on the seat of a chair from the back of which the great fish hangs.

I will permit myself a personal digression to illustrate the similarities that might not register for nonartists, or for artists who have never seen these paintings in person. I have spent hours in front of Chardin's *Ray* in the Louvre and Soutine's *Rayfish* at the Metropolitan Museum of Art, and have drawn both in countless sketchbooks. The two paintings have taught me a great deal about composition, illusion, how to contrast dark and light. Both taught me that one should not draw the objects themselves, but how the light allows the artist to see the object. Soutine placed a pitcher with a spoon sticking out of its neck to the left of his ray, just as Chardin had. And also like Chardin, he didn't paint a line to communicate the edge of the pitcher, but only the shadow behind it. The difference in effect is the difference between naming a feeling and describing it.

In comparison to Chardin's virtuosic rendering, a triumph of visual mimesis, Soutine's pitcher doesn't seem accurate or delicate. On the contrary, that detail of the painting looks almost crass because of the pitcher's distortions. But in truth the artist established the object with care, indeed with delicacy. Notice how he, like Chardin, renders the shadows behind the pitcher in order to establish the pitcher itself. And the orange streak that runs from the base of the pitcher up to its mouth and around the lip was a thoughtful aesthetic decision. This is not mere energy; it is intelligent energy. Intelligent energy is the mystery and miracle of Soutine's work. Even when the excitement is clear, it is undergirded by a strenuous subtlety and deliberation. Soutine is able to permit himself intense energy and color because of the careful, powerful scaffolding that organizes his canvases. This scaffolding is at the heart of his development away from the Céret style.

Soutine's delight in the colors of the ray overwhelms his canvas, whereas Chardin's colors are luscious but controlled. The richness and joyousness of the reds in the fins, where Chardin used pale pinks, whites, and blues, define the difference. Soutine's red looks like rubies. He could never have copied Chardin's painting because Chardin was not excited by the same elements of the creature that Soutine was. Chardin taught him that this was a subject worth being stimulated by, and he taught him how to arrange the ray such that the canvas would be balanced, but he could not teach Soutine how to look at it, how to be fascinated by it, and how to turn that fascination into a visual expression.

In the summer of 1927 Soutine visited Zborowski and his wife at their seasonal rental on 17 Boulevard Chanzy, in Le Blanc, a commune in central France. Initially, Soutine was meant to paint inside the house, but the plan was scrapped almost immediately. The dead animals he dragged inside and left to decay filled the whole house with an unbearable stench. The Polish sculptor Dniprovsky, who was also staying with the Zborowskis, became good friends with Soutine. He remembered, "When he first arrived we gave him the big salon with stylish furniture. . . . Soutine laid out poultry or game on the table in the salon to serve as models and left them to putrefy while waiting for inspiration to seize him so he could commence painting. A terrible stench wreaked from the room."[6] Horror and exasperation on the part of the other occupants forced Soutine to relocate to a small shed in the garden that served as his studio. There he painted a number of his renowned chicken paintings.

The difference in temperament between the paintings Soutine was looking at for inspiration and his own interpretations is far more acute in the poultry series. It is far-fetched to argue that Soutine was quoting Chardin by choosing to paint hanging fowl, since the subject is a common one, whereas the rayfish was obviously inspired by Chardin's enormous *Ray* at the Louvre. Soutine would have seen several paintings that depicted recently shot fowl, and none of them were charged with the same energy his are. Of the three series, Soutine dedicated the largest number of canvases to poultry, conceivably because chickens and turkeys were easier to come by than enormous dead rayfish and carcasses of oxen. He painted twenty-one such paintings.[7]

These birds are the most energetic of his still lifes. They may even be the most energetic of any of his paintings. The movement in the canvases is certainly reminiscent of the movement in his most ecstatic landscapes. In almost all these works, a single bird is the only identifiable object in view. (In one instance, a duck hangs above a smattering of what look like red peppers—though they are called tomatoes—and against a backdrop showing a bit of brick wall.) But the solitary birds whirl in such a way that the dynamism devours the entire canvas. Thus the three series make up an interesting arc: the ray with several objects surrounding the fish, which together form a kind of triangle; the fowl, which whirls about the whole canvas; and the beef, which presides over the painting but does not fill it in the same way.

Which brings us to the beef series: six paintings of whole beef carcasses hanging from hooks, and three variations with part or all of a carcass arranged differently. The viewer's eye moves to the cavernous pitch between its ribs and the surrounding darkness in which the beast hums but does not whir.

Tonally, Soutine's carcasses do not resemble Rembrandt's. The drama of the subject is commensurately intense in both, but the communication of that intensity is managed differently. Still, "interpretation" is not too strong a word for Soutine's versions, because the decision to dedicate an entire canvas—and these are among the largest canvases in Soutine's oeuvre—to that single massive body was an enormous risk. It was a risk for Rembrandt, too, and he had to come to the decision on his own. Nonpainters may find it difficult to grasp the challenge of selecting subjects and deciding where they go on the canvas. Paulette Jourdain recalls that for this series Soutine used two different carcasses: an ox and a cow.[8] Both unfortunate beasts were suspended the same way. He strung them up by their hind legs on cords.

The cavity of the ribcage is the focal point of Soutine's carcass canvases as it is of Rembrandt's. This gaping body, its crimson geometries, the complexity of its structure, and the luscious beauty of the colors that make it up were an education for Soutine. The hours he spent with the carcasses taught him how to paint in a new way, how to compose a painting the center of which was determined for him by the body of the animal. Starting the following year the effects of this education were strikingly apparent. The decision to focus the entirety of an enormous canvas on a carcass taught him how to localize energy, and afterward Soutine's relationship to energy matured rapidly. His still-life canvases began to radiate comparatively gently in a circular motion outward from the center toward the edges, offering viewers a point of entry, a way into the painting, the way the Cagnes landscapes did. The rest of the canvas was not dead or even soft. In the beef carcass paintings, the backgrounds are charged, but they hum with an energy that forces concentration away from them and toward the center of the work.

By 1924 Soutine was finally able to rent a proper apartment and a separate studio. When he was not filling the shed outside 17

Boulevard Chanzy in Le Blanc with dead fowl of various sizes, he lived in two bourgeois apartments in Paris, first on rue Delambre, then on Avenue du Parc de Montsouris. He rented a large brick studio on the rue du Saint-Gothard, "just a few steps from Parc Montsouris and so right next to his home," Paulette Jourdain recalled. It was in this studio that he painted the entire flayed-beef series.[9] The smell, of course, did not delight his neighbors. They complained relentlessly but to no avail. The French art historian Pierre Cabanne wrote:

> Soutine, haunted by Rembrandt's *Flayed Ox*, had bought an enormous quarter of beef from the abattoir of port Brancion and hauled it to his studio at night to paint it. Unfortunately, at the end of a few days of work, the meat turned green and started to give off a pestilential odor. Secretly, Soutine went back to the slaughterhouse to get a bucket of blood which he intended to throw over the meat in order to restore its rosy color. This he did. Alas! The blood pooled on the floor and, drop by drop, dripped between the badly laid floorboards into the downstairs neighbor's home. Terror seized the entire neighborhood: "Murderer! Someone slit Soutine's throat!" the neighbors bellowed. We rushed to the "victim's" house and found him wading in a pool of blood frantically painting an enormous canvas.

The Vaugirard abattoir, the closest to Soutine's studio and likely the source of the body, was located right next to La Ruche. These were the beasts he'd heard braying while he tossed and turned on the bottom floor of the Beehive when he first arrived in Paris. His studio was about three kilometers from the abattoir, all the way across Montparnasse. If Soutine carried the carcass himself, he would have lugged it for the better part of an hour—probably longer, given his infirmity—and then up the stairs to the second floor. Modigliani once observed that Soutine painted meat best when he was hungry. He would have been voracious after that trek![10] And he made this journey in the late 1920s, during the Années folles—when the city teemed with glamorous American expats. It is comical to imagine Josephine Baker gyrating at the Folies Bergère across the Seine, and Hemingway downing daiquiris at Le Select just blocks from Soutine's studio, while the artist, soaked with sweat and drenched in the blood of a dripping carcass, hauled it across the city. It was a feat he would have only undertaken for Rembrandt. His obsession was so great he regularly traveled from the Gare du Nord to the Rijksmuseum to pay respects to Rembrandt's masterpiece *The Jewish Bride*, about which he once said, "Color has become the delicate instrument of the spirit." Soutine always spoke of that painting with his hand on his heart.[11]

Zborowski's assistant Paulette Jourdain visited Soutine's studio while he was painting the legendary carcass. She watched in shock verging on horror as he tossed buckets of blood on the decaying ox. Suddenly they heard a knock on the door. "It's the Hygiene Services," a voice announced. Soutine turned white as death. "Be nice!" Jourdain pleaded. "You can see clearly that he's painting it! He must be allowed to finish this canvas!" She managed to inspire pity in one of the officials.[12] A man in a doctor's coat came forward with a syringe and instructed Soutine to watch as he injected the carcass with ammonia to slow bacterial growth. The next day officials were sent over to disinfect the entire studio, and then Soutine was permitted to continue his work. From that day on Soutine always carried a syringe of ammonia. He would plunge the needle repeatedly into the bodies of ducks, turkeys, chickens, and oxen, which would become stiff as wood without losing any of their coloring. But when Soutine threw the bodies out, local dogs would dive into the trash cans, eat the poisoned animals, and die.

The drama of his work was mitigated by periods of rest. Jourdain, who traveled with Soutine and the Zborowskis to Le Blanc, watched his disposition transform when he took breaks from painting. He calmly sat and read Balzac, Dostoevsky, Valéry, and books of mythology and philosophy. When the weather was fine he went for walks in the village and visited the ancient churches. For the first time in his life, Soutine could afford tranquility.

CHAPTER 7

Companionship

SOUTINE DID NOT NEED ALL THE FINGERS ON A SINGLE hand to count the number of people with whom he could have conversations about his work and his passions. He met and formed lasting bonds with two of them during the 1920s. One was the critic Élie Faure; the other was Madeleine Castaing, who would play a larger role in the development of his legacy and career than any other person, including his agent, Zborowski. Zborowski was aware of her influence and did not like it.

A dealer has a complicated relationship with his painters. His job is to identify an artist before anyone knows his name and keep him after it's up in lights. The investment in an unrecognized painter gets returned once success is secured, but only if he continues to give the agent a cut of all he sells. Zborowski's early displeasure at being saddled with Soutine in order to hang on to

Modigliani had now faded to a memory. His task post-Barnes was to keep his star artist happy and therefore loyal to him. This was not an easy thing to do, particularly with an artist as ornery as Soutine. Other people—patrons and agents—began to notice that Soutine was gifted. Soutine was introduced to the posh art dealer René Gimpel at the opening of Zborowski's gallery. Zborowski knew that Gimpel was in a sphere above the Montparnasse bohemia, an emissary of a wealthier and more powerful Paris. Zborowski must have noticed how attentive Gimpel was to Soutine. And then there was Jonas Netter, whose affections for the artist had always been manifest, and Henri Bing, who gave Soutine his first solo show in September 1927. It boded well for Zborowski that Soutine missed the opening of his own show because he was vacationing with Zborowski in Le Blanc.

Zborowski was shrewd. He gave Soutine something invaluable: a personal chauffeur whose job was to drive the restless painter to any village that struck Soutine's fancy. It was an ingenious strategy. Soutine's habitual peripateticism was by that point well developed. He quickly became dependent on the driver, a Monsieur Daneyrole.

Few people spent more time with Soutine than Daneyrole, and hardly anyone else had as much opportunity to study his working habits. "He hated to be seen painting," Daneyrole remembered. In fact, he said, Soutine repeatedly painted a specific tree in Vence (see inset page 6) because there was a corner in the square where he could work without anyone seeing the canvas. "This tree is like a cathedral!" he would exclaim as Daneyrole drove him back to the spot again and again.

Soutine also forced Daneyrole to read:

Rimbaud, Seneca's Letters to Lucius. . . . With him I wasn't just a driver. We would talk, we would discuss the evolution of humanity, and the future of the world. He had suffered so much, that Soutine! By the time I knew him, his life had already turned around. He could sell his paintings for ten thousand francs. But he remained extremely suspicious. "They used to leave me starving, but now, because people know my name, they come to lick my boots." He was wounded by injustice, by all injustice. . . . His door was always closed to sycophants. But he didn't yell at everybody! He knew how to be diplomatic occasionally.[1]

Imagine the scene: Soutine packing his brushes, paints, and canvases into the car, clambering into the back seat, and then arguing with Daneyrole about Seneca as the two men drove the six hours from Paris to Vence. It's a beautiful drive. The city gives its frenzy over to miles and miles of open fields. Centuries-old stone and stucco buildings are nestled in acres of greens and yellows. Occasionally the pair would pass a medieval castle falling into dignified disrepair. Soutine loved these trips, and he took advantage of his mobility, traveling incessantly in and out of Paris in the late twenties while his reputation swelled. In 1928, Soutine included, alongside Modigliani, Chagall, and Utrillo, in *L'Expressionisme Française* at the Galerie Alice Manteau in Paris.

Around this time, Soutine developed a friendship that would yield true intellectual and artistic companionship, the only one of its kind he ever had. It also led to his only heartbreak. Élie Faure, born in 1873 in Sainte-Foy-la-Grande, a city on the Dordogne in southwestern France, was a medical doctor as well as a celebrated art critic and historian. He moved to Paris for secondary school, where his artistic education began and continued throughout his life, sustained by frequent trips to the Louvre. Faure studied philosophy with Henri Bergson in college before going to graduate school to study medicine. After graduation he worked as an anesthesiologist. In 1902, he began publishing essays of art criticism, which first appeared in Georges Clémenceau's socialist literary magazine *L'Aurore*, for which he wrote regular reports on the salons.[2] Faure and his friend the artist Éugène Carrière taught an art history course for five years at the Popular University, the first of many Faure would give at various universities. These lectures formed the basis for his seminal books on art history, published between 1909 and 1924 in four volumes: *Antique Art, Medieval Art, Renaissance Art,* and *Modern Art,* and published by Georges Crès et Cie. This work was the first of its kind in France—a survey from ancient to contemporary art history—undertaken at a time when France was just establishing chairs for the study of art history, a discipline that had previously existed only on the fringes of academia.

Faure and Soutine began exchanging letters in 1927 and grew increasingly close over the next three years. Their friendship was as intense as any romance, not least because Faure had the capacity to appreciate Soutine's peculiar painterly genius and articulate it better than any other writer before him—better even than Soutine himself. Faure wrote a monograph about his friend, published by Crès et Cie in 1929, which was the most brilliant and beautiful analysis of Soutine's powers published during the artist's lifetime. Faure's mastery of language matched Soutine's mastery of paint. In their respective fields, the two men were equals.

Faure's monograph was written by a man intoxicated by the bold bloodiness of Soutine's brush. Trained as a surgeon before becoming an art critic, Faure understood Soutine's fascination with pulsating innards. Faure, too, found the insides of a living creature as beautiful and vibrant as the wind in the trees. More than that, he saw God in the shimmers of blood and bones. The monograph is hot with religious fervor: "I will be accused of a lack of 'spirituality' if I write that physicality in painting is the whole of painting, consequently the whole mind. But I write it anyway, being sure to be right. I say that if this fire burns at the hearth of matter, as vile as it is, it will radiate to the limits of spiritual space, being the spark of God. Soutine is the rare 'religious' painter known to the world, because Soutine's work is among the most carnal that painting has expressed."[3]

Faure's admiration would have been precious indeed to Soutine. Faure was the most influential art intellectual in Paris, closely connected with all the significant contemporary painters, including Matisse, Signac, and Derain. But most important for Soutine, Faure was a great art historian whose province was the study and appreciation of the Old Masters. He was the first to write a long consideration of Cézanne, and this was the company in which Soutine longed to be placed and recognized. It was enormously exciting for him to be able to discuss his own painting with a critic able to appreciate the work of Cézanne and Rembrandt. Faure's eye and his erudition made him an invaluable asset to Soutine; he was able to critique Soutine's paintings using the same frame of reference and standards that Soutine himself had. An authority on the very painters Soutine revered could meet him where he was, offering a recognition and appreciation that truly mattered to him.

It was no doubt Faure's influence that catalyzed the artist's first expedition to Amsterdam to see what would become his favorite painting, Rembrandt's *The Jewish Bride* (now known as *Isaac and Rebecca*). He may have visited the painting as many as three times during the year he and Faure became close. Later that same year he traveled to London to see the Rembrandts on display there. On that trip he wrote to Faure from Kent. We do not have the letter, but we can imagine its contents: the excitement and relief with which Soutine must have described to his friend the riot of color and textures that his idol had bewitched into coherent beauty. It must have been a joy for him to discuss his pilgrimage with someone capable of understanding its import. Soutine also depended on Faure for more than intellectual nourishment: Twice the critic wrote checks to help him pay his rent.

Tragically, in March or April of 1930, a mysterious quarrel occurred between them, permanently ending their intimacy. Many of the letters they exchanged have been lost, but those that remain from the period of their misunderstanding offer a moving portrait of both men:[4]

1930

Soutine,

You are atrociously unjust, something you will regret—I hope so, for your sake—when calm has returned to your heart. No one in my home has made sport of you, we have both been victims of circumstance and of a common imprudence in which I see nothing that can diminish the respect in which I hold you and that you owe to me as well. How can you judge us so harshly? If I did not know how to read you, if I weren't sure that you must have suffered intensely to refuse to understand what happened, I would accuse you in turn of surrendering yourself to resentments unworthy of nobility, to wounded vanity. You are so overwhelmed, then, that you do not sense the distance between ourselves and those who have never seen anything in our friendship but a goldmine? And such is your estimation of my daughter, to say nothing of myself? I would blame you even more than I do if you were to deceive yourself to this extent about her and about me.

Yet you are not a base man. I know you better than you know yourself. Even now your letter no longer exists in my memory. It is you, yourself, who would be "offended" if you realized what it reveals about the present state of your soul. And I would suffer not at all from your renunciation if I thought for a minute that it represented your real nature. It is within yourself that you will seek forgiveness and I like to think that you will find it there. On that day, I will receive you as a man in whom "admiration" has become, since the time that I met you, the necessary complement of our friendship. If in this friendship you yourself have felt only "admiration," I would regard that as a sufficient reason to withdraw both of them from you, for that would show me that there was only an exceptional painter where I thought I had found a man. And that would be so much the worse not for me, but for you. Until the day—which I hope will be soon—when you realize that humility is the supreme conquest and refuge of pride.

I do not want to think for a minute that, should you feel a desire to see me again one day, you would use this foul pride to flee from realizing this desire. If when this day arrives you should hesitate, it would be because you still insist on disregarding all that I have been to you. I will wait for you, then, with confidence, months and years if necessary. You were, you still are, aside from my two sons, the only man I love. I am fifty-seven years old. I could die without your having forgiven me for a wrong that no one in my home intended to do to you, and for which I, for my part, forgive you your ugly interpretation. But if I die without your having come to tell me that you were mistaken, not for my sake but for your own, my soul will be tranquil in the conviction that one day you will regret not having reconciled with me. And in this conviction lies the proof of the affection, of the respect and "admiration," that I persist in feeling for you, if only you will let me. From afar, your painting will tell me whether you remain the man that I still see in you.

In the meantime, I remain your only friend, and your solitude is my suffering.

Élie Faure

Soutine to Faure
April 28, 1930
Sunday
Monsieur,
I have thought and reflected much on your letter and I prefer her making sport of me to all this admiration that you throw in my face. Just when I've been so offended it's wrong to talk of painting.

And your feelings of friendship, what can you mean by them at such a time? Future conversation, then, no longer makes any sense.

But rest assured that I have wonderful memories of some moments.

C. Soutine
26 Passage d'Enfer

Soutine to Faure
147 Blvd St Germain
December 5, 1930
Dear Monsieur Faure,
I have indeed received your two letters. I thank you for them. Frankly, I feel awkward. Memories of the past years are still fresh. It would be very difficult for me to see you at this time.

Please accept my sincere regards
Soutine

Soutine to Faure
Sunday February 8 [1931]
Dear Monsieur Faure,
Forgive me for the delay in returning your Balzac volume, but I was sick with a bad case of the flu.

Very sincerely,
Soutine

Faure to Soutine
Paris 147 Blvd St Germain
April 20, 1931
My dear Soutine,
I have just become the owner of your large plucked bird that I used to call the "crucified turkey" and that I recently came across by chance.

This by way of saying that I have not stopped loving you, for I had to make a sacrifice totally incommensurate with my present resources, "business" going as badly for me as it possibly could. But I couldn't resist. Thus I have you a bit closer to my heart.

I hope that you are doing well. I saw some beautiful recent canvases by you, which make me think that you remain the profound man that I knew and the first—far and away—among living painters.

It would be a great joy for me to see you again. I hope you won't refuse me this. As of today the way is entirely open to you, and will remain so.

Come whenever you like, write me whenever you want.

I remain, tomorrow as yesterday, the best of your friends.

Élie Faure

Soutine to Faure

Monday, May 13, 1935

Dear Monsieur Faure,

I received your very cordial letter, which touched me deeply. I thank you for it. I have been traveling.

If you like, I could meet you in a café.

Until I have the pleasure of seeing you again.

Soutine

My address 26 Av. d'Orleans (portico)

Soutine to Madame Faure

[Late 1937]

Dear Madame,

I was struck and very moved by the death of Dr. Faure. I have

an impression of sadness that will stay with me for a long time.
I also regret not having seen him again and spoken with him.

Trust in my sincerity.
Ch. Soutine

The details of the drama remain shrouded in mystery forever—all the relevant parties are now dead, and none ever gave a complete account—but one can surmise the gist of the trouble from these letters. It appears that Soutine had developed deep affections for Élie Faure's daughter Marie-Zeline, but was rebuffed. His bruised heart and ego were so wounded that he severed all meaningful connections with the Faure family.

In his unpublished memoir, Michel Kikoine recorded a version of the story that Soutine had shared with him and his wife:

Soutine was timid in the extreme, to a degree difficult to imagine. One winter's evening, myself, my wife, and Soutine were all gathered around a fire that was almost extinguished, it was smack in the middle of the heroic period, we scarcely ate anything, and only once a day. That evening Soutine, a bit depressed and forthcoming, told us the story of his amorous drama. For some time he had been frequenting an eminent family whose daughter was the focus of his dreams. . . . He came to realize that he loved her quite seriously and that he wanted to share his life with her. But he dared not declare the torch he bore her; time passed, and when he saw her he never broached the subject, so she treated him as a good companion. One day he resolved to speak to the mother of the young woman and avow his feelings to her. She promised to keep his secret. A bit later the father also became privy to the confidence. Plans were laid, an apartment was sought, furniture was even bought, and still the young woman knew nothing. Finally, at the urging of her parents, he summoned his courage and resolved to speak to the young interested party. She listened with kind attention and then broke into gentle laughter, telling him that he should have spoken to her much sooner, for a few days earlier she had agreed to be the wife of her cousin, who was an aviator. Later it was learned that her happiness was short-lived, for her husband was killed in a plane crash. Soutine shared in the distress of the one he loved.[5]

In his letters, Faure repeated several times that he continued to be Soutine's only real friend. This would have been presumptuous if both men had not been quite certain of its veracity. There was no one else who ever came close to understanding Soutine's work or loving him precisely because he understood his work so well. The loneliness Soutine experienced after losing Faure must have been sharpened by the three years during which their friendship had thrived. And that relief would have been a precious thing even for a man less lonely than Soutine. Faure had provided a particularly sweet intellectual companionship. It is rare in the life of a serious artist to find another person capable of enriching their understanding of art. Loneliness haunts genius, and Soutine was trying to do something through painting that no one else was attempting or even interested in discussing. His entire life was in service to that project.

Until Élie Faure, the only people who could influence or alter Soutine's relationship with his craft were dead. They could not stand beside him in front of his canvas and say, "Ah, this stroke is brilliant," or "In this painting you are repeating tendencies from your earlier work." Even if he was not the sort of artist who required intellectual collaboration, it must have been painful to have no one he respected well enough to discuss his work with.

The question "What is art for?" is asked far more often than it is asked seriously, by far more people who can sound out the words than who have a sufficiently sophisticated understanding to grasp the gravity of the subject. Soutine lived in a period when many people—some brilliant, most ridiculous—relentlessly repeated answers to that question that he believed to be drivel. But Faure answered it the same way Soutine did. Both men were naturally fascinated by vitality, by the luscious beauty of living things. Soutine's lifelong goal was in some ways the same as Faure's—to understand energy, to capture it. Consider the balm that Faure's friendship had provided and the ache that its loss left behind.

It is a special honor for a great work of art to be recognized for what it is. Some paintings hang on museum walls for centuries, genuinely understood by only a handful of eyes. It is a kind of miracle that a person capable of understanding Soutine's work lived in his time and place, that they met, and that they were able to talk to one another. Of course, when such people cross paths, either love or torment ensues, and in this case Soutine paid for one with the other. Around the time he first became friendly with Faure, he was also developing a relationship with Madeleine and Marcellin Castaing, one that would prove transformative. When Faure cast him off, the Castaings picked him up.

Madeleine Castaing was an extreme figure, reveling in her eccentricity. Picasso called her the most beautiful woman in Paris (there could hardly be a greater authority on the subject). By the time Soutine met her, she was a fixture of the Montparnasse party circuit. Her journey to Paris was more straightforward than his had been. A child of the Third Republic, she shared none of Soutine's temperament, upbringing, values, or worldview.

Born in Chartres in 1894, the year after Soutine, Madeleine came from a bourgeois family that bequeathed her a fortune. Her childhood was easy, even glamorous. Her maternal grandfather, Rodolphe Burgues, was a sophisticate who cofounded *La Presse*, a political journal with an enormous social influence, alongside the celebrated journalist and politician Émile de Girardin. He was also close to the French symbolist poet Théodore de Banville, who, along with other, similarly exciting friends, gathered at the family estate and shouted at one another about politics and philosophy while downing bottles of absinthe. Little Madeleine would listen in rapture at the door.

Madeleine had obsessive tendencies. When she kindled to something, she burned white hot. From a young age she loved only two writers—Chateaubriand and Proust—and according to the writer Maurice Sachs, who attached himself to her later in life, she had read practically nothing else. He wrote of her, "She had only one husband about whom she was quite mad (and this is already less usual than one might think), one friend, one admiration in painting." Hers was a conscious, cultivated monomania. Sachs noted in his memoir that Madeleine proselytized for her idols, insisting that obsessive attention was the best way "to savor people and things, and almost managed to convince me of it."[6]

This obsessive streak was fully developed when, at fifteen, she fell in love with a man fifteen years her senior. She had caught sight of him during a layover between trains while departing for vacation with her mother. The gentleman, Marcellin Castaing, was serendipitously seated in the adjoining compartment in the subsequent car. Once her mother had fallen asleep, Madeleine slipped through the compartment doors, stood before him, and made her affections known. Marcellin Castaing (whom she preferred to call Marcel, as if playacting that she was married to her beloved Proust) was the scion of a wealthy family from Toulouse.

They married in 1915, when she had reached the ripe old age of twenty. Madeleine always claimed that she had wed in a Grecian robe, bare legged and in sandals, like the figures on the frescoes adorning the Parthenon. (Never mind that there are no frescoes on the walls of the Parthenon.) Marcellin became *sous-préfet*, the highest official of an arrondissement, in Amiens, a city in northern France, and later an attaché to a prefecture in Nancy, near Luxembourg. Madeleine found this life intolerably boring. After giving her beloved husband two sons, she considered herself well acquitted of her duties to him and insisted that he give up administrative life and relocate the family to Paris, where she believed she had always belonged. Marcellin acquiesced, and the family of four took up lodgings on rue Victorien-Sardou.

It was during this stretch of her life—in 1923, immediately after the Barnes purchase but before it had fully transformed Soutine's financial situation—that Madeleine first met Soutine. She and her husband were dining at La Rotonde with the artist Pierre Brune—the same Brune who, along with Frank Burty Haviland, had tempted Picasso to Céret. (He also founded the Céret Museum of Modern Art with the help of Picasso and Matisse.) A disheveled Soutine stumbled into the café. Brune told the Castaings that a destitute artist in desperate need of their generosity had just walked through the door. Marcellin approached Soutine, and the three of them made plans to meet at the artist's studio.

When they were seriously delayed for their appointment, Soutine, tired of waiting, left the studio and ran into them in the street. Obviously annoyed, he offered to turn around and take them to look at his paintings, but the couple did not have time. Marcellin offered 100 francs as a sort of down payment and suggested he give Soutine a promissory note for the rest and then come back another time. Soutine took the bill and threw it on the ground without saying a word before storming off. The Castaings had not yet learned that Soutine's ego swelled as his stomach shrank. Their charity had insulted him.

The next few years were full of drama for both parties. Soutine became a star, and Madeleine Castaing became a jealous and tormented wife. Marcellin was an avid adulterer, the sort of man who takes pride in his philandering, developing it like an art. Madeleine knew of his appetites and ignored them so long as no lust blossomed into romance. She told the private investigator she had hired to tail her beloved that he need only warn her if Marcellin returned to the same bed with regularity. The dreaded report came: Her husband sought refuge at a set hour each week with a particular prostitute. Madame Castaing devised a scheme. She paid the prostitute for Marcel's hour, and when he arrived, he found his wife where he had expected his mistress. This delighted him; he admired her courage. She vowed she would be both whore and wife to him if he promised not to stray. He made this vow eagerly, but without solemnity or seriousness. His wife was unconvinced. She no longer felt safe staying in Paris. The couple left the city to vacation in Châtel-Guyon, a beautiful spa known for its thermal baths, where Madeleine spent some time plotting the next chapters of their lives. As chance would have it, they met Soutine again while they were there. Zborowski had decided he needed a rest cure.

By the late twenties, Soutine was entering a period in which he would go for weeks, even months, without painting at all. This was partly due to his stomach ulcers, which caused him increasing pain. But long pauses in production were bad for business, and one of Zborowski's tactics to get Soutine's creative juices flowing was to send him to the spa town. The driver Daneyrole recalled, "I took him for his cures to Châtel-Guyon where he had his own masseur, and where he would visit with the Castaings. Zborowski paid for everything."[7]

The Castaings filled the void in Soutine's life left by Élie Faure's absence. While his initial introduction to the couple had occurred years earlier, it wasn't until they met again in Châtel-Guyon that their mutual fascination and attachment developed.

At about the same time, Madeleine had resolved to relocate her family from Paris to Léves, not far from her childhood home in Chartres. She wanted her husband to herself, and as it turned out, she wanted Soutine too. When the Castaings reconnected with Soutine they had recently purchased one of his great *Choir Boy* paintings for no less than 30,000 francs—an enormous sum, much larger than any other price his paintings had fetched at the time.[8]

The intensity of Madeleine's attention transfixed the artist. He permitted himself to be acquired by the Castaings. "For five years the three of us did not answer a single letter," Madeleine wrote.[9]

She exaggerated slightly—of the five years she and her husband spent in Léves, Soutine lived with them for only three. In 1933 she and Marcellin moved back to Paris. The three of them still spent a good deal of time in Léves, and the couple permitted Soutine to stay there even when they were in the city. But in those first three years, the Castaings devoted themselves entirely to the artist.

More and more of the responsibility for his care was usurped by the Castaings from Zborowski. Tensions mounted between the competing parties as the couple spent hours every week searching for the kinds of canvases Soutine liked, scouting out landscapes for him to paint, hunting down Céret paintings for him to destroy, and oohing and aahing over the new works he permitted them to see. Many of the costs that Zborowski had absorbed for Soutine suddenly became the Castaings' responsibility. They bought him brushes and paints, and they purchased as many of his paintings as Zborowski would allow, though the agent still had first pick of the bunch. He and Paul Guillaume remained the only competition the Castaings had over "ownership" of the artist.

Then, in 1932, Zborowski tragically died of a heart attack at age forty-three. Soutine had had a falling out with him in 1930, and since then the Castaings had gradually taken over Soutine's business affairs. Zborowski's death finalized the transition. The better part of Soutine's last decade was spent in their care.

The Castaings were society people, and they introduced Soutine to a glittery milieu. Modigliani and the composer Erik Satie had both been close friends of theirs. By the time Soutine entered their lives, those celebrities had been replaced by others, such as Jean Cocteau and the author Maurice Sachs—who was so addicted to Madeleine's charms that he and his lover, Henry Wiggins, moved next door to be closer to her.

In his memoir Sachs recalled meeting Soutine twice: "The two times I saw Soutine, I was moved by his soft, wild gaze. . . . He was noble and at the same time had the hunted air of some proud, solitary animal horrified by the footsteps of man, but never sacrificing the secret laws or pride of its race. . . . I found in his canvases a terrible, involuntary distortion, undergone in fear and trembling, that all his efforts aimed at taming."[10]

The Castaings offered Soutine his first, and ultimately a permanent, entry into a Parisian cultural universe that was primarily Christian and, if not overtly then at least subtly, anti-Semitic. This became clear much later, when the Nazis occupied Paris and Madeleine Castaing's newly opened interior decorating company flourished. Such prosperity would not have been possible without some degree of collaboration with the Nazi regime. The Castaings themselves did not despise Jews, but the anti-Semitism ingrained in French culture was not inconsistent with their way of life.

Soutine suddenly found himself in a community of people who did not share his lifelong fear of the hatreds—whether latent or manifest—that curdle every elite circle. Moving in high Parisian social life meant being in close proximity to anti-Semitism, always lurking a few whispers away. Soutine read newspapers and listened to the radio, and he took politics seriously. His life experience had taught him that Jews were particularly vulnerable, and most of those he knew protected themselves by remaining within Jewish communal life. It must have been bizarre to find himself so far removed from that world. It must also have been exciting.

In any case, anti-Semitism did not prevent his patrons from supporting him. The Castaings had the opportunity to study Soutine's work habits with obsessive constancy. Over the decade during which they nurtured his talents, he never permitted them to watch him apply brush to canvas, but they learned the rhythms of his artistic metabolism, which were erratic and exacting. Soutine could only paint when compelled by some inner necessity, when some force seized him. While waiting for the creative convulsion that he called "the miracle," he would brood in sterile frustration for long stretches, growing increasingly anxious that the thunderbolt might never strike again.

The Castaings knew a great deal about Soutine's painterly eccentricities. All painters have their preferred surfaces—some favor raw, unprimed canvases; others cardboard, burlap, or wood. Soutine's preference was unusual: He wanted to recycle abandoned eighteenth-century paintings because he liked the textures left behind by the covered images. The Castaings scoured flea markets for these prized canvases, these precious bits of junk. Once supplied with a satisfactory canvas, Soutine meticulously prepared his paints, assigning each one its own brush space on the palette and its own brush. "It all depends on the way you mix color, catch it, place it," he told the couple. He preferred to finish a painting in a single session, ensuring that the speed of application was evident in the energy of the finished work. If dissatisfied, he would tear the paintings to shreds.

There was a time when greedy collectors and dealers began paying thieves to scavenge Soutine's trash for discarded canvases, which they stitched together. Fakes—or salvaged works "edited" by some other painter—circulated in the market freely. René

Gimpel once told Soutine he had visited the Tate in London and suspected that the museum had a fake Soutine on display.[11]

Soutine had a habit of unintentionally yet mercilessly torturing his models. He was extremely particular about what he wanted to paint, and once he settled on a subject, he could not bear for his model to move for the duration of "the miracle." This proved especially difficult in his execution of *Woman Wading*. He had set out to create his own interpretation of Rembrandt's *Woman in Her Bath*, and the Castaings trotted around Chartres with him looking for a model with precisely the right shape and aura. When Soutine at last set his sights on a particular peasant woman, he enlisted the Castaings to convince her suspicious husband that there was nothing untoward about his wife posing for a strange man while ankle deep in a stream, wearing only a nightgown raised above her knees.

Mid-session, gray clouds darkened the sky, and a heavy rain began pelting sitter and painter—to the horror of the former and to the apparent glee of the latter. He painted on, undeterred, in the light of sporadic bolts of lighting, while his model shrieked and begged to take cover. Like a man possessed, he shrieked back for her to stay put, refusing to stop before he was satisfied with the work. The result was a magnificent painting, which, like so many of Soutine's canvases, has disappeared into a private collection.[12]

The figure at the center of the painting stands upright, head tilted forward and arms akimbo, holding her skirt. The water below reflects her body, her clothing, and the grass that lines the stone steps behind her. A dark blue arch curves overhead. The shady landscape feels cool and wet, almost cave-like, accentuating the woman's warmth. Soutine rendered her exposed flesh in smatterings of yellow, green, red, and blue. Her shimmering dress, draped over her bare shoulders, mixes strokes of white and primary colors, its shadows rendered from a rubbed-down pink. Unlike in Rembrandt's original, there is not one stretch of pure, unalloyed color. Decades earlier Baudelaire imperishably described the style:

> An intoxication of pencil or brush, almost amounting to frenzy. This is the fear of not going fast enough, of letting the spectre escape before the synthesis has been extracted and taken possession of, the terrible fear that takes hold of all great artists and fills them with such an ardent desire to appropriate all means of expression, so that the commands of the mind may never be weakened by the hand's hesitation; so that, in the end, the ideal execution may become as unconscious, as flowing, as the process of digestion is for the brain of a healthy man after dinner.[13]

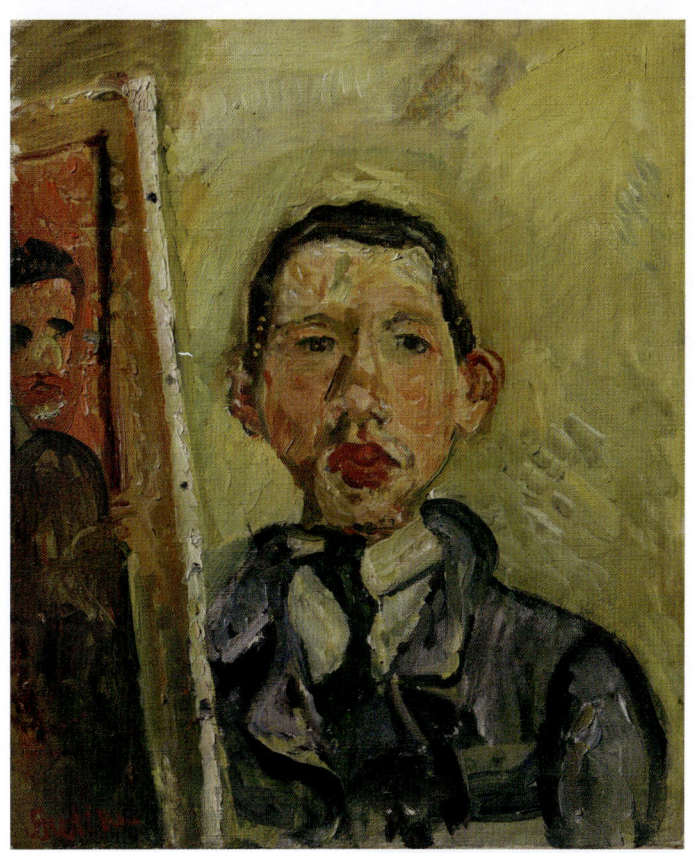

Self Portrait, c. 1918.

(Princeton University Art Museum/Art Resource, NY)

Bouquet of Flowers (Bouquet de fleurs), c. 1918, oil on canvas.

(The Barnes Foundation)

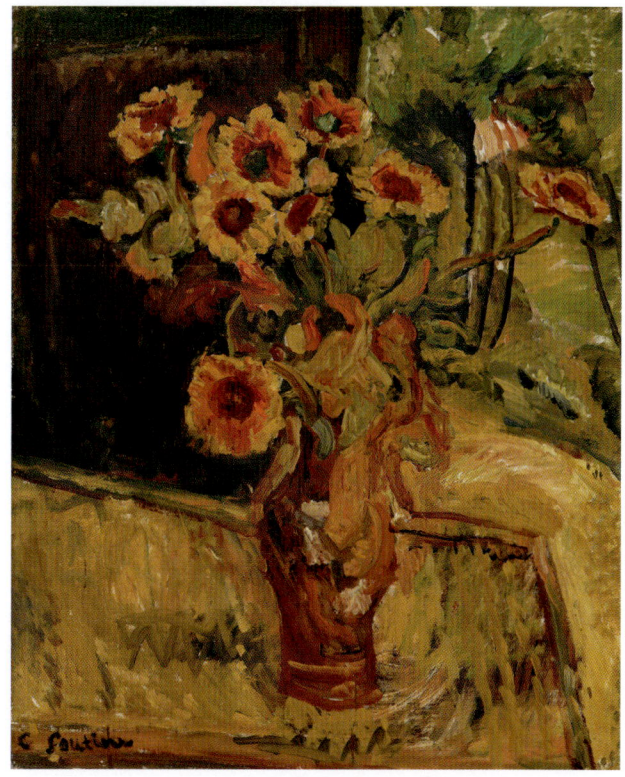

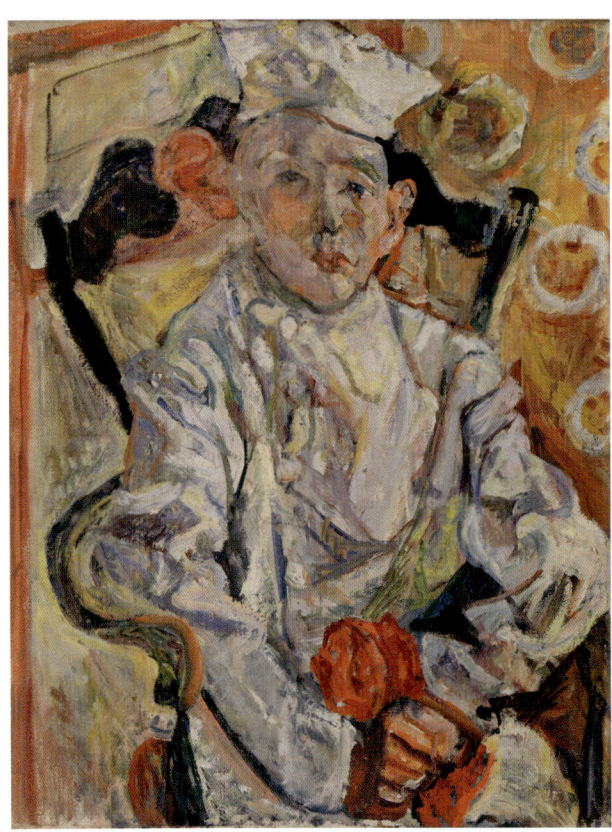

The Pastry Chef,
c. 1919, oil on canvas.

(The Barnes Foundation)

The Hill at Céret, c. 1921.

(Digital Image © 2009 Museum
Associates/LACMA. Licensed by
Art Resource, NY)

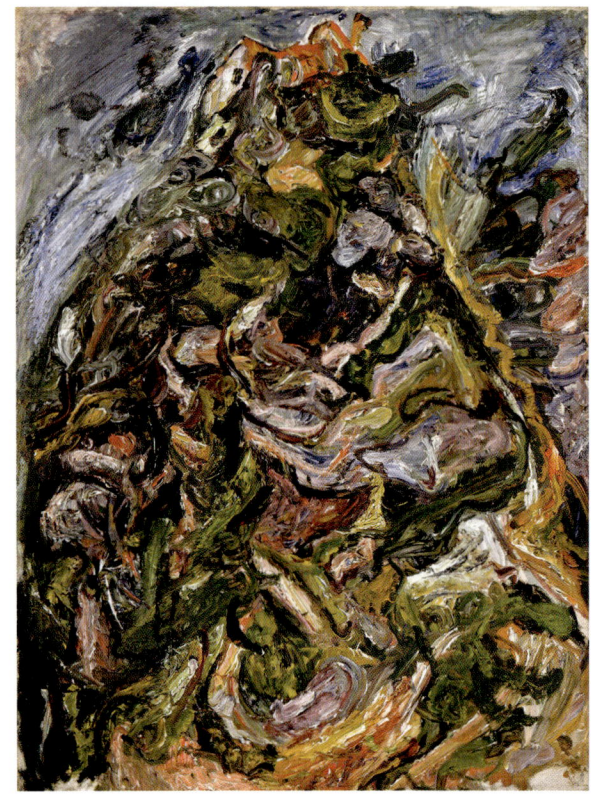

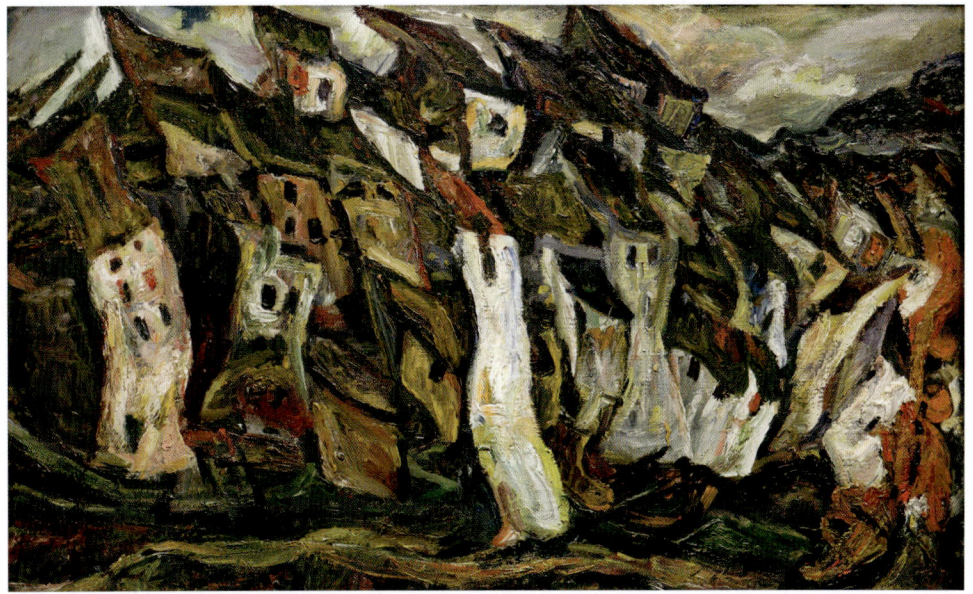

The Houses, c. 1920–1921. (Photographie numérique)

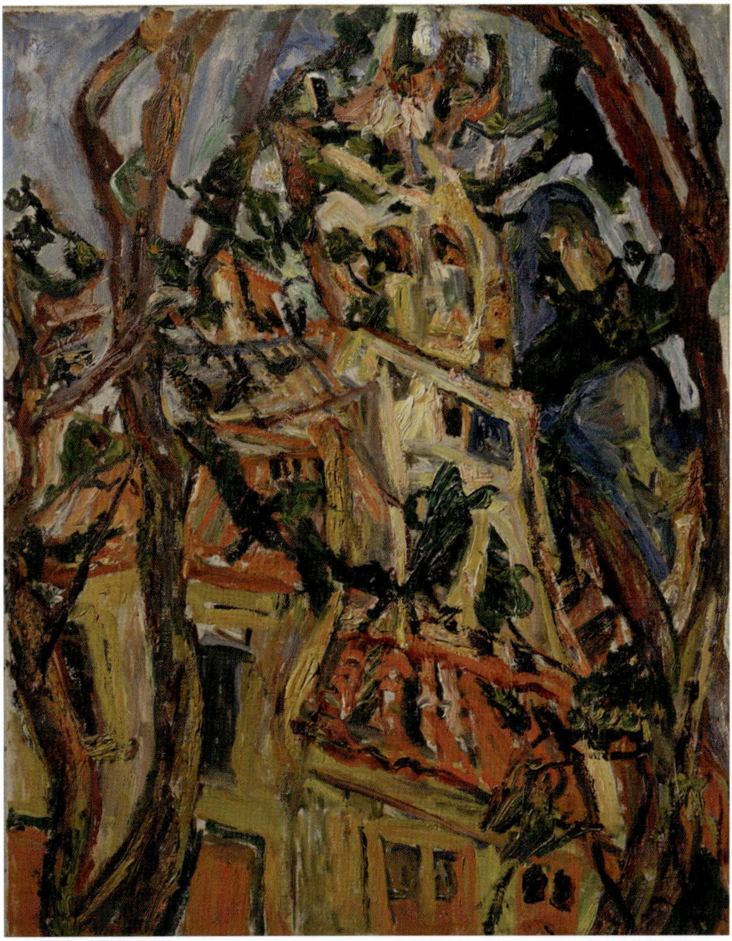

Red Roofs, Céret,
c. 1921–1922.

(The Henry and Rose
Pearlman Collection/
Art Resource, NY)

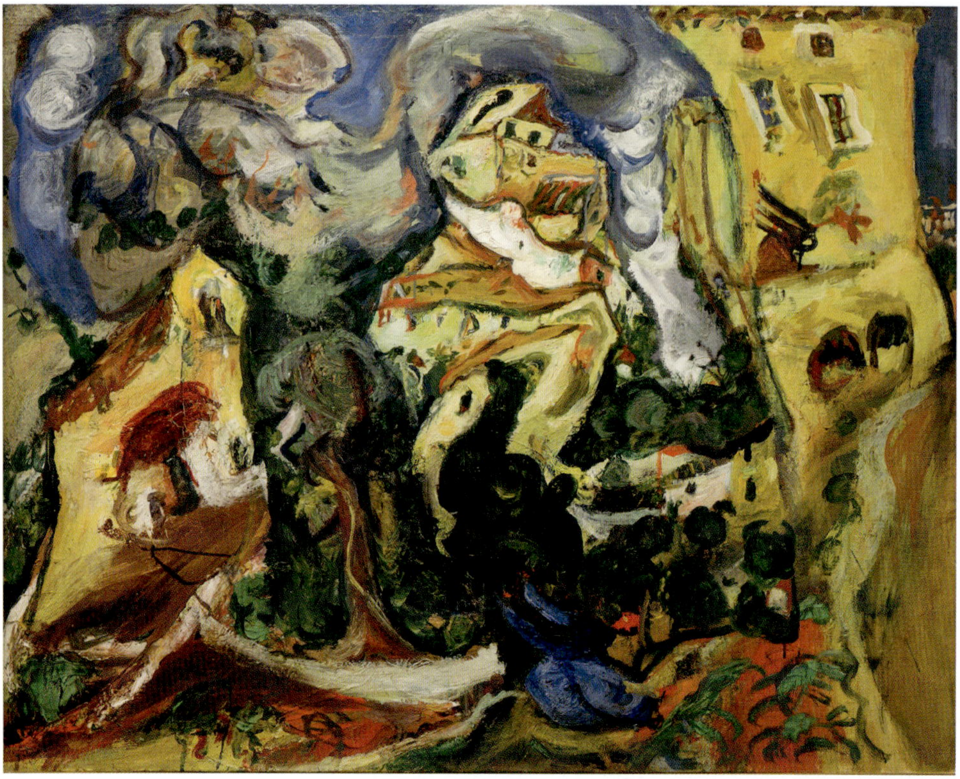

The Village, c. 1923.

Still Life with Rayfish,
c. 1923.

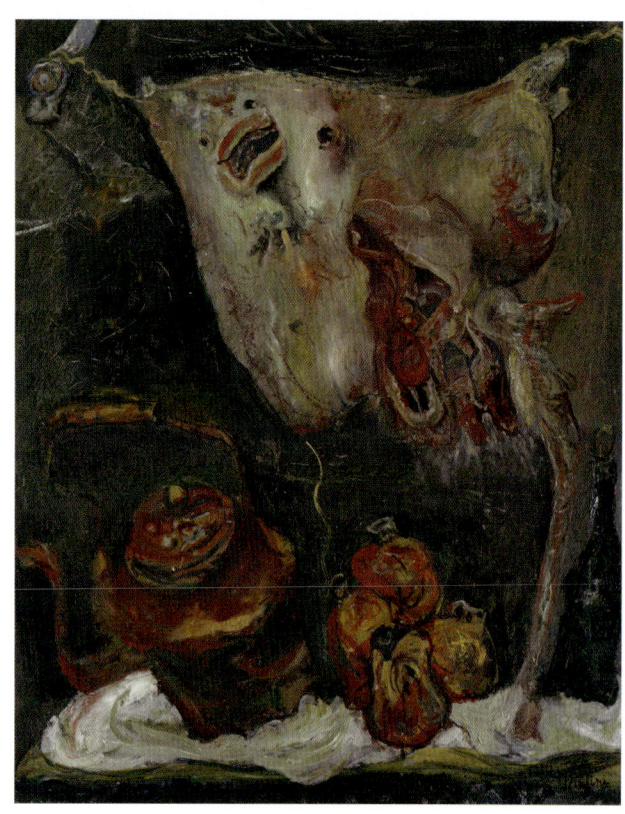

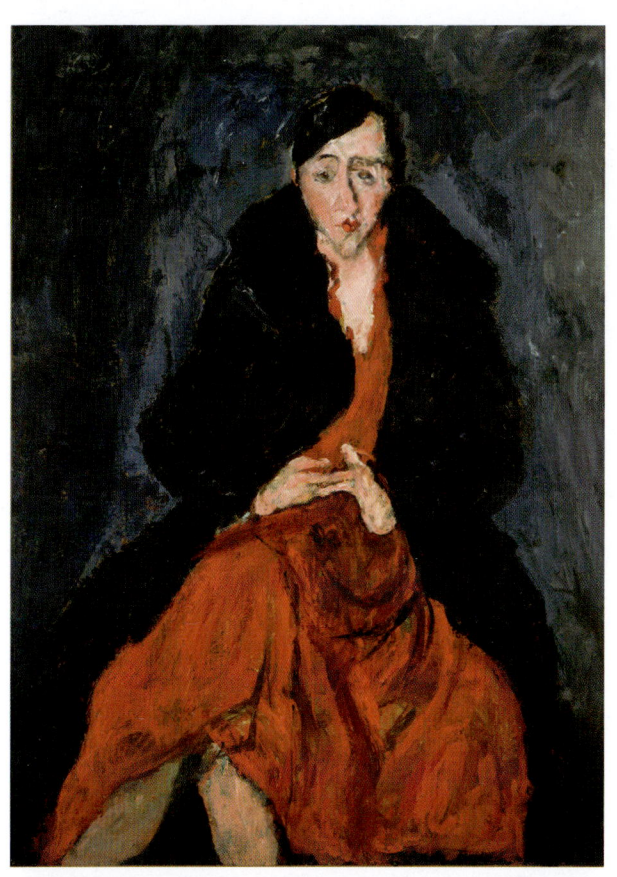

Madeleine Castaing, c. 1929.

(Image copyright © The Metropolitan Museum of Art. Image source: Art Resource, NY)

BELOW:

The Two Pheasants, c. 1924–1925.

(Open Art Images, Public Domain)

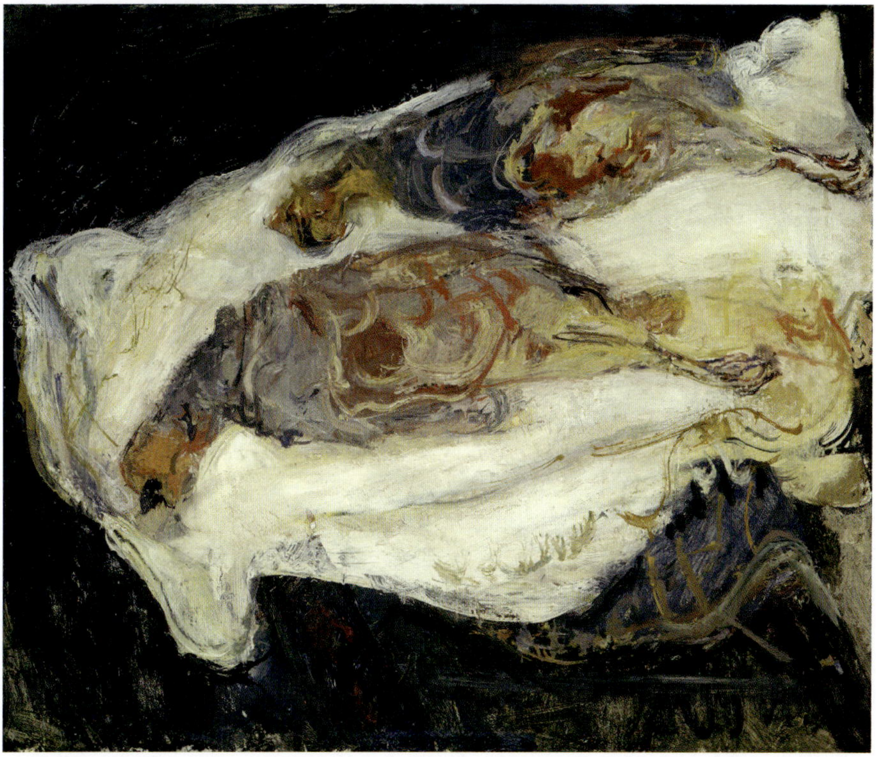

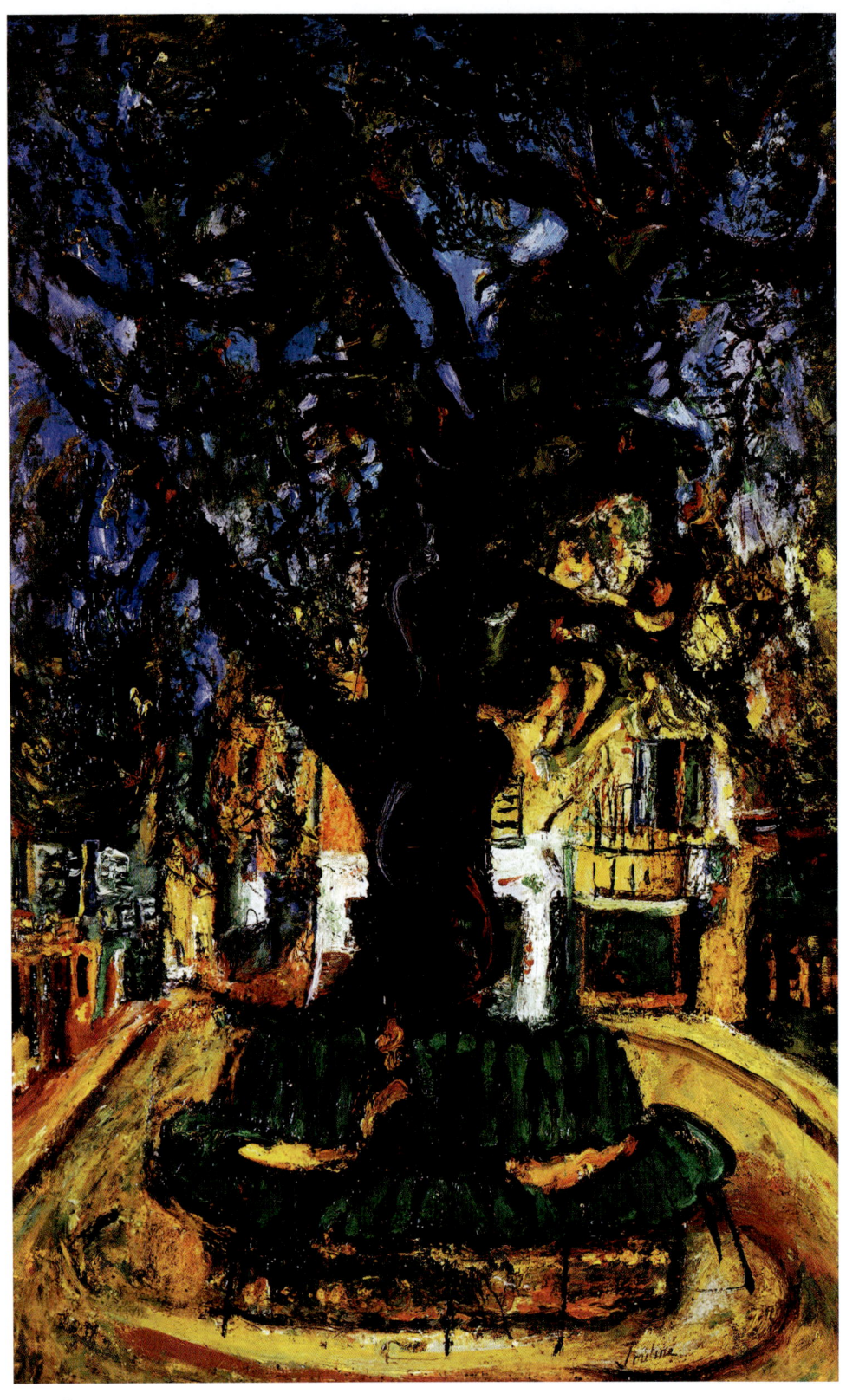

Small Town Square in Vence, c. 1929. (© DeA Picture Library/Art Resource, NY)

The Bellboy, c. 1928.

Woman in Profile, c. 1937.

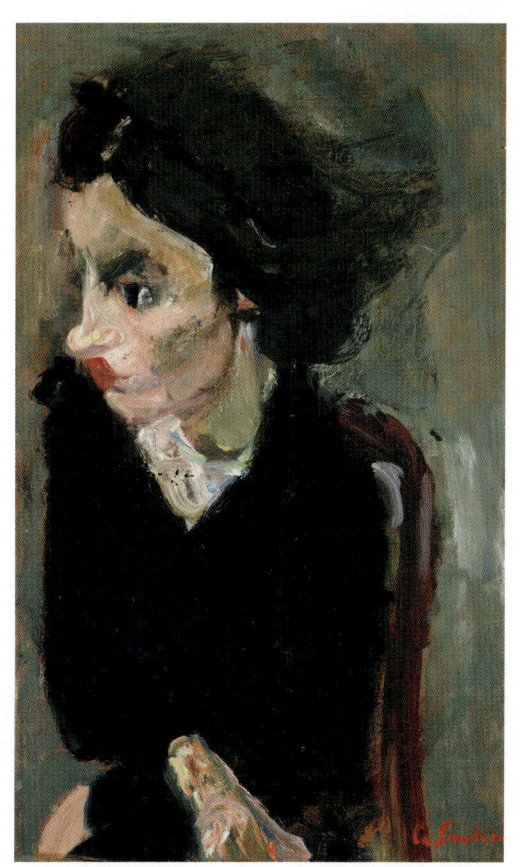

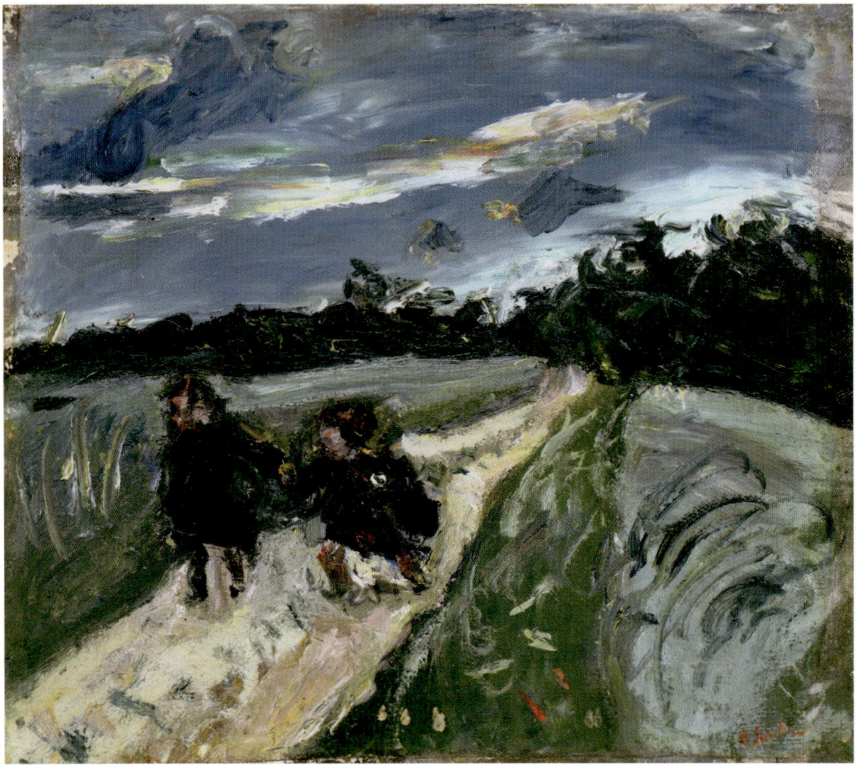

Return from School After the Storm, c. 1939. (The Phillips Collection, Washington, DC)

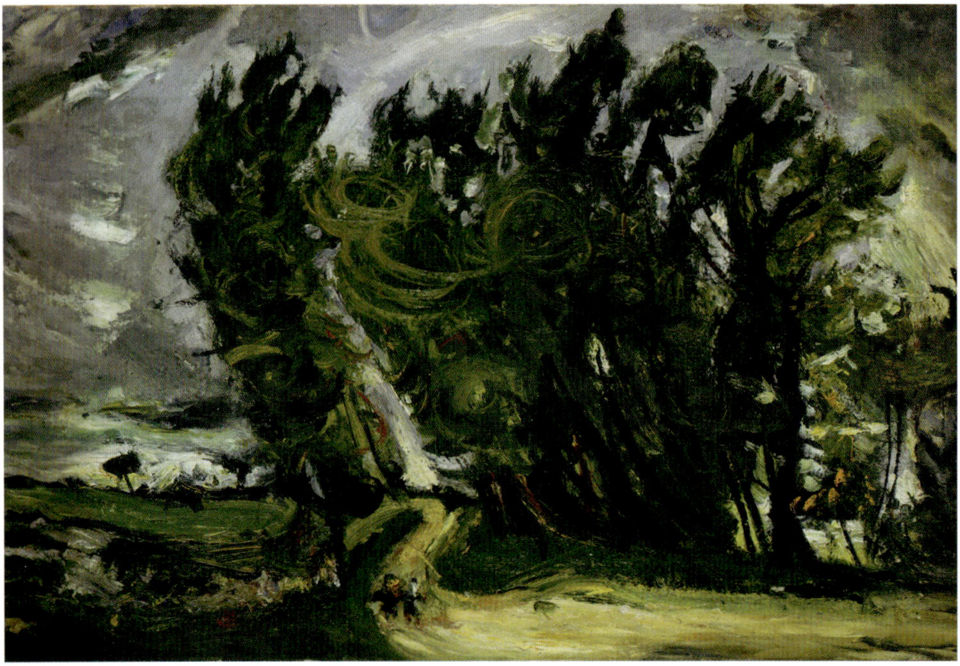

Windy Day at Auxerre, c. 1939. (The Phillips Collection, Washington, DC)

CHAPTER 8

Love at Last

ADOLF HITLER LEFT VIENNA FOR MUNICH IN THE SAME year and season that Soutine arrived in Paris. The young Hitler, born just four years before Soutine, had spent the previous five years in Vienna, later recalling, "I owe it to that period that I grew hard."[1] How unnerving to think that Soutine's early strides forward were made in step with Hitler's. In May 1913, both men were just lost boys in unfamiliar cosmopolitan centers. A decade later, the year of Albert Barnes's major purchase of Soutine's works, Hitler was part of a failed coup in Germany. He and his coconspirators were sentenced to five years in prison, of which he served only one. The first mention of Adolf Hitler in *The New York Times* alerted readers to his early release. He had been busy in prison: During those months behind bars he completed *Mein Kampf* and would spend the next eight years preaching its putrid politics. The message resonated. With Hitler at the helm, by September 1930 the Nazi Party rattled the globe by winning 6.4 million votes in the national election, making it the second-largest party in Germany.

The world was beginning to notice that a strange new evil was incubating in Germany, but if Soutine was paying attention there is no record of his alarm. He was by then a bona fide member of the Parisian elite. As Nazi membership lists swelled and poison swirled through salons and evening parties across Europe, Soutine sipped champagne at the Castaings' and visited cafés to give young artists the opportunity to flatter him.[2] It was a beautiful time to be in the City of Light. Josephine Baker had recently arrived and was immediately hired by Les Folies Bergére, where she danced topless in her infamous banana skirt while the adoring crowd cooed, "La Baker!" in rhapsodic delight. There were moments, amidst the crush of gyrating bodies or the hours spent in the Castaings' living room exchanging pleasantries with Cocteau—who later flourished in occupied Paris—when Soutine forgot he was a Jew. And there may have been awkward, even bruising stretches—say, while listening to Maurice Sachs snarl about the Jewish pollutants in Paris—when he could not forget. If the recollection didn't come to him on his own, it would be forced upon him later.

Two months after the Nazis' shocking electoral victory, Soutine participated in a curious episode in Paris that attests to the height of his celebrity. In 1928 a mysterious woman named Maria Lani appeared in the city, claiming to be a famous German movie star. She was accompanied by a man who went by various names, including Maximilian Abramowicz, Maximilian Ilyin, and Mac Ramo, and who claimed to be the writer and producer of a film in which Lani was to star. The mysterious duo called the project *The*

Woman of the Hundred Faces, and said they had come to Paris to ask the greatest modern painters to each contribute a likeness of Maria Lani. Within two years she had sat for the "most important, most expensive and most dangerous" Parisian artists.[3] On November 3, 1930, Soutine and fifty other artists' works appeared in the exhibition *Fifty-One Portraits of Maria Lani* at the Galerie Bernheim. Shortly thereafter, Lani and her strange accomplice disappeared. Years later, they absconded to America with all of fifty-one of the paintings and sculptures from the show, which they sold to galleries in New York and Chicago.

Not until they had disappeared from the scene did it become clear who they were. Lani had been a Czech secretary, and Abramowicz was her husband. Cocteau, who had been their great champion and had secured their entry into the glitziest circles in the city, wrote in his diary, "Abramowicz dreamed up the story that this little unknown, this nobody, was a celebrated German actress. He begged us all to do her portrait. He exhausted us. . . . [This was the] Triumph of an imposture."

Soutine's contribution to the show was the only one of his paintings ever to have been exhibited in prewar Germany. It was displayed in a group exhibition at the Galerie Alfred Flechtheim in Berlin in 1930. (Flechtheim, a German Jewish dealer, was among the first great champions of European avant-garde art. Penniless, he fled Germany for Paris six months after the Nazis came to power in 1933, and he died in London in 1937.) The Nazi second-in-command, Reichsmarschall Hermann Göring, saw the Soutine hanging there and became obsessed with tracking down and destroying the Jew who had painted it, along with every other Soutine canvas. The painting is now in the permanent collection of the Museum of Modern Art in New York. If you visit the collection while the painting is on view, you can get just as close to it as Göring once was.

In the early 1930s, Soutine went back and forth between Paris and Léves regularly; the Castaings permitted him to use their home whenever he wished, whether they were in residence or not. After Zborowski's death in October 1932, Madeleine Castaing gradually became Soutine's acting agent, managing his sales and speaking on his behalf to gallerists, patrons, curators, and the like. Soutine's productivity slowed considerably in these years. His manic bursts of work grew less frequent and were over more quickly. "There were two Soutines," Madeleine said, "the Soutine of painting and the Soutine of idleness. The one was as exaggerated as the other."[4] It was true that he was painting less, and that he had become unproductive during a period of critical and professional recognition. His first solo exhibition in the United States, at the Chicago Arts Club, was held in 1925. Two years later the celebrated Leicester Galleries in London held a retrospective of his work, and in 1929 Lincoln Kirstein, a giant of American modernism, included Soutine in a show at the Harvard Society of Contemporary Art in Boston.

The Leicester Galleries was a groundbreaking institution in England. Originally founded as an ordinary conservative venue in 1902, it became a champion of the avant-garde during the 1910s. It was the first gallery in Britain to exhibit works by Cézanne (1925), Degas (1922), Gauguin (1924), Léger (1926), Matisse (1918), Morisot (1930), Picasso (1919), and Van Gogh (1923). In response to growing anti-Semitism in the 1930s, the gallery hosted exhibitions of Chagall in 1935 and Soutine two years later. In 1941—at the height of the Second World War—it dedicated an exhibition to Paul Klee, another Jewish artist hunted by the Nazis.

It was a dangerous time to be a minority in Europe, but—as humanity has occasion to relearn every few decades—endangered minorities find ways to convince themselves that they are not among the hunted. Soutine had traveled far from the small village where he was born and where he and his community were painfully conscious of their lack of means and protection. He spent the early days of World War II forgetting where he came from.[5] But in 1934, Soutine received a reminder in the form of a letter from a ghost from Smilovichi. One of his sisters had managed to track him down, evidently not for the first time—the letter suggests they had been in sporadic communication. She wrote in Yiddish. Soutine would have had a hard time making out the words:

My dear brother Chaim-Itzhak Soutine,

I, your youngest sister, Etel, write you a greeting and wish you happiness in life. I, together with my beloved husband and my daughter Nekhomele, am with our mother. Until now, dear brother, we have been living miserably. Our father has been dead for three years. It has been two years since our brother Yankel passed away. We are like lost sheep in the great world. Now, dear brother, you are like a ray of sunshine—lighting up our dark lives. We thank you, dear brother, for the present that you have sent us. Mother also gave us a few francs. Dear brother, I myself am a weak person, I have a serious condition: it's called diabetes. It's incurable and I must keep a strict diet. Until now I was not able to do that, because we live very poorly. But now, dear brother, as mother gave me a few francs, I have some kind of support for my sickness.

Now, dear brother, I am turning to you to save us, as I have no other recourse. Please forgive me that I bother you so much, but it has come to a point that I must share everything with you—who can be closer than a brother? Only you, my dear, can be my savior. Our daughter is neglected, I rarely look out for her because I am always too weak. She is especially dear to me, since for five children she is the only one who survived, may she live for many years. Dear brother, it is very difficult for me to ask, but I ask you nevertheless if you can please help us with a few francs, in all my future life I will always say that you were my savior. I wish you health, your sister Etel Tzukerman. My husband and daughter send their regards.[6]

Two years later Soutine received another letter, this one from his mother, Sarah Soutine, which was mailed from Smilovichi to his hotel at 26 Avenue d'Orléans. The contents of the letter and whether he ever responded to it or to the former missive are unknown.

Soutine moved from apartment to apartment in the 1930s, restlessly replacing one home with another. A lease in the Passage d'Enfer that was signed in 1930 was replaced with a sojourn in a hotel on the Boulevard Raspail, followed by an address on the Avenue d'Orléans in 1936, and another from 1938 to 1939 at 18 Villa Seurat, an artist residence just twenty minutes on foot from the cemetery plot where he would be buried half a decade later. The street buzzed with other artists. Dalí, Derain, and Gromaire had all lived there at one time or another, and Henry Miller and the sculptor Chana Orloff were Soutine's neighbors when he moved in.

Miller attempted to make Soutine's acquaintance several times but always found the artist shy and rushed. It's a shame—the two would have kindled to one another. Of his own spiritual development, Miller wrote:

> Here is my genealogical line: Boccaccio, Petronius, Rabelais, Whitman, Emerson, Thoreau, Maeterlinck, Romain Rolland, Plotinus, Heraclitus, Nietzsche, Dostoevsky (and other Russian writers of the Nineteenth Century), the ancient Greek dramatists, the Elizabethan dramatists (excluding Shakespeare), Theodore Dreiser, Knut Hamsun, D. H. Lawrence, James Joyce, Thomas Mann, Élie Faure, Oswald Spengler, Marcel Proust, Van Gogh, the Dadaists and Surrealists, Balzac, Lewis Carroll, Nijinsky, Rimbaud, Blaise Cendrars, Jean Giono, Céline, everything I read on Zen Buddhism, everything I read about China, India, Tibet, Arabia, Africa, and of course the Bible, the men who wrote it and especially the men who made the King James version, for it was the language of the Bible rather than its "message" which I got first and which I will never shake off.[7]

He and Soutine would have had much to teach one another. The pantheon of one's personal gods is as perfect a record of their soul as a person can produce, and Miller and Soutine frequented the same churches.

Chana Orloff became a close friend of Soutine's. "It didn't take long for us to get to know each other," she said. She met a version of Soutine much changed by money and high society: "His meticulous appearance shocked those of us who saw the horrific state of his apartment!" Soutine would sometimes walk into his friend's home and express delight at the delicious smells wafting from the kitchen. Invariably, she said, "He would sit at the table and eat too much, then suffer from indigestion. If he met me the next day on the street he wouldn't even greet me." Soutine once confided to his friends that he had at times been so poor that he could not afford even to buy a shirt. "He told us how he managed to go out during that period: he would replace the shirt with underpants whose legs served as sleeves, gracefully tying the belt into a collar, and he would wear a tie on top. As if to prove the improbable utility of the underwear, he gave us a demonstration which was hilarious." Orloff said that Soutine would fain ignorance of the Russian language and culture, which they shared. To prove to herself that this was a performance, Orloff once misquoted Pushkin on purpose in his presence. Immediately Soutine corrected her, from which she confirmed her suspicion that he knew not only Russian but also much of Pushkin by heart.[8]

Soutine was living in Villa Seurat, in a two-floor apartment coated with dust, splattered paint, and cigarette butts, when he met Gerda Michaelis, a German Jew from Magdeburg who had escaped to Paris just as Hitler was coming to power. She was hardly the only Jew to seek refuge in France after Hitler's rise in Germany. The painter Wassily Kandinsky, the composer Arnold Schönberg, and the writers Joseph Roth, Hannah Arendt, and Walter Benjamin all did the same. While he was in Paris, Benjamin lived catty-corner from La Ruche on rue Dombasle. (For a while Arthur Koestler lived in the same building.) Small plaques testifying to both dwellings wink at one another from adjacent corners in Montparnasse.

Michaelis had never been particularly interested in religion—hers or any other—and in college she gravitated toward socialism. In 1930, she married a Christian architect with similar political loyalties. The marriage was pleasant enough, but that period in history did not permit Jews to forget their origins, no matter their personal spiritual predilections. The number of brownshirts in Germany metastasized in tandem with growing unemployment and inflation. As soon as Hitler came to power he wasted no time implementing racial laws that stripped Gerda Michaelis's father, along with all other German Jews, of their jobs. Nazis endeavored to solve the housing crisis by evicting Jews from their apartments and replacing them with Aryan families. Jewish activists in political parties were interned in concentration camps. Michaelis, scared, was determined to flee to France. Her husband was fond of her, but not fond enough to protest or to accompany her: A prudent divorce was hustled through, and Gerda went to live with a friend who had already seen the writing on the wall and fled Germany for a small village in Normandy.[9]

Michaelis, who arrived penniless, quickly became painfully bored. Her friend helped her secure work as the companion to an old woman, but the work was dull, and Gerda suffered from terrible loneliness. One night, in a fit of recklessness, she took the train to Paris and made her way from the station to Le Dôme Café, which she had heard about back home. The place was overflowing with Germans, and she joined their company with eager relief. It was there, one afternoon in 1937, that a friend introduced her to Chaim Soutine.

"Everything about his body pleased me," she wrote. She moved in with him immediately and loved him forcefully and totally—as a man, not as a painter. His work was never what interested her. Other than the stock of materials he used to paint, little in their apartment attested to his professional life—a startling fact considering that for everyone else, and for all time, Soutine was first and foremost a painter. But she did not experience him that way. He had "many books by Balzac, a few Russian novels, and the essays of Montaigne, but not a single monograph about him—not the one by Élie Faure or the one by Waldemar George. He didn't have any catalog from any of the shows of his in Chicago or London or New York." And he never talked to her about his former lives: "Of Modigliani, a friend from his youth, he hardly ever spoke to me. And he didn't mention La Ruche, that famous house on the rue Dantzig where he met Chagall, Zadkine, and a few others. The names 'Léopold Zborowski,' 'Paul Guillaume,' 'Albert Barnes,' which are so often cited in works related to Soutine, he never once pronounced in my presence. I didn't know till much later the outsized role they each played in his life." Throughout their entire relationship, she remained mostly ignorant of his oeuvre. They passed the two years before the war in happy companionship: "We had abolished our respective pasts of our own volition, and we shut our eyes to the future. We tried not to hear the rumblings which announced the approaching storm."

Their life together settled into a routine. He painted and she cleaned. On weekends they visited the Louvre and the flea market, where Soutine would buy the old, discarded paintings that he used in place of fresh canvases. He loved attending boxing matches, and she often went with him. Every once in a while, he took the train to Amsterdam to visit his beloved Rembrandts at the Rijksmuseum. In those fleeting days of calm and contentment, Soutine did not want for money, but he was perpetually fearful that he would lose everything and was almost pathologically tightfisted. "The most trivial expenses worried him. Like a miser he agonized over small, daily purchases especially those concerning food." It reassured him to keep cash on his person. The idea of opening a bank account never occurred to him. "He wouldn't part with his money for anything in the world. On the whole he carried his money around with him. But, since he realized this practice had its drawbacks, he chose to stash away parts of his fortune in hiding places. This was how I happened to find a large sum stored in a samovar which I found at the back of a cupboard with an assortment of random knick-knacks."

When Michaelis, whom Soutine lovingly referred to as "Garde" because of the assiduous care she provided him, pointed out to him that this was a very irresponsible way to handle his money, Soutine scoffed, "What is the best way to keep money safe, then? Can't you see that the banks could suspend payments overnight?" He explained to her that he was terrified of thieves because in his neighborhood in Smilovichi burglaries occurred frequently. This fear was so pronounced that he invested little in his wardrobe—he was paranoid about thieves pillaging his clothes. He kept one or two shirts and a pair of pants, and when any garment showed signs of wear he would throw out the offending article and replace it with a new one. He absolutely refused to own more than one pair of shoes, and if they needed mending he had to stay home barefooted until the cobbler had completed his work. "The entire time we were together I only ever saw him in one outfit: a navy blue, double breasted suit—the very one he's wearing in all the photographs."

By the time they met, the days when Soutine could not afford to bathe were long past. Perhaps the rumors about his early dandyism, when he was first flush with cash, were true, but when Garde knew him Soutine had reached a happy middle ground: He was well kempt. The same could not be said for his apartment, which was filthy when she arrived. She threw herself into the maddening work of scrubbing and rearranging his home, and he appreciated her efforts—so long as she left his paintings alone. He kept them locked up in a cupboard, zealously and eternally hidden from view. Otherwise, she had total freedom to organize as she liked. The cigarette butts that had littered every surface were swept away, replaced with ashtrays located at regular intervals around the rooms.

A bathroom was across from his bedroom, but before her arrival Soutine had been afraid to work the gas to heat the water, so he had taken cold showers. Against his wishes, she operated the gas herself, and "when he saw that the water was running hot from the faucet he was delighted and wanted to take the first bath himself." He took excellent care of his teeth, which were strong and very white, and of his thick, handsome black hair, which he had a terrible fear of losing despite not being remotely threatened by baldness. He cut his hair himself, an old habit left over from a period when he could not spare the francs for a barbershop. She thought he did a beautiful job.

Michaelis was madly in love with Soutine, but she never mistook his companionship for reciprocal romantic attachment. "The truth is that nothing interested him but his work," she wrote. "I was lucky, if we can put it that way, that he was sick and that he needed me. If not for that, I don't believe he would have attached himself to any woman."

Whether this was true or not, it is certain that, above all, she worried terribly about his poor health. When they met he was subsisting on a very strict diet, which he followed meticulously. If it spared Soutine from greater suffering, he paid the price in diminished strength. Chana Orloff recalled that he endured terrible stomach pain—at times so intense that he slumped against a wall, head down, waiting for the pangs to pass.[10] He ate no meat, fish, or eggs, surviving mostly on boiled potatoes, plain pasta, and vegetable soup. He drank nothing but milk—she never saw him touch wine or beer. His early alcoholism had long since faded into a bitter memory. He detested strong drink. All this austerity had reduced him to skeletal proportions and, Garde thought, sapped him of energy and happiness.

Despite persistent duress, he refused to see the doctor Garde had found for him, an Austrian Jew named Tennent who had lived next door to her in her previous apartment, and who, like her, had fled his hometown in the wake of Hitler's rise. He and his family were working toward passage to the United States. In 1937, the same year Garde and Soutine met, she persuaded Tennent to covertly examine Soutine during an arranged social gathering. After doing so as discreetly as possible, he asked her to obtain X-rays of Soutine's stomach. Somehow she managed to badger Soutine into complying. Once they were acquired, the doctor delivered a daunting prognosis: Soutine had a severe, likely incurable stomach ulcer. His body was too weak for surgery. While treatment might slow the disease's progression, he doubted

Soutine had more than five or six years to live. He urged them to begin treatment immediately and to "hope for a miracle."

The doctor prescribed a diet rich in meat, eggs, fish, and butter—luxuries that Soutine had been deprived of for years. But Soutine, suspicious of Tennent's motives, rebuked Garde for seeking his counsel: "Your doctor is a charlatan! He pretends that I have a stomach ulcer! I am sure that this isn't true. He just wants to frighten me into following his treatments, which will never end, and which will destroy me." In a rage he grabbed the packet of medications that Garde had purchased and threw them to the ground. Garde was desolate, caught between inviting Soutine's rage by raising the subject again and watching him rapidly weaken as the condition worsened.

Madeleine Castaing proposed a solution: She acknowledged to Soutine that doctors can make mistakes but insisted that he consult with a specialist to see if the prognosis was corroborated. He acquiesced, and Castaing selected the well-respected Professor Gosset. When he confirmed Tennent's diagnosis, Soutine apologized to Garde for his furious protests. At last he consented to the regimen she had tried to implement, and over time his health showed considerable improvement. As an expression of gratitude and apology, Soutine painted an unforgettable portrait of the doctor's wife—a tribute to the family. This painting now hangs in the Phillips Collection in Washington, DC.

Soutine painted the portrait in 1937 (see inset page 7, *bottom*). It is one of the few among his portraits in which the subject is neither centered nor looking straight ahead. She is positioned close to the left edge of the canvas, slightly hunched, with her arms crossed on her lap and drawn close to her chest, as if she were cold. The background remains mostly bare, revealing a browned canvas beneath a thin skin of bluish paint, which appears to have been rubbed on dry rather than applied in a wet coat.

The woman's hair and shirt are both black but not the same black: The blue of the background appears to have been blended into her hair, and the strands are rendered in the same dry rubbings, reminiscent of charcoal (though certainly not charcoal). Her clothing is a richer and gentler black. She is thin. Veins and harsh shadows stand out on her exposed hand in scrapes of blue, green, and red paint, and also on her face, which is cut with a high cheekbone and a harsh jaw juxtaposed starkly against the greenish flesh of her neck.

The woman in the painting appears worried, and the subject of the painting certainly was, with good reason. She and her husband read the same newspapers that Soutine and Garde pored over together in the spring of 1938. They saw photos of Hitler on the balcony of the Hofburg Palace in Vienna, proclaiming the death of Austria after the Anschluss, and tried their best to habituate themselves to the growing ambient terror. An eerie silence permeated Paris. It seemed particularly pronounced and unbearable to Soutine on Sundays, as it contrasted so starkly with the bustle of the Sundays before the Anschluss, when the city clattered with activity.

The two took to escaping to the countryside on weekends. They would hire a group taxi to Fontainebleau, Chantilly, Versailles, or the Chevreuse Valley, where they would disembark and scout out a suitable spot for Soutine to set up his easel and paints. Each time, Soutine would issue the same ritualistic decree: "Above all, do not watch me while I work." Garde would laze about in the grass with a book or a magazine, occasionally taking her life in her hands by peeking up from the pages to catch a glimpse of the artist at work. From these surreptitious glances, she noted with awe that he never did a single preparatory drawing; he attacked the canvas directly. His favorite paints speckled the ground at his feet, with droplets of vermillion, cinnabar, and silvery-white dotting the grass where Garde had lain. He would work for two or three hours, stopping only when he was too tired to continue. They would pack up the supplies, scrupulously handling the canvas so as not to disturb the wet paint, and return to Paris—this time in a private taxi, to protect the painting.

Once back in the city, he would take the unfinished work to his studio and continue working on it until he was satisfied. If, after hours of frustrated effort, he remained dissatisfied, he would shred the canvas with a razor blade he kept for that purpose. This same impulse compelled him to show freshly completed works, once dry, to established agents like Hessel, Kaganovitch, or Rosenberg, and try to persuade them to exchange an old painting of his for a new one. If he succeeded, he would take the procured canvas home and destroy it.

This was how the pair spent the summer of 1938. As it drew to a close, cool winds matched Hitler's chilling march across Europe, and Soutine seemed to hasten to the newspaper each morning a little faster than the day before. August bled into September, and France and England signed the Munich Agreement with Hitler on September 30, sacrificing Czechoslovakia in exchange for a phony promise of peace.

Like everyone else in Paris, Soutine scoured his memory and network for contacts who might help ensure his security should things worsen. The most politically powerful of his patrons was Albert Sarraut, a center-right, opportunistic politician who had served as prime minister twice during the Third Republic, and, in 1939, was acting minister of the interior. (A year later, he voted to empower Marshall Pétain to establish the Vichy regime.) An art lover, Sarraut had several Soutines in his private collection. The artist appealed to him to renew his visa, and Sarraut readily agreed, even putting Soutine in touch with his chief of staff, André-Louis Dubois. This greatly soothed Soutine's anxieties—he lived in perpetual fear of administrative authorities and was acutely aware of the vulnerability his refugee status exposed him to, as well as the protection that government bureaucrats could offer. He began calling on Sarraut or Dubois regularly, just to reassure himself of his security. This would prove useful later—though not useful enough.

In the midst of all this drama, Garde became aware of a disturbing personal history of Soutine's that had been kept from her. It turned out that he had a daughter. Soutine had no relationship with the child and never mentioned her, but one day he received a letter that visibly rattled him. When pressed to explain, he told Garde, "It's an old story. . . . Apparently I have a child."

Garde was shocked. "How old?" she gasped.

Soutine didn't know precisely. "Perhaps ten years old."

"A boy or a girl?"

"A girl. I don't know her at all. I don't want to know her. Anyway, there is no proof."

He was angry, and Garde was afraid to ask further questions. But he volunteered, "The mother is Russian. I despise her. She lives with a Polish tailor now. I believe he has recognized the child."

Garde was extremely disturbed. He had only recently told her that if the two of them were to have a child together, he would marry her. How could he want nothing to do with the daughter he already had? But when she tried to ask him these questions, he demanded that she never raise the subject again.

After Soutine's death Garde met the daughter and her mother. The girl, Aimee Soutine, looked strikingly like her father. She painted, too, though not remotely in his style, and signed the paintings with his last name. Garde was acutely conscious of how despicably Soutine had treated both the mother of his child and his own daughter. A story, the veracity of which she could never confirm, tormented her deeply. She had heard that at one point the mother had gone to Soutine and begged him for money. Irate, he had refused her several times. She kept returning, pleading for help, until finally, overcome with fury, he held up some thousand-franc notes, thundered that he could give them to her if he wanted to but preferred to burn them, and then threw the fistful into the fireplace, watching them crumple to ash.

Nevertheless, Garde had committed herself to Soutine, and her loyalty was unflappable. He was all she had. She considered caring for him her highest and only calling. It was therefore a relief to her when, after his initial protestations, Soutine reversed his habits and began seeking medical treatment almost compulsively. After 1939, when Dr. Tennent managed to secure passage to the United States, Soutine had to find new professionals who could ease his anxieties. He started seeing two doctors: Dr. Guttmann, whom Madeleine Castaing's friend Gosset had recommended, and Dr. Abramy. He became neurotically dependent on their advice, seeking it ritualistically as a calming practice. They prescribed the same cocktail of medications ("bismuth, papaverine, Laristine Roche"), and Abramy advised that the invalid get some air in the country. This last recommendation permanently and dramatically altered Soutine's and Garde's lives.

Chapter 9

Storm Clouds

On the strength of his doctor's advice, Soutine and Garde left Paris in the summer of 1939 for a visit in Civry-sur-Serein, a small village about 220 kilometers southeast of Paris. Another artist, Udo Einsild, had recommended the spot to them. They left in August. It was the last time the pair would ever leave the city together. En route, Soutine painted what is now one of his most famous post-Céret landscapes, *Windy Day at Auxerre* (see inset page 8, *bottom*), which has been part of the Phillips Collection in Washington, DC, for the past six decades.[1] It is a relatively small landscape, measuring 19¼ by 28⅝ inches, and does not require the drama of its origin story to take a viewer's breath away.

The stretch of yellowing-brown dirt road extending from the bottom right corner to the middle grounds the painting. Two small forms, apparently children, hold one another on a path stretching back and to their left. The grass beside the path flows left to right in pleasing, solid swoops, and the path itself cuts through the green in a curve that winds but does not writhe. Trees, clustered on the right side of the painting, whirl above the figures, and a sky of riotous whites and blues threatens overhead. The scene is a portrait of the wind. The trees are rendered with brushstrokes pushing up and to the right, except for dramatic, turbulent swirls that communicate how the branches are being tossed in the wind. On the left, conflicting greens layer one another, painted as though a slight incline falls from left to right toward the center of the picture, where the children struggle against the wind. The wind whips the leaves of the trees with a force that contrasts with the gentler movement of the children beneath them. The leaves loop and swing. The children are sweet, touching—Soutine managed tenderness. He never had before.

Soutine was not a social or political allegorist, and the clouds over the children's heads were not symbolic of encroaching disaster. However, consider the chilling date of its acquisition by the present owner: Duncan Phillips bought the painting in 1943, the same year Soutine died, and just four years after it was painted. An ocean and a universe away, it was hung in Washington while Soutine's body grew cold in a plot at Montparnasse. For a full year after the burial, six feet above his corpse, Nazi boots marched to and fro in the same Paris where he and Garde had spent their fleeting happy days.

Upon their arrival in Civry-sur-Serein, Soutine and Garde stayed in a small, uncomfortable apartment that belonged to a woman named Madame Galand. A row of poplar trees ran down the center of the village, and Soutine returned to paint them several times. It was here that he developed a startling relationship with a new subject: children. He painted a number of canvases of two children walking side by side along the path beneath the swaying trees. Garde recalled that she bribed the children with chocolate to persuade them to stay still long enough to be painted.[2]

At the beginning of their stay in Civry, Soutine regularly took the train into Paris for business and to consult with the doctors on whom he had grown so dependent. On one of these trips, his marrow-deep paranoia got him into a spot of trouble: Two gendarmes were roaming the train, looking for a thief who had slipped through their fingers. When they spotted Soutine sitting hunched over with his hat's brim pulled low, covering most of his face, they were convinced they had found their man. As if to confirm every fear Soutine had about men in uniform, he was carted to the nearest police station. Desperately, he insisted that if they would just call his old friend, the dependable Léon Zamaron, at the police prefecture in Paris, Zamaron would vouch for him. At last they made the call, and Soutine was permitted to go free.[3]

A few weeks after Soutine and Garde decamped to Civry, on August 23, Stalin and Hitler signed their nonaggression pact. On September 3, France and England declared war on Germany. By then Soutine and Garde had been outside Paris for almost a month and wanted to return to the city, but due to the war, Garde was now a citizen of an enemy country, and the mayor of Civry treated her as such. He assigned them to new living quarters—a one-room house—and forbade them from entering Civry or departing for Paris without his permission. Cut off from his doctors, Soutine grew increasingly nervous about his health. It took two weeks for him to secure a pass to Paris, leaving Garde behind to await his return alone. This became a pattern, an unbearable back-and-forth that continued for months. His condition was so severe that he often collapsed in his Paris apartment, which prolonged his stays. Tormented by weakness and the logistics of securing passes between Paris and Civry, Soutine was frequently kept from Garde for long stretches. She subsisted on whatever money he had left with her before his departure, her boredom punctuated by fear and longing.

They endured these conditions for almost eight months. Finally, in April of the following year, Soutine smuggled Garde out of Civry under cover of darkness. They packed their bags and, at eleven o'clock one night, left the small home where they had been sequestered. They walked for miles, careful not to speak to one another. When they passed the last house and reached the trees Soutine had spent so many of the preceding months painting, their anxiety slowly dissipated. They reached the train station at one in the morning. The outside of the building was totally camouflaged due to the war, but inside things were normal. Soutine bought their tickets, and they boarded as if life were as it should be. Huddled together in their third-class compartment, they sighed with relief as the train pulled out. The adrenaline that had fueled their long, terrifying hike left their bodies, and they slumped into one another, exhausted, and fell asleep. They switched trains at La Roche and watched eagerly as Fontainebleau came into focus in the gentle sunlight. When they reached the outskirts of Lyon, Soutine took Garde in his arms and whispered, "You are saved." Jews fleeing *into* Paris in the spring of 1940 labored under the delusion that safety was a luxury they still enjoyed. How long before Soutine would realize the severity of that miscalculation?

Garde was perturbed by the state of things at 18 Villa Seurat. During Soutine's stays in the apartment since September, he had restored its original disorder. Once again, the patient woman set about sweeping his cigarette butts off the floor and returning the home to a livable condition. Soutine watched appreciatively, repeatedly promising that he would keep her forever, that they would never be separated again. Rumors swirled that France was losing the war, that the Luftwaffe's bombardment was too power-ful to counter. Soutine rushed to the kiosks every morning to glean what he could from the newspapers. Despite the fact that the news was heavily censored, it was clear that the prospects were not good. They worried aloud to one another that France would be defeated. And then what would happen to them? They clung to one another, with no idea that their time together was running out.

On May 14, Garde opened the newspaper and gasped in hor-ror: All German women were expected to report to the Vélodrome d'Hiver the following morning, where they would be transported to an internment camp in the Pyrenees. That last night together, they repeated promises to find one another as soon as they could, to write, to wait until the war was over before resuming life as before. The next day they took a taxi across Paris to the vélodrome, where they had attended so many boxing matches together. He kissed her goodbye, and she disappeared behind a mass of uni-formed bodies.

Soutine returned to the diminished rhythms of the life he had once lived in Montparnasse. Modigliani was long dead, but Kisling was still in Paris, and the pair had maintained the friendship that had begun all those years before in Minsk. Nearly thirty years had passed since they first sat on the wicker chairs outside La Rotonde.

Madeleine Castaing worried that Soutine would not be properly looked after without the doting attentions of a woman. Only a few months after Soutine and Garde said goodbye, she took it upon herself to introduce her precious painter to someone new. In the summer of 1940, while sunning herself outside Le Dôme Café with Maurice Sachs and Soutine, she waved over a young woman named Marie-Berthe Aurenche. Marie-Berthe was a tragic figure, plagued by depressive tendencies all her life. She was the younger sister of Jean Aurenche, the celebrated screenwriter responsible for the scripts of many great films, including Marcel Carné's masterpiece *Hotel du Nord*. He was their parents' favorite. They had not wanted a daughter, and the weight of that knowledge burdened her. She had attempted suicide repeatedly by the time Soutine met her.

Marie-Berthe was very beautiful. Her first job was as a teenage model for Chanel. When she grew tired of modeling she worked at the Van Leer art gallery, where she met her first husband, the surrealist painter Max Ernst, in 1926, at his first significant exhibition. She was only twenty years old. Ernst, a German divorcé fifteen years her senior, was old enough to horrify Aurenche's father, which, her brother later theorized, was her primary intention. Aurenche père hired private detectives to track down his daughter and arrest the artist guilty of consorting with a minor. Marie-Berthe and Ernst folded into the surrealist circle in Paris, never bothering to leave the city, and somehow managed to evade detection for quite a while.

One day, to the delight of the surrealist gang, Aurenche père and a group of hired agents burst upon the couple while they were about to exit a taxi to join their friends at a café on the rue des

Beaux-Arts. In a flash of courage, André Breton shouted, "I'm Max Ernst! I'm Max Ernst!" The friends who had gathered on the street hastily confirmed this pronouncement, and the police hauled the entire party, sans taxi riders, to the station. At that point Breton revealed his true identity.

Max and Marie-Berthe fled to Île de Ré, an island off the coast near La Rochelle, where they stayed for six months. The following year—1927—they married. The marriage lasted twelve years, during which Marie-Berthe became a member in good standing of the surrealist world. Rumors swirled that André Breton based the character Nadja, from his canonical novel of the same name, on her, and Luis Buñuel gave her a small role in his seminal film *L'Age d'Or*.

Ernst remembered their years together happily; Marie-Berthe less so. In 1937, at the great surrealist exhibition in London organized by Roland Penrose, Ernst met Leonora Carrington, a painter the same age Marie-Berthe had been when they first met. The two began an affair with so little discretion that Marie-Berthe heard of it in Paris. When she arrived in London for the exhibition, she wore a slip with a slit that ran the length of her body, and nothing underneath. "This is the appropriate dress for an abandoned woman. She deserves no better," she bellowed as she stepped off the train. Upon returning to Paris, she jumped into the Seine, survived, was hospitalized, then leapt out a window, breaking both her arms. Drugs and alcohol would replace the suicide attempts that never succeeded.

This was the woman Madeleine Castaing introduced to Soutine in the summer of 1940. Maurice Sachs, sitting beside the matchmaker as the introduction took place, accused her of imprudence for pairing a disturbed woman with a sickly Jewish artist notorious for his short temper, in a city under Nazi occupation. Sachs's warnings proved misplaced. For the few years they spent together, Soutine and Marie-Berthe made one another happy—or as happy as a Jew and his lover could be in a country under Hitler's thumb.

Marie-Berthe was immediately smitten with Soutine. He seemed youthful, commanding. He reminded her of Rembrandt's self-portrait in the Louvre, with "the same aspect of power and goodness." She admired his mouth, "round and thick, and with a singular charm, active like a child's, changing its expression rapidly," and his eyes, "curious and deep and black." She found his hands "strikingly beautiful, white, simultaneously fine and muscular" and enjoyed the sound of his voice, which had the calming warmth of ardent sincerity. Marie-Berthe was surprised to find him so polite and soft spoken, and so carefully dressed—his legend had misled her. She wondered, "Was this the man so often described as savage and brusque?"[4]

By the time they were introduced, the French government had already surrendered to the Nazi army. On June 11, Marie-Berthe and Soutine left Paris for Bordeaux, joining about a hundred thousand other Jews, most with nowhere to go. Soutine stayed in the occupied zone. Jews who remained in Paris were prohibited from owning businesses, bicycles, or radios. They could not enter libraries or attend movies or concerts. Yellow stars were stitched onto their shirtsleeves. Nazi uniforms and flags filled the streets of the capital. The Louvre was closed, all the paintings in its collection having been transferred to small museums outside the city before the surrender. When the Nazis forced it to reopen, only sculptures were left on display.

Marie-Berthe and Soutine took to one another. In the early days of the Nazi occupation, she clung to him despite his ill health and his Jewishness, a combination that made him doubly dependent on her. His prospects were bad. Castaing had been right—he needed help. He needed the ferocious loyalty of a woman in love. Marie-Berthe rose to the occasion, though she could not have known what was being asked of her. It took her a while to discover how sick he was. Gradually, over months spent in Nazi-occupied Paris—to which they had returned, swiftly and imprudently, shortly after leaving—she came to understand the severity of the pain he was in.

Life could have been normal for Marie-Berthe. Had she wished, she could have enjoyed Edith Piaf and Maurice Chevalier performing onstage—they were in Paris, entertaining their Nazi patrons. She could have gone to the movies too. The theaters had reopened and were screening French and German films. The Paris Opera House, one of Hitler's favorite buildings, was among the first entertainment venues to reopen—for non-Jews only, of course.

Germany did not have to instruct France to discriminate against its Jews. A powerful minority of the French population did it on their own, eagerly and with gusto, from the first opportunity. This hostility exploded after the German conquest. It was in France, after all, that modern anti-Semitism had been developed in the years after the Dreyfus Affair and the establishment of L'Action Française. On August 27, 1940, France repealed the Marchandeau Law, an amendment to an 1881 law that had prohibited any press attack "against a particular race or religion when it is intended to arouse hatred among citizens or residents." French newspapers rushed to print anti-Semitic screeds in a hysterical spirit "bordering on delirium."[5] The French were so quick to unleash torrents of Jew hatred they had long been forced to suppress that German soldiers had to intervene when Frenchmen attacked Jews in Paris. Their intervention was grudging, to say the least. On September 10, the chief of staff of the German military command in France issued the following directive: "Inasmuch as belonging to the Jewish race is not a matter of identity papers, there will be grounds for turning away at the demarcation line all persons whose name or physical appearance suggests they are Jewish, if they cannot prove that they are not Jews."[6]

The Vichy regime was the rump French government headed by Marshal Philippe Pétain, a hero of the Great War. The French government was forced to flee Paris and set up shop in the southern spa region of Vichy, taking refuge in empty hotels. The Vichy government presented itself to the French people as a buffer between them and Nazi Germany, claiming that by allying with the Germans, they could spare the French people from the worst of Nazi policies. The truth, as Robert Paxton irrefutably demonstrated in his authoritative book on the subject, is that Vichy had very little power to act autonomously. Regime officials did most of what they did because Berlin indicated that they should. But there was one fundamental exception: Vichy enthusiastically enacted anti-Semitic legislation of its own accord. The passage of these laws was not compelled by Germany; Philippe Pétain and his government did not need to be told to discriminate against French Jews. As Pétain himself said, "Germany was not at the origin of the anti-Jewish legislation of Vichy. That legislation was spontaneous and autonomous."[7]

The laws passed by the Vichy regime were designed to keep Jews from holding public office, strip them of citizenship, and relegate them to second-class status. Denaturalization laws were enforced beginning on July 16, 1940—hardly a month after the regime began. On October 7, all Jewish citizens of Algeria were denaturalized. On October 3, the first Jewish Status Law was passed, excluding Jews from military service, the press, commercial and industrial activities, and the civil service. This applied to all French territories, including Algeria, Tunisia, and Morocco. On July 1, thousands of Jews were expelled from the occupied zone and relocated to the south. In July of the following year, a second law was passed requiring all Jewish businesses to register with the government and excluding Jews from all commercial and industrial professions.

As a result of these policies, by the summer of 1941 Jews had no income and were forbidden from owning radios, changing residences, or leaving their homes except during designated hours. A French office was established to track down, round up, and deport Jews to concentration camps. Similar policies were instituted in Algeria, Morocco, and Tunisia.

The discrimination was not merely legally coercive. It was cultural as well. The Institute for the Study of the Jewish Question was founded in May 1941 to create and distribute anti-Semitic propaganda. Its most significant event was *The Jews and France*, a massive multimedia exhibition that opened in September 1942. Based on the research of George Montandon, a professor of anthropology and the author of books such as *How to Recognize a Jew* (published in 1940), the exhibition aimed to portray Jews as powerful, thuggish pollutants corrupting France. At its center stood an enormous sculpture of an old, bearded Jew with a hooked nose, clutching a globe, symbolizing the threat of world domination.

And yet Soutine stayed in Paris.

After France surrendered, all Jews in the country were required to register at police stations. Their identity cards were stamped "Juif." Chana Orloff recalls catching sight of a perturbed Soutine staring at his card on the steps outside the police station. "What's wrong?" she asked. "They've smudged my Juif!" he told her, showing her the blurred letters.[8]

A sign reading "Juif" was to be hung in all Jewish shop windows. A census of Jews in the city was handed over to the head of the Gestapo in Paris. Any non-French inhabitants considered "redundant" to the French economy could be interned among groups of foreign workers. Prefects were given the power to detain foreign Jews in special camps or in assigned residencies.

Marie-Berthe was desperate to find a place where Soutine could be safe. She wanted to bring him to the free zone, but he refused to go. "They don't have milk in the free zone," he insisted, to the bafflement of his friends. He responded similarly when wealthy American patrons offered to try to relocate him to the United States: "There are no trees to paint in America," he said.[9] In truth he had tried several times to get passage to America, but the police refused his requests repeatedly since he had no Russian identity papers.

He kept his apartment on Villa Seurat but relocated to a hotel, where he explained to the clerk that he needed a room for a short while because his air conditioning was broken. This was the first of many increasingly desperate moves he made around the city while trying to evade Gestapo agents. He and Marie-Berthe moved in with her parents, but this was a short-lived arrangement. Her parents didn't like it and neither did Soutine. Marie-Berthe appealed to Marcel and Anne Laloë, who had a large apartment at 26 rue des Plantes, about a five-minute walk from the graveyard where Soutine would be buried in just two years. The couple were old friends of Marie-Berthe's first husband. In the early summer of 1941, she knocked on their door in the middle of the night—hours past curfew—and told them she had brought with her a famous artist who was being hunted by the Gestapo. The Laloës were star-struck by Soutine, a painter they had long admired.

They agreed to offer the couple refuge in a guest bedroom. On the streets outside, Nazis and French police were tracking down Jews, dragging them to Drancy, and from Drancy deporting them to Auschwitz. For months Soutine remained hidden in the apartment, leaving once each evening to accompany Laloë for his nightly walk. But it couldn't last. The building concierge had noticed the extra guest and asked for an official list of all the people staying with the family. It was a criminal offense to hide a Jew in Paris. Soutine had to be moved.

The Laloës were friends with a man named Fernand Moulin, a veterinarian and the mayor of Richelieu, a commune in the Loire Valley. Though Richelieu was in the occupied zone, it was largely farmland and had fewer troops stationed there. Moulin agreed to help. He installed Soutine and Marie-Berthe in Champigny-sur-Veude, a village on the outskirts of Richelieu with a population of about 830. They stayed at the Hotel-Restaurant du Commerce for a full year before moving from rented room to rented room, eventually settling in a tiny hotel called the Café Saint-Louis.

Champigny was a beautiful place to die. And because Soutine painted his last works in that remote stretch of landscape, it is there that Soutine the artist died. His body made its way back to Paris, but he left his final palette in Champigny. Some neighboring farmers kept it for decades after his death.

In his last two years, he returned to his frenetic painting habits as if he knew he was running out of time. Marie-Berthe waited for him in their small rented apartment while he painted an average of eleven hours a day, until it was too dark to see any longer. "When he came home he would have to change—his shirt was drenched in sweat even when he worked in the coldest weather," she wrote.[10]

Soutine's late paintings are their own chapter. They evince a new capacity, a delightful complicated beauty, that took him until his final years to develop. They have their own rhythm. All Soutine's best works vibrate with a common energy, internal to the painting and complete unto itself. Paintings fail if parts of them feel out of step with the rest of the work, as if painted on a different frequency. When Soutine succeeds, his paintings are unified; when he fails, patches of the painting feel as if he could not maintain the intensity at the same register—as if they are stretching but cannot reach. But the energy—his last energy, you might say—in the works from the final decade of his life is different in kind from what vivified his early works. In these late works, there are separate vectors of energy, each in harmony with the others, complementary rather than tangled. In earlier periods, and most obviously in Céret, the vectors are distinguished by their direction but not by their intensity. In the late landscapes, even the wind is rendered with a more sophisticated control, expressed with varying emphases.

Just as Cagnes was different from Céret, just as the carcass paintings were different from the fowl canvases, Soutine's late works represent yet another phase in his development, another period in the evolving romance between Soutine and paint, the true love of his life. The late works have their own tones, emotions impulses, and appetites. In them he achieved unprecedented calm and delicacy. They are the fruit of a particular effort, the effulgence of a specific iteration of the man who never had the chance to outlive them. Soutine was not permitted to discover what would have come after Champigny. It would have been different, vital, coursing with his gorgeous power. How unjust, improper, and tragic that his body was sapped of life too early for him to push forward toward what would come next. He was betrayed by his sickly body, so unprepared for the demands of this world—a world to which his spirit was entirely equal. It is as if the demands of his spirit were too extreme for flesh and blood.

In a great act of service, the Laloës provided paints and canvas when Soutine ran out, visiting the couple to make their deliveries. The Castaings came only twice, and on the second visit they argued so bitterly with Soutine that they left and never returned. The fight was over a particular canvas. They had seen Soutine midway through a painting of one of his favorite subjects, a great oak tree in Richelieu. Madame Castaing declared that they would buy it when it was finished, but when they came to collect it, it was clear that Soutine had drastically reconceived the canvas. It wasn't the painting they had expected or wanted, and they told him they wouldn't take it. When he offered a different one in its place—a beautiful painting of two pigs, gently rendered in pale pinks on a bed of delicious vermillion green—they refused it as well. Monsieur Laloë took the second canvas to Paris and sold it to the dealer Louis Carré. From then on he became Soutine's primary buyer.

On one of the Laloës' visits, Soutine and Madame Laloë returned home to find Marie-Berthe crouching over a portrait Soutine had painted of her, attempting to make the likeness more becoming. She was a vain woman, unused to seeing her features distorted by her partner's probing but unflattering brush. Soutine ripped the canvas from her hands and furiously cut it to ribbons with a pair of scissors. Such flashes of anger grew rare as his health declined. When the Laloës visited again at Christmas in 1942, they found him much altered. He walked with a cane and was beset by frequent spasms of pain. He wondered whether he could return to Paris to consult with Dr. Guttmann. That winter, Marie-Berthe wrote to her friends, "He has an appearance that worries me. He is all white. . . . For three weeks he has eaten only milk. Usually his attacks do not last as long as they do now."[11]

By July, Soutine was too sick to travel. On the last day of the month, a local doctor advised that he go immediately to the hospital in Chinon, nineteen kilometers away. Marie-Berthe put a cross around his neck and signed him into the hospital as Charles. When Laloë visited Soutine in the hospital, Soutine was "immobilized in his bed, indifferent to visitors, and emitting a long, endless moan that tore at the heart."[12] The doctor told Soutine that surgery was necessary. Marie-Berthe made the decision to return him to Paris for the procedure. The doctor in Chinon later insisted that he had permitted the journey to Paris only because he believed the two were married. If he had known otherwise, he would have performed the surgery himself in Chinon.

Early in the morning on August 6, Soutine, Marie-Berthe, and a Dr. Lannegrace climbed into an ambulance with a black and white flag on its headlights. The flag signaled a medical emergency, a precaution they hoped would prevent German troops from stopping them. The ambulance reached Paris the next day, arriving at a private clinic at 10 rue Lyautey. The surgeon operated on August 8. Soutine died at six o'clock the following morning. He was buried in Montparnasse Cemetery two days later, on August 11, 1943.

Soutine was fifty years old when he was taken to Paris for surgery. Hitler was six years older when he shot himself in the mouth two years after Soutine's death. Think of what that madman accomplished in those six years—how many lives he cut short, how many miracles of human creation and capacity he stole from us. Countless lives filled with drama and genius equivalent to Soutine's were erased from our collective inheritance.

There are worse crimes than the obliteration of genius, but it is a loss from which humanity never fully recovers. The fruits of human greatness take all of us to cultivate, analyze, metabolize. And yet, how much mediocrity exists alongside the rare brilliance that is our birthright? What a sin to have allowed even a little of what we are given to be squandered—at any time, in any place, from any people.

CHAPTER 10

Goodbye

GARDE NEVER HAD THE OPPORTUNITY TO SAY GOODBYE to Soutine. Three years earlier, on November 8, 1940, Madeleine Castaing had written to her, informing her that she would arrive at the Carcassonne train station the next day at 2:32 p.m. To ensure that Garde would show up, she signed the letter, "Castaing-Soutine." The trick worked. When Garde arrived at the station, she was perturbed to see that her beloved was not there. Her spirits did not improve when Madame Castaing told her that Soutine, having returned to his former haunts in Montparnasse, had not only rekindled old friendships but also made a new one.[1]

The news about Marie-Berthe Aurenche rattled Garde considerably, which was what Madame Castaing intended. She knew she could manipulate Garde in ways that were not possible with Marie-Berthe. Castaing told the heartbroken woman what

Maurice Sachs had said the day she first introduced Soutine to Marie-Berthe: "What imprudence! You've signed his death certificate!"[2] She revealed that Soutine was living with Marie-Berthe in her father's home. But he longed for her, Castaing assured her. He believed Garde was the only one who could truly take care of him. He asked for her and rejected Marie-Berthe, who, in comparison, treated him poorly. Castaing advised Garde to wait until the end of the war and, in the meantime, not to lose heart, implying that Soutine would be eager to reunite with her as soon as the anti-Jewish regulations were lifted.

Castaing returned to her glittering life in Paris, and Garde remained in hiding in the unoccupied zone, thinking of Soutine trapped in Nazi-occupied Paris, where the regulations did not ease but spread like a disease. She followed the news, watching from afar as Paris devolved along the same path as the Germany she had fled a decade earlier.

Madeleine Castaing visited Garde again the following year, bringing news of all that had transpired in Soutine's life. She claimed that Marie-Berthe was neglecting him, and also that she was filthy—her clothes always stained, ripped, and dirty—and mentally unstable. Castaing said the pair fought constantly, mostly about money. When enraged, Marie-Berthe would taunt Soutine publicly, shouting that he was a "dirty Jew," knowing he would give in to her demands out of fear of being identified by the Gestapo. Sometimes their feuds escalated into physical altercations. And yet, Castaing was told, they loved each other deeply.

By 1942 Garde believed that Germany would lose the war, but she knew the loss would be slow and agonizing. At the end of that year, Madeleine Castaing wrote to urge her to move on, telling her that the past could not be rekindled. Garde remembered what Dr. Tennent had told her four years earlier—that Soutine's condition could worsen at any time, that constant care was essential, and that he would likely only survive another few years. She wryly reflected that she, too, was just as likely to be alive when peace finally came as Soutine was. The Jews of Europe, she thought, shared a common prognosis of doom.

In November, the Germans occupied the free zone, by then called the southern zone. While on a day trip to Perpignan, Garde and a friend, another German Jew named Ruth, were rounded up and placed in an internment camp. For reasons Garde never understood, she was released after a few days, but she never saw Ruth again. It was rumored that all the Jews in that camp were deported to Germany.

In 1943 Castaing wrote to inform Garde that Soutine's health had deteriorated dramatically and urged her to try to make her way to Paris. A neighbor who had taken a liking to Garde revealed that she was in the resistance and could help procure false Aryan papers for her. The papers were obtained, and Garde became Marie Dupas, French, born in Saint-Marcel on June 10, 1910. Castaing sent her money for travel and offered her a place to stay. Garde booked a train to Paris at the end of June.

When Garde arrived at Castaing's house, her host told her that the last time she saw Soutine, he had been asking for her: "Garde is the only one who knows how to save me. If I stay here I will die soon." Gratifying, certainly, but also worrying. What Garde wanted most was to visit Soutine, but if it was true that he had said such things about her to Marie-Berthe, it would make a visit not only extremely awkward but probably impossible.

Garde also knew that in Champigny, Soutine was safe—he didn't even have to wear a yellow star. It would be reckless and stupid for him to visit Paris. There were constant roundups, widespread poverty, and posters plastered all over the city inviting French workers to go seek employment in Germany. It was best for Soutine to stay put.

Garde moved from apartment to apartment in Paris. Madeleine told Soutine that Garde was in the city; she kept him updated with Garde's new address whenever she moved, in case he decided to write to her.

From Garde's memoir, *Mes années avec Soutine*, we learn that on August 11, at about eight o'clock in the morning, she received the following letter, dated ten p.m. the night before: "I urgently need to see you tomorrow morning before you go to work. Please call me tomorrow 8 ½. Suffren 16-42. Marie-Berthe Aurenche-Soutine."

Garde knew that such a letter could only mean that Soutine was dead. She called.

"Madame Marie-Berthe Aurenche?"

A voice on the other end of the line said: "It's me."

"This is Garde. I received your message. Tell me the truth. Is Soutine dead?"

"How did you know?"

"You would never have called me if he were still alive."

"That's true. I want to tell you that in his final days he asked for you several times. I couldn't make up my mind to call you. We had to operate. We couldn't save him. He died the day before yesterday. The funeral will be held at Montparnasse Cemetery, come at two o'clock, we will meet at the main door."

For the rest of her life, Garde recalled the shock of that telephone call and the horrifying realization that he was dead—that she would never see him again. He had been dead for an entire day before Marie-Berthe wrote to her.

Picasso attended the funeral, which was a small gathering. Madeleine Castaing did not attend, nor did anyone else of notable fame. Garde briefly spoke at the ceremony. Afterward, Marie-Berthe asked Garde if she wanted to accompany her to the hospital, where she had some legal matters to settle. That way, Garde could visit the room where Soutine had died. Death had rendered any rivalry between the two women absurd. They arranged to meet the following Saturday.

On the appointed morning, Garde received a letter: "I am too tired to go. I will wait for you to come to me at your earliest convenience. Affectionately, Marie-Berthe." Garde went to Marie-Berthe's home immediately and found her unwell and in bad spirits—which, she would learn, was not unusual. Marie-Berthe explained that she had to return to Champigny to vacate the home she and Soutine had shared. She invited Garde to go along. The prospect of seeing the place where Soutine had spent the last two years of his life overwhelmed Garde.

Soutine's two lovers spent four or five days in Champigny together. Marie-Berthe pointed out the places he had loved: the café where they had brought him cups of milk, the famous chapel, the hotel where he had stayed upon first arriving. For the first time, Garde was able to really look at Soutine's paintings. In life, he had grown agitated and angry if she lingered too long over a canvas. Now she was free to sit and study them.

Marie-Berthe had other plans for them. Desperately in need of money, she believed that the paintings Soutine had left behind in Champigny were rightfully hers to sell. "Do you know any Soutine enthusiasts who would be interested in buying them?" she asked Garde.

"What about Madeleine Castaing?"

Marie-Berthe shook her head. "I have my reasons for not wanting to let her know about these. Do you know of anyone else?"

Garde suggested the wealthy industrialist Jacques Guérin, who agreed to make the journey to look at the paintings.

One evening, in a stroke of generosity, Marie-Berthe handed a painting to Garde. When Garde expressed surprise, Marie-Berthe replied, "Do you expect me to behave as if I don't know how he felt about you?" It was a kind gesture, but a month later Garde received outraged letters demanding she return the painting. Rather than acquiesce, she decided to go into hiding. This was a wise decision regardless; Paris was no place for a Jew, even with Aryan papers.

Garde survived to publish her memoir in 1973. She was, to put it mildly, lucky. When the Germans invaded France in 1940, Paris was home to 175,000 Jews. By the time Soutine died in 1943, only 60,000 remained. By then, the Nazis had begun deporting Jews from orphanages, nursing homes, and hospitals. At the beginning of 1944, they extended their reach to include Jews with French citizenship. By the time the Allies liberated Paris on August 25, 1944, at least 50,000 Parisian Jews had been slaughtered by the Nazis.

Before World War II, the concept of a "French Jewish community" did not exist in the minds of most French citizens. The only distinction that mattered to them was whether a Jew held French citizenship. Yet within the Jewish population, there were many differences, and these shaped how they experienced the war's horrors. Of the roughly 330,000 Jews located in the country before the German invasion, about 90,000 were members of families that had lived there for generations.[3] Emancipated by the Constituent Assembly in 1791, they had been granted full citizenship. They saw an ideological harmony between the liberal values of the French state and the universalist messages they discerned in their Bible. Their Judaism had developed in concert with their identity as French citizens. By contrast, recently naturalized Jews brought with them diverse religious traditions from other lands. The waves of Jewish immigrants fleeing eastern Europe in the late nineteenth and early twentieth centuries were distinct from those who moved to France after the peace treaties that ended World War I, and all of them were different from Jews like Garde who fled Germany when Hitler first came to power.

Moïse Kisling, who arrived in Paris from Kraków three years before Soutine, was another of the lucky ones. He volunteered for the French army, then fled to America when France surrendered and the Nazis occupied the country. Until 1946 the Kislings lived next door to Aldous Huxley in Southern California. Then they returned to France, where Kisling died in his home in 1956. Unlike the works of many of his friends, his paintings survived the Nazis and now hang in museums in France, America, Japan, Switzerland, and Israel.

Others were less fortunate. Georges Kars was born in Kralupy, Czechoslovakia, in 1882. At eighteen, he left home to study art in Munich with Heinrich Knirr and Franz von Stuck. In 1905, he traveled to Madrid, where he met Juan Gris and was deeply influenced by the works of Goya and Velázquez. Kars was settled in Montmartre by 1908. During World War I, he served on the Galician front and endured Russian captivity. After the war he returned to Paris, where he renewed friendships with many residents of La Ruche, including Marc Chagall.

Kars had the refined dexterity of an academic painter, but his works are spiced with the styles and moods that dominated Paris in his day. The deep blacks of Goya and Velázquez darken his still lifes and portraits, which also bear the influence of Cézanne. He was enriched by cubism but not overwhelmed by it. His portraits especially display his skills as a colorist. His most exciting works are his drawings, some so vivid it is as if he just put down his pen.

When the Nazis occupied Paris, Kars fled first to Lyon and then to Switzerland. In 1945, probably after hearing that many of his relatives had been murdered by the Nazis, he killed himself by jumping out the fifth-floor window of his hotel. When his widow died in 1966, his atelier was sold at auction. Many of his paintings were acquired by the French collector Pierre Lévy and the Swiss collector Oscar Ghez. Upon Ghez's death in 1978, he bequeathed 137 works from his collection, including those by Kars, to the University of Haifa.

Moissey Kogan was born in Bessarabia on March 12, 1879. A precocious childhood interest in chemistry gave way to a passion for drawing and sculpture, which led him to the Academy of Fine Arts in Munich in 1903. The great critic Julius Meier-Greafe, who was instrumental in introducing the achievements of Manet, Cézanne, Van Gogh, and other painters, encouraged Kogan to make a pilgrimage to Paris and visit Rodin, which he did in 1905. Rodin advised the young artist to dedicate his life to sculpture. Three years later Kogan returned to Paris and settled down at La Ruche, where he joined the group of artists known as Les Dômiers.

Most of Kogan's works depict nude female figures, and they evince the influence of Rodin and Maillol, both of whom admired him in turn. Like theirs, Kogan's bodies are full, fleshy, and sensuous, yet simultaneously austere and formally pure. In every form—drawing, woodcuts, textiles, and primarily sculpture—his line is consistently delicate without sacrificing force. Terra cotta, bronze, plaster, and wood were his preferred mediums.

Kogan eventually became one of the greatest French neoclassical sculptors. His work was first admitted into the illustrious Salon d'Automne in 1907, after which he served regularly on its jury. In 1909 he showed at all three exhibitions of the Neue Künstlervereinigung München (NKVM) in Munich, where he formed close ties with Jawlensky and Kandinsky. In 1925 he was elected vice president of the sculpture committee of the Salon d'Automne, a great honor for an émigré artist.

He kept a studio near La Ruche at the Cité Falguière (where both Modigliani and Soutine had once lived) from 1926 until his death in 1943. In 2002, art historians in Germany discovered Kogan's name on a list of deportees to Auschwitz. The official documents detailing the circumstances of his death were destroyed by the Nazis during their evacuation and liquidation of the camp. It is a matter of record, however, that Kogan was on Convoy 47 from Drancy to Auschwitz. Along with 801 others, he was likely taken to the gas chambers upon arrival on February 13, 1943. Many of his works were destroyed by the Nazis in their "Degenerate Art" campaign.

Rudolf Lévy was born in Germany in 1875. He enrolled in carpentry school but left to study painting with Heinrich von Zügel at the School of Fine Arts in Munich in 1899. In 1903 Lévy moved to Paris, where he joined Les Dômiers. He studied at Matisse's academy from 1908 to 1910, taking over as head when Matisse left. Lévy frequently returned to Germany, where he befriended Alfred Flechtheim, who exhibited the Dômiers many times in his gallery.

During the First World War, Lévy happened to be in Germany and was conscripted into the German army. After the war he returned to Paris but often traveled to North Africa, where he befriended Max Ernst and Oskar Kokoschka. In addition to painting, Lévy was a gifted writer, penning novels and poetry in German and French.

When the Nazis came to power, Lévy was in Germany, but quickly moved to Majorca and then to the United States. In 1937 he visited Naples with other German artists and remained in Italy for the next two years. He was in Florence in 1939, attempting to escape to America, when SS officers arrested him and transferred him to Milan. On April 5, 1944, he was deported to Auschwitz in Convoy 9. He was murdered five days later. Most of his paintings and writings were destroyed by the Nazis.

Roman Kramsztyk was born in Warsaw in 1885. As a young adult he studied painting in Kraków for a year, befriending several artists, including Henryk Kuna and Leopold Gottlieb. Several years later these men would form the Society of Polish Artists, known as Rytm. Kramsztyk studied at the School of Fine Arts in Munich before moving to Paris, where, in 1911, his work was accepted at the Salon d'Automne.

He lived in Paris for four years at the start of the First World War, after which he spent the rest of his life traveling between Paris and Poland, where he became quite famous. His work was entered into the art competition in the Summer Olympics of 1929.

Kramsztyk was visiting family in Warsaw when the Germans invaded Poland in 1939, sealing his fate. In October of the following year, when the Warsaw Ghetto was established, Kramsztyk, along with all other Jewish residents of the city, was imprisoned within its walls. There he assiduously documented events in a sketchbook. His drawings of the ghetto are the most haunting and memorable of all his works. In one, gasping children with hollow cheeks cling to a father with dead eyes; they are delicately, achingly rendered. In another the skeletal head of a young boy, staring hopelessly into space, is conveyed with Dürer-like grace.

In that hell, while doing his grim duty to document the extermination of his own people, the Parisian innovations—the frenzied colors and contorted perspectives—were of no use to Kramsztyk. He drew what he saw. Sometime between August 6 and August 10, 1942, during the liquidation of the ghetto, he was shot and killed by a Ukrainian SS officer.

Adolphe Féder was born on July 16, 1886, in Berlin. He became involved in the Bund Labor Movement in 1905, which led to him fleeing Berlin for Geneva, where he remained briefly before moving to Paris in 1908. There, Féder became one of the most active members of La Ruche. He studied at Académie Julian and later with Matisse at his academy. In the 1920s, he did illustrations for *Le Monde* and *La Presse*, and for books by Rimbaud and Joseph Kessel.

When the Second World War broke out, Féder stayed in France and joined the underground in Paris. He and his wife, Sima, were betrayed, and they were arrested on June 10, 1942. They were interned for four months in a military prison on the rue du Cherche-Midi. Four months later, Féder was transferred to Drancy, where he managed to produce many oil-pastel drawings and watercolors of life in the internment camp.

Féder's landscapes and still lifes that predate his internment at Drancy show the influence of Cézanne, though Féder preferred hotter and more luscious colors. The heat disappears in his works from the internment camp. Perhaps this was due to a lack of supplies, though there was a place to buy paints inside Drancy. Féder was not an exceptional draftsman; he was an illustrator. But his rudimentary skill somehow makes his drawings from 1942 and 1943 profoundly moving. His Drancy works differ in medium, color, subject, and location, but each person depicted has the same crushed expression. There is no light in their eyes, nor any sign of hope, anger, or even sadness. These are, without exception, portraits of despair.

Féder was deported to Auschwitz, where he was killed on December 13, 1943. Sima Féder survived the war and donated a number of his drawings to Beit Lohamei Ha-Getaot, or the Ghetto Fighters' Museum, in Israel.

There are many more such biographies from La Ruche. In 1942 and 1943, the École de Paris was decimated. But at the Beehive, life, like art, went on, as it did in the rest of the cold world.

Epilogue:

Afterlives

THE THREE WOMEN WHO TOOK CARE OF SOUTINE DURING his truncated life had far less involvement with him than Esti Dunow, the sole guardian of his legacy now. As a recognized expert on Soutine's paintings and coauthor of his two-volume catalogue raisonné (the third of which is forthcoming), Dunow has dedicated fifty-two years to studying Soutine's work. Though born five years after the artist's death, she has spent more time immersed in his paintings and legacy than anyone else, including Soutine himself.[1]

Her scholarship on Soutine began in earnest while she was a graduate student in the 1970s in New York. In some ways, though, Soutine's and Dunow's stories intersected even before her parents met. Her father, Moshe Dluznowsky, crossed paths with Soutine when they both lived in Paris. Like Soutine, he traded eastern Europe for Paris and fell in love with the city. But from there, the two men's lives diverged—one ended, and the other wound its way from Europe to the United States. Dluznowsky was fortunate enough to escape France and build a new life in America after the world he and Soutine had shared was destroyed.

Esti Dunow's loyalty to Soutine's oeuvre is a result of her deep esteem for his paintings. Dunow herself is a painter. She believes that painters have a special devotion to Soutine, one that non-painters cannot fully understand. And this belief is confirmed by her decades of experience in the studio and the gallery (two very different art worlds indeed), where she has encountered fellow Soutine-lovers who experience the same awe and joy before his canvases that she does. Standing in front of a Soutine makes artists want to paint. Only other artists can understand this.

However, there is another essential element of the Dunow-Soutine story. Because Dunow's father was in Paris when Soutine was, and because he made it out, and also because his daughter would come to be responsible for the stewardship of Soutine's afterlife, it is impossible not to notice that Soutine himself should have survived past fifty. There is another version of history in which he did. Dunow has spent all these years studying Soutine's works and thinking how absurd it is that his "late paintings" were painted when he was in his forties—middle-aged!

In retrospect the swoop of the past feels inevitable, like a pre-determined kinetic force—but in truth the brute force of history spares some and snuffs out others without rhyme or reason. Why didn't Soutine leave Paris, as Dunow's father did? A slip of paper, a lack of foresight, insufficient imagination—whatever the causes, they were no doubt myriad and brutally banal. It is easy to imagine an alternate history in which Soutine and Moshe Dluznowsky passed one another first on the streets of Paris and again by chance some years later on the Upper West Side. This biography could have been longer; it could have ended with final chapters on Soutine's second life in the States. But Soutine's last canvases were painted in his fifth decade, and Moshe Dluznowsky's daughter has only ever been able to wonder—like the rest of us—what he would have painted had he gone on living.

For these reasons, the parallels between the lives of Soutine and of Dunow's father are worth noting. They underscore how easy it would have been for Soutine's story to have ended differently. Dluznowsky was born in 1903 in Tomaszów (now known as Tomaszów Mazowieck), a small city near Łódź, Poland. In 1820 the owner of the town, Count Antoni Ostroski, had offered Jewish weavers and merchants plots of land in the hopes of improving the town's economy. In 1831 the Jewish community was granted rights to establish a synagogue, a ritual bath (*mikveh*), a hospital, and a cemetery. That same year, the defeat of the Polish uprising by the Russian Empire resulted in the confiscation of Ostrowski's property. He fled for France, but the Jews he had invited remained, and by the 1850s the original dozen or so Jewish families had swelled to a community of nearly two thousand people. By the time of Moshe Dluznowsky's birth, that number had increased fivefold. For the duration of his life there, the Jews of the city were tormented with anti-Semitic persecution.[2]

Dluznowsky spent his childhood about eleven hundred kilometers from Soutine's hometown, in a city ten times larger than Smilovichi. Before the Anschluss, Jews accounted for roughly 30 percent of Tomazsów's population; about thirteen thousand Jews lived there just before World War II broke out. In March 1941, two thousand Jews from Plock were relocated to Tomazsów. On April 27, 1942, a hundred Jews were rounded up and shot, and on October 31, seven thousand were deported to Treblinka, where they were slaughtered. Another seven thousand were killed in Treblinka three days later. Tomazsów was converted into a forced labor camp for the thousand or so Jews left. They remained there until the ghetto was liquidated in May 1943. All who were still alive were transferred to Blizna and Starachowice, where most perished. The Nazis were thorough: Almost all the Jews who had lived in Tomaszów between the wars were exterminated. When Dunow visited her father's hometown decades later, hardly any trace of its once vibrant Jewish life remained. It had all been erased.

Moshe Dluznowsky was the youngest of six children raised by traditional religious parents. Unlike Soutine, who spent no time as an adult in his home country, Dluznowsky served in the Polish army. While making dinner for his children decades later, he would joke that he had been the best cook in the Polish army. After his service he moved to Paris with two of his siblings. Though he and Soutine never became friends, Soutine would have met Jews like Dluznowsky—Jews who had spent their adulthoods in the eastern European countries where they were born.

Moshe was the only member of his immediate family to survive the war; relatives that remained in Poland and the siblings who went with him to Paris were all murdered. He, his sister-in-law (named Chavileh), and her four daughters survived.

Dluznowsky didn't like to discuss his early life; he preferred to talk about the part of his past that took place in Paris, his favorite city. He and Soutine had that in common. His children, Esti and Henry Dunow, learned what little they could about their father's family from the aunt who had also immigrated to the United States. For example, Dunow's aunt told her that Moshe's father, Henukh, had been dressed in white until he turned thirteen because his mother had suffered a number of miscarriages. This was apparently a form of superstitious protection practiced by the Jews of eastern Europe.

Dunow never considered Soutine's biography the most compelling part of his legacy. For her, the paintings take precedence over everything else. But for art historians and art critics, and for the many Jewish Soutine admirers she has met over the years, interest in Soutine's Jewishness amounts to a kind of obsession. Soutine scholarship is rife with wild considerations about how his Jewish identity influenced his work.

Dluznowsky's and Soutine's families had likely practiced the same kind of Judaism, one shaped as much by cultural heritage and social participation as by religious faith. Esti's father studied in a religious school just as Soutine had; neither had received a secular education. In fact, Dluznowsky was born the same year Soutine abandoned his Jewish studies to go work for his sister's husband in Minsk. But unlike Soutine, Dluznowsky committed himself to enriching Jewish culture. He became a Yiddish writer, an act that was a social and political statement, a conscious choice to root himself in Jewish tradition. By contrast, Soutine chose to situate himself in the lineage of painters he revered, forging an artistic identity that was enough for him.

By the time Dluznowsky reached Paris, he had already begun his career. He stayed in the city until just before the German army entered Paris—so he was there for about a decade. Those were the most formative years of his life, during which he found his voice as a writer and became a member of a vibrant Jewish artistic community. The survivors of that community, and its memories, remained his true social world for the rest of his life. Unlike Soutine, Dluznowsky stayed within Jewish circles in Paris and became fast friends with several people Soutine had known well during his early years there. Dluznowsky's dearest friend was Emmanuel Mané-Katz, who had met Soutine on his first day in Fernand Cormon's studio at the École des Beaux-Arts. Dluznowsky himself met Soutine a few times, though by the time he arrived in Paris, Soutine had long since traded his Jewish friends from La Ruche for Madeleine Castaing and her crowds. The two men were never close, but they knew each other well enough to say hello.

Like Soutine, Dluznowsky loved France. Even after relocating to New York and starting his third life there, he continued to identify primarily as a Frenchman rather than an American—a Jew first, but a Frenchman before any other nationality. This despite the fact that his own brother and sister had been deported by the French and killed in Auschwitz.

From the affection with which her father told her stories about Paris, Esti Dunow had trouble fully comprehending the degree to which the French had betrayed their Jewish neighbors during the war. As a teenager she attended the premiere of *The Sorrow and the Pity* at the New Yorker Theater on Eighty-Ninth Street. The five-hour, two-part documentary exposed the Vichy regime's collaboration with the Nazis and the role ordinary French citizens played in that evil partnership. It ruptured the comforting illusion, cultivated by most French citizens (including Prime Minister Charles de Gaulle, for whom the myth was politically expedient), that most of the country had robustly resisted the Nazis throughout the war. Directed by Marcel Ophuls and released in 1969, the film was the first work to force the French to confront their own complicity in the Nazi regime. It shook the country, sparking riots in the street. It is tempting to speculate that Soutine himself, the brilliant arriviste, might have been among the rioters.

Sitting in the theater in New York—an ocean and two and a half decades removed from the hell—Esti Dunow was startled by her own shock. She had known the facts regarding French collaboration with the Nazis, but the film made plain just how profoundly the country her father still loved had betrayed her family. She felt almost guilty. Dunow had been raised to despise the Germans and the Poles, but now she realized that the French had never been subjected to the same contempt. It wasn't that her father had misled her or distorted history, but the feeling he communicated about his time in Paris was never one of contempt or fear or anger—it was a sense of freedom. And it was this freedom, this novel exuberance felt by so many Jews for the first time upon reaching that capital of liberation and excess, that Moshe Dluznowsky shared with Chaim Soutine.

For both of them, and for so many others with similar origin stories, Paris offered their first chance to live in a secular world. Wasn't that what Modigliani and Zadkine and Lipschitz and Pascin had all sought on the streets of Montparnasse? A sense of full membership in the modern world? For Esti's father, the richness, the joy, the friendships, and the memories of living in a creative epicenter with other recently emancipated Jews simply overshadowed the subsequent betrayal. He never spoke a word against the French.

Like Soutine, Moshe Dluznowsky had lived in Montparnasse. His brother Avrum and his sister-in-law, Chavileh, had set up house across the Seine in the Jewish quarter known as the Marais, and although he visited them there, for the most part he spent his days in the same parts of the city where Soutine had lived. Dunow visited Paris in the 1970s, while her parents were still alive, walking alongside her father through the streets he still adored. Her parents introduced her to their surviving friends, many of whom still lived in the same places. On that trip, Dunow befriended a whole community of Yiddish writers.

Later, when she began her work on Soutine, she returned to Paris for three months of research, spending much time with her father's friends as well as with more recent émigrés from eastern Europe who had folded into the Yiddish community in Paris. At that time, just as decades before, a small world of Yiddish-speaking Jewish painters and artists still existed—theater people, miniaturists, sculptors, poets. In some ways it felt like living in the world that Soutine and her father had lost—like the hurricane of human brutality that had destroyed it had never occurred.

In 1939 Dluznowsky made it out of Paris to Marseilles, where he managed to gain passage on a boat to Morocco. He spent at least a year there, documenting Jewish life and taking photos with a small Brownie camera that were later published in Yiddish papers in America. This was a year before Pearl Harbor, while US President Franklin Roosevelt was teetering on the brink of war, unsure of how prepared the country was for conflict. He sought propaganda to support military action, anticipating that Japanese bellicosity might force the United States into the war. By 1938 immigrants from Europe faced waits of up to two years for a US visa, but in 1940 Roosevelt issued special visas for journalists to help cultivate prowar sentiment in America. Dluznowsky, a journalist, benefited from this policy. The pile of press cards he had accrued during his time in Morocco all but saved his life.

Dluznowsky joined the swelling but small community of Jewish refugees in Manhattan. Most were artists whose work was a statement: a commitment to the cultivation of secular Jewish culture. (Would Soutine have been part of that community? Or would he, in New York, have preferred to distance himself from his coreligionists, just as he had in Paris?) Dluznowsky met and married Berta Klebanow, who had come to America from Minsk as a small child. The couple moved into a small apartment in a shared brownstone on Seventy-First Street between West End Avenue and Broadway. Soon after their daughter was born, the family moved to 246 West End Avenue, into a building partly owned by the writer Zalman Shneour, a celebrated Hebrew poet and Yiddish novelist and one of Dluznowsky's closest friends. His daughter Renee was a flamenco dancer, and Dunow used to spend hours with her, going through her trunk of costumes.

Berta came from a family of staunch Yiddishists who were very active in the storied Workmen's Circle. The organization, founded in 1900, served as a mutual aid society, providing recent Jewish immigrants with vital resources such as life insurance, unemployment relief, health care, and community. She was an impressive woman, educated and imposing. Moshe used to repeat with pride that his wife spoke the most beautiful Yiddish. She was one of the first female teachers in the Yiddish high school. The other teachers were old, bespectacled, and deeply respected men, and Berta was a twenty-something woman.[3]

Moshe and his wife were raising a family in an American metropolis where Soutine's reputation was already fully developed. As Dunow grew up, her parents took her to galleries and museums that featured paintings by the artists her father had crossed paths with in Paris, Soutine among them. By the time Dunow was old enough to visit museums herself, however, Soutine's reputation in America had waned from its apex. In the twenties, thirties, and forties, Soutine's paintings lined gallery walls across the United States. He was regularly displayed in New York, usually in group exhibitions alongside other members of the School of Paris, and his name was well known in other major American cities as well. His first large exhibition anywhere in the world was at the Arts Club of Chicago in 1935. The next year, two successive galleries in New York, the Valentine Gallery and the Mrs. Cornelius J. Sullivan Gallery, held solo shows for him. He was also included in two group shows in the city. Those who regularly attended galleries and museums knew his name, and he became an increasingly influential force in the American art world during the first half of the twentieth century.

In 1929 Lincoln Kirstein included Soutine in an exhibition about the School of Paris at the Harvard Society for Contemporary Art, which Kirstein had founded that same year. The following decade was, in terms of sheer number of shows per year, the busiest for Soutine, both during and after his lifetime.[4] Yet the apotheosis of his prestige in America occurred in 1950, when he became the second member of the School of Paris (after Chagall) to be given a retrospective at the Museum of Modern Art, the new mecca of the American art world.[5] The other French painters who had received solo shows at MOMA before him were Matisse (1931), Toulouse-Lautrec (1933), Léger (1935), Van Gogh (1935–1936 and 1937), Picasso (1939–1940), Dalí (1941–1942), Rousseau (1942), Chagall (1946), Bonnard (1948), Nadelman (1948), and Braque (1949). A tradition was being codified, and Soutine occupied a privileged place in it. Modigliani did not get a retrospective at MOMA until the year after Soutine did.

MOMA was founded in 1929, ten days after Black Tuesday and at the onset of the Depression, the reverberations of which would later rattle Paris, and Soutine with it. It was a bold time, financially and socially, to champion challenging art. Chosen as the first director of the institution was Alfred H. Barr Jr., a young man who had recently been a professor of art history at Wellesley. Barr was a proselytizer of the avant-garde. MOMA was established just a few years after Albert Barnes's infamous disaster of an exhibition in Philadelphia, where the public reacted with such violent dislike for modernist painting that Barnes locked away his entire collection, a treasure the rest of the art world has been laboring ever since to release. So it was significant that, less than a decade later, Alfred Barr was able to consecrate the newly founded institution to precisely the kinds of paintings that had so horrified Barnes's viewers. The first solo exhibition was a retrospective of Henri Matisse, whose paintings had enraged attendees of the Armory Show of 1913.

A year after the Matisse retrospective, Barr held a group show called *Painting in Paris from American Collectors*, which included three of Soutine's canvases. Barr began the work that Monroe Wheeler, the curator of Soutine's 1950–1951 retrospective, would continue. By the 1950s, the New York City painters were coming into their own, World War II having freed them from the long shadow of Parisian culture. The same year Soutine died, Peggy Guggenheim commissioned Jackson Pollock to paint a mural for her apartment vestibule. This was his first large-scale commission, and it inaugurated the movement that would soon be christened abstract expressionism. That same year, Mark Rothko and his friend and comrade-in-arms Adolph Gottlieb showed a few paintings together in an exhibition held by the Federation of Modern Painters and Sculptors. Their works elicited a snarky review by *The New York Times* art critic Edward Alden Jewell, remembered now for his incapacity to appreciate the vertiginous genius on display under his nose. Rothko and Gottlieb penned an acerbic response to his review, published a few days later by the *Times*, that serves as the first explicit manifesto of the abstract expressionist movement.

Today, if Americans esteem Chaim Soutine, it is in no small part because Willem de Kooning told them to think highly of him. In a 1977 interview, De Kooning named Soutine as his greatest influence, and this utterance secured Soutine's status in this country more than anything else. Since then Soutine has been interpreted by art-focused Americans primarily as a harbinger of twentieth-century American painting. In 1998, the Los Angeles County Museum of Art hosted a show that cast him as a prophet of the New York School; in 2006 Cheim and Read held an exhibition in New York in which Soutine's paintings were hung alongside those of De Kooning, Richard Diebenkorn, Louise Fishman, and others who had benefited from his tone and touch. In 2021, the Barnes—home to the second-largest collection of Soutine paintings in the world, and whose founder played the primary role in vaunting Soutine from impoverished obscurity to fame—held an exhibition called *Soutine/*

De Kooning, which explored the affinity between the two painters. De Kooning anointed Soutine, and we heeded his decree. Only our gods can select new ones; we are parochial. But then, so was De Kooning. He saw himself in Soutine's work and ignored the parts of Soutine's oeuvre that did not nourish his own.

There is certainly an affinity between Soutine's brushwork and purity of color and the project De Kooning set for himself. But noticing likenesses between two artists can blunt one's capacity to recognize either one's idiosyncrasies. It is both knowing and obfuscating to look at Monet and see Joan Mitchell or to recognize Brancusi in the Cycladics. And the fact that a viewer knows enough to draw these associations can be as much a stumbling block as a source of enrichment. Sophistication can lacquer the senses. It can dull us. In precisely this way, a veil of analogy shrouds Soutine from American viewers who see him primarily as a harbinger of abstract expressionism.

Soutine's paintings are wholly dominated by a single overwhelming impetus, which is indeed markedly like "all-over" painting. The phrase, coined by the critic and cultural commissar Clement Greenberg, was initially used to describe drip paintings by an artist named Janet Sobel but later was broadly applied to the abstract expressionist school over which Greenberg believed he presided. Jackson Pollock saw Sobel's paintings and was moved to imitate her. (This detail teaches us more about Pollock than it does about his muse.)

Like many members of the New York School, De Kooning was smitten by MOMA's Soutine retrospective. Art critics and art historians alike flocked to the galleries, and so did painters. As the artist Charles Cajori put it, "In the late 40s and 50s, the time of the

MOMA show, Soutine was central to the ongoing understanding of what painting was. He was understood as a pillar." The painter Jane Freilicher remembered years later, "Soutine is a painter one can't forget. I can still recall the MOMA exhibition of 1950. A vivid light, a mixture of pathos and joy. That was his unique gift."[6]

The poet John Ashbery's account of the show is especially full and illustrative:

> I hadn't realized it, but my arrival in New York coincided with the cresting of the "heroic" period of abstract expressionism, as it was later to be known, and somehow we all seemed to benefit from this strong moment even if we paid little attention to it and seemed to be going our separate ways. We were in awe of De Kooning, Pollock, Rothko and Motherwell and not too sure of exactly what they were doing. . . . I could see all of this entering into Jane's work and Larry's and my own. And then there were the big shows at the Museum of Modern Art, whose permanent collection alone was stimulation enough for one's everyday needs. I had come down from Cambridge to catch the historic Bonnard show in the spring of 1948, unaware of how it was already affecting a generation of young painters who would be my friends, especially Larry Rivers who turned from playing jazz to painting at that moment of his life. And soon there would be equally breathtaking shows of Munch, Soutine, and Matisse, in each of whom regardless of the differences that separate them one finds a visceral sensual message sharpened by a shrill music or perfume emanating from the paint, that seemed to affect my painter friends

like catnip. Soutine, in particular, who seems to have gone back to being a secondary modern master after the heady revelation of his MOMA show in 1950, but whose time will undoubtedly come again, was full of possibilities both for painters and poets. The fact that the sky could come crashing joyously into the grass, that trees could dance upside down and houses roll over like cats eager to have their tummies scratched, was something I hadn't realized before, and I began pushing my own poems around and standing words on end.[7]

For the abstract expressionists searching for a way out of representational painting, Soutine was an important rung on the ladder. They needed his example for their own purposes—the sort of influence and inspiration many artists depend on. New York School painters like De Kooning sucked abstract expressionism from Soutine's paintings and reinterpreted the singular artist as a prophet of their own movement. They nourished themselves with the aspects of his work that provoked them. What they could not understand or what was not useful for their project got reinterpreted, smoothly fitted into an understanding of art that corroborated their own Hegelian philosophy: Art moved upward out of figuration toward abstraction. They considered Soutine at his most artistic when he was most like them, which is to say when he strayed from representation. But this is to consider Soutine so partially, so impishly, that the artist's great, consuming project becomes beside the point: ignored.

And so the quality in Soutine that drew painters to him in the 1940s and 1950s, while abstract expressionism was being developed, contained within it the inevitability of his fall from the center of the pantheon when, having used him for their purposes, American artists moved on. Even at the time of the great MOMA exhibition, there were signs that Soutine's status was unsteady. Consider the review that the art critic Clement Greenberg wrote of the MOMA show in his influential column in *Partisan Review*. Greenberg, the greatest theologian in the church of abstraction and the picture plane, was a brilliant and despotic critic who lorded it over New York's art world in the second half of the twentieth century. The rise and fall of his scepter ignited or foreclosed myriad artistic careers. He defended his favorites vociferously and endeavored to condemn others to obscurity. Those who assisted in forcing art in the direction of his Hegelian orthodoxy were praised; those who deviated from it were lambasted.

When Greenberg was eighty years old, he recalled that, as a five-year-old, he once found an injured goose, picked up a shovel, and beat it to death. "Geese can attack small children . . . but I don't think that's why I did it. It was cruel." That cruelty, the vehemence that laced his writing, altered the art world he lived in and also the one he bequeathed to, among others, a young Esti Dunow, studying art history in New York some fifteen years later. He was more responsible than any other figure for the fact that, by the time she began her studies, it was absurd to study artists as manifestly representational as Soutine. When he lived, Greenberg worked behind the scenes with gallery owners and museum curators to have shows canceled, and when he couldn't achieve his preferred outcomes he slashed artists in ink. In 1944, Greenberg decreed that "the future of American painting depends on what [Motherwell], Baziotes, Pollock, and only a comparatively few others do from now on." (Baziotes! Who?) Morandi, by contrast, he dismissed as "just a bottle painter."[8]

Given the role that Greenberg's thought—and the thought of those like him, who considered art important only if it conformed to a certain theory of art history—played in condemning Soutine to the outer limits of art history, it is worth explaining what it was and why Soutine did not fit into it. Greenberg decreed that art history had reached its apex with abstraction, that "modern figurative art" was oxymoronic, that contemporary representational painting was tantamount to an aesthetic decline. He theorized that modernism itself was "the intensification, almost the exacerbation, of this self-critical tendency that began with the philosopher Kant." After Kant, every discipline was forced to justify itself on its own terms: "The essence of modernism lies, as I see it, in the use of characteristic methods of a discipline to criticize the discipline itself, not in order to subvert it but in order to entrench it more firmly in its area of competence. Kant used logic to establish the limits of logic, and while he withdrew much from its old jurisdiction, logic was left all the more secure in what there remained to it."[9]

Greenberg's grasp of Kant on logic was a little shaky, but his point was this: Just as logic should restrict itself only to subjects that can be properly understood using logic, so art should concern itself only with what naturally and totally falls within its jurisdiction. A painting cannot breathe or move, so it should not reproduce living things. Do not imprison a bird in a fish bowl, and do not compress a human figure onto a canvas. "Realistic, naturalistic art had dissembled the medium, using art to conceal art; Modernism used art to call attention to art."[10] (Is anything less Soutine-like than such an edict?)

Slowly, beginning with Manet, according to Greenberg's account, painters began to respect the properties of their medium, allowing their paintings to celebrate those properties rather than conceal them. The many -isms that overflowed from the cornucopia of modern art—cubism, orphism, futurism, constructivism, and so on—were a result of this inward-looking self-critical impulse, said Greenberg. All of them flourished in the Paris in which Soutine worked—and he dutifully and consistently ignored them.

Greenberg knew that, for the most part, these artists were not consciously avowing a theory of history when they stood before their canvases. An aching to paint more profoundly and powerfully is what led them toward abstraction, and they inadvertently fulfilled an alleged historical imperative without noticing they were doing so. There are different ways of defining success in art. One of them—but not the only one—is to reach the vanguard of human expression and push past it. Greenberg offered painters with that sense of frontiersmanship a direction, an articulable goal. It doesn't have to be condescending or patronizing for a critic to name and champion or condemn the ideas that relate to contemporary painting. Some critics humbly acknowledge that even the art they criticize is beyond their capabilities to create, but Greenberg was not one of them. He often repeated that "all artists are bores." It is not surprising that he viewed them as blind pawns in the grip of historical forces they obeyed without comprehension. (In the movie *Pollock*, Jeffrey Tambor, playing Greenberg, deliciously captures his superior, ex cathedra attitude. He turns to the lost and struggling painter and, in his condescending baritone, chastises him, "You're retreating into imagery, Jackson!")

Greenberg believed that contemporary artists, rather than working in service to an artistic ideal, grow weary of, and then overthrow, the dominant style of the day. Art history, as they tell it, is a tale of permanent revolution, to borrow Trotsky's phrase. Viewed on a small scale, it appears as if every reigning style is the bastard child of the previous one, and that artists whore after the new, always eager to topple the old. But the new decays and becomes antiquated as soon as the most recent revolution succeeds, and the rebels themselves calcify into the establishment. (Corporations in the mid-twentieth century swiftly began acquiring abstract and abstract expressionist art.) Somehow, a providential force shepherded all these revolutions toward abstraction, as if a Hegelian demiurge were pulling the strings. As Meyer Schapiro acidly summarized the idea:

> The theory of imminent exhaustion and reaction is inadequate not only because it reduces human activity to a simple mechanical movement, like a bouncing ball, but because in neglecting the sources of energy and the condition of the field, it does not even do justice to its own limited mechanical conception. . . . And a final goal, an unexplained but inevitable trend, a destiny rooted in the race or the spirit of the culture or the inherent nature of art, has to be smuggled in to explain the large unity of a development that embraces so many reacting generations.[11]

For all his intellectual rigor, Greenberg was, like all prophets of history, something of a mystic. He operated as if he had a privileged perception of the esoteric workings of art's destiny. His theory of art history is stupendously dogmatic and, considering the extraordinary variety of art that was produced in his own time, it makes little sense. It misrepresents, omits, or expels all the artists that disrupt its smooth linear narrative—most unfortunately, the modern painters whose accomplishment was precisely to throw into doubt the distinction between representation and abstraction because their work contained both. Soutine, for example.

Greenberg's theory of art, when taken to its conclusion, becomes absurd. He argues, as Schapiro puts it, "that representation is a passive mirroring of things and therefore essentially non-artistic, and that abstract art, on the other hand, is a purely aesthetic activity, unconditioned by objects and based on its own eternal laws." Let us consider both propositions. First, "that representation is a passive mirroring of things and therefore essentially non-artistic." It is true that there is a kind of virtuosic academic style, stultified by study and devoid of originality. Soutine and his fellow students in Minsk and then Vilna and then Paris started out in their classrooms tracing gypsum skulls and learning the rudiments of painting in precisely this way, with the goal of verisimilitude. Most students never evolve beyond this, and there are still legions of artists who make a career producing what laypeople consider "real" art because it looks like a photograph. Artists as original and exciting as Titian, Rembrandt, Manet, Cézanne, Matisse, Derain, Soutine, and Balthus began their careers producing realistic drawings and canvases. But all of them turned away from that early academic style and created figurative paintings that were radical and singular—not *reproductions* of reality but *interpretations* of it, and exceedingly original and painterly ones.

"A passive mirroring of things"? Hardly. Not a single stroke on the weakest paintings of any of those artists is merely veristic or essentially nonartistic. Even Greenberg couldn't bring himself to say that Soutine's paintings were lifeless—he said instead that they were not successful.

And the second claim, "that abstract art, on the other hand, is a purely aesthetic activity, unconditioned by objects and based on its own eternal laws," was meant to snap the cord of communion between the canvas and the world around it, a cord without which Soutine's paintings would be impossible. In any case, even for painters for whom physicality is less or differently essential, that cord cannot be snapped. There is no way to produce any kind of art that is unconditioned by objects. There is no way to *view* any kind of art that is not informed by our experience. There is no view from nowhere. Every aesthetic is developed through an interaction with the world.

Color and form are all that painters have to create an aesthetically pleasing work, but color and form can best be studied in experience. This does not mean that they should be used only mimetically, to copy the world. But abstraction emerged out of the discoveries of representation, as in Kandinsky's crinolines, in cubism's geometries, in Brancusi's *Bird in Space*, and of course in the movement in Soutine's entire oeuvre. Many abstract painters believed that their rejection of representation was not a rejection of the world, but a deeper grasp of it—just as Soutine believed that he strayed from naturalism in order to approach some essential quality of his subjects.

The abstractionists were correct—their departure from one reality was a way toward a different sort. Their sense of that truth is one of the reasons we linger before their works. Joan Mitchell's paintings are vivified by a fantastic energy. They convey a teeming movement, even though canvases cannot move. Jackson Pollock was simulating sensations and rhythms that he knew only through experience. If we can "read" such paintings, if they are coherent to us, it is because we have an eye for rhythm and order that was learned from existing shapes and incidents in the world of material forms and living things.

The balance, the fittedness, and the rhythmic consistency that we find in, say, *Blue Poles* are taken from the cognitive experience of both the painter and the viewer. An abstract painting must be as cohesive, complicated, and brilliantly ordered as a skeleton. Conversely, you don't need putti or apples to capture the lived world. The problem with "a purely aesthetic activity" is not its aspiration to high art but its aspiration away from life. Greenberg's Platonism bears little relation to what artists actually do. He once said that the first mark of paint on a canvas was an adulteration, since it disrupted the perfect two-dimensionality of the canvas. It would be impossible to produce an art that conformed exactly to what Greenberg wanted without being sterile. Greenberg, Barr, and the other teleologists shrunk art in the name of its own climax. The future they demanded was shriveled rather than expansive.

And Soutine did not fit into the grand official teleology, as Greenberg set out to explain when, after having visited the MOMA retrospective, he put pen to paper. Armed with his theories and his tyrannical tastes, Greenberg articulated a theory of reading Soutine that has held sway ever since. In the January/February 1951 issue of *Partisan Review*, Greenberg began by admitting that, before this retrospective, Americans' access to Soutine's works had been decidedly limited:

> Soutine was until recently on the periphery of our attention here in America—not so much disregarded as overlooked. We had got used to think of Miró as the only significant painter to issue directly from the School of Paris after 1918. When Soutine chanced to come into focus he was viewed with respect only we did not see enough of him. Lately we began to suspect, when we thought of it, that he might be the greatest of the Expressionists since van Gogh; but we had not seen the right things yet. . . . Since I have not got [to the Barnes], the current exhibition at the Museum of Modern Art of seventy-five oils representing all periods of his career gave me my first real opportunity to verify those expectations. They were disappointed.[12]

Greenberg's curmudgeonly tendencies are not, sadly, reason enough to dismiss him. Even when he is wrong he is intelligent, and his heresy-hunting at least tells contemporary readers what their world believed. Hence, in this tightly packed first paragraph we learn that Soutine was already considered an expressionist—a superficial and erroneous designation that Dunow has spent decades refuting. When viewers entered the MOMA exhibition doors, they expected to determine whether or not Soutine rose to fill the shoes that Van Gogh—the great expressionist—had left empty. But Soutine, who spent much of his life insisting against Van Gogh's influence on his work, had his own shoes and strangely sized feet. This was simply not the proper question to ask.

We also learn that whatever the School of Paris meant to the art cognoscenti of 1951, it was not the same thing that it meant across the ocean in Paris, or across the decades now. Miró did live in Paris, but so did Dalí and Brancusi and Picasso—none of whom would be called members of the School of Paris today, though Greenberg certainly would have grouped them together. It seems that in New York, "School of Paris" simply referred to the Parisian avant-garde. One of the essential qualities—the Jewishness—goes unmentioned. Greenberg also talks of Soutine as if he sprang fully formed in Paris in 1918, though he could not have been unaware of Soutine's origins, since Monroe Wheeler named them in the exhibition catalogue. (Greenberg himself had the good fortune to be born in New York to Jewish immigrants who had already made the journey overseas and so spared him memories of an unhappy childhood in eastern Europe—one abstraction of indisputable worth.)

Greenberg goes on to say that Soutine manifests a capacity for greatness that he repeatedly fails to realize. Soutine "asked, perhaps, too much of painting." He did not bow to the strictures that the medium imposed on artists, he did not aspire to "a minimum of decorative organization . . . until near the end of his life." He continues, "What Soutine wanted of painting seems to belong too much to the province of poetry or music, and beyond any art of space." This is perceptive. What is untrue is Greenberg's conviction that the standards he sets are the only ones by which a proper analysis of the work can be made. But there are other, more appropriate standards. Greenberg believed that it was a critic's job to stand before a work and determine whether it succeeded on his terms and based on his expectations. This is an entirely valid approach to take, and many fine critics employ it. Another is to ask what the artist is trying to do. Greenberg concedes, however obliquely, that Soutine's drive, his project, is beyond Greenberg's comprehension. If that had been an admission rather than an indictment, it would have been wise.

There is much in Greenberg's influential essay that reveals an almost reluctant appreciation for Soutine's work—an appreciation that might have led another writer to question whether there were virtues beyond those he championed. He writes that Soutine is "coarse yet sensitive at the same time," and that "he was one of the most painterly painters there ever were, one of those who succeeded best in converting the substance of pigment into signified emotion." He concedes, "There may be more sap and juice in the paint of a French master; van Gogh's brushstrokes are more articulate and harmonious; but no one has dealt more intimately than Soutine with the tactile properties of oil paint—its consistency, grain, weight—and at the same time used them so exclusively for optical effect." All of this is high praise and correct.

Greenberg's powers of discernment were of course remarkable. It's what he did with his exquisite observations that require careful handling. He writes, for instance, that Soutine's "dream of the heights of painting saw the declamatory and grandiose design and subject-handling of the Old Masters married to the violent and distorting immediacy of Post-Impressionist art, Rembrandt's pathos embodied in the instantaneous response and sensation of Expressionism. Only an outsider and newcomer could think this could be done, only someone arrogant, and hypnotized by the *pompier*'s notion of sublimity, yet committed to the directness of modern art, in spite of himself, by his own instinct for painting."

He is again in every instance technically correct and even wise. The biting implication that Soutine's arrogance is tantamount to an unfortunate hubris is the problem. Which great artist was not arrogant? Which great artist did not demand from painting what had never been demanded before? Rembrandt was an insider who grew to want more from painting than the establishment of his time could bear, and he was ostracized for it. Were Goya's demands academic? Did El Greco mind the line?

For Greenberg, the difference between Soutine's objectives and those of other radical painters is not in the degree of the radicalism, but in Soutine's failure to realize his personal vision and at the same time make a legible painting. Greenberg insists again and again throughout his review that Soutine was attempting to "transcribe [his] emotion in all its immediate, 'existential,' extra-aesthetic truth." This again misinterprets Soutine as an expressionist. It is quite true that Soutine was attempting to express in paint something alien to paint, but this was empirical vitality, not personal emotion.

The misinterpretation explains Greenberg's analysis of Soutine's development: He agrees with Monroe Wheeler's assessment that as soon Soutine became more technically skillful, he became less tormented and less capable of expressing torment in paint. This sapped him, according to Greenberg, of his essential painterliness: "He had bought his 'brilliance of style' by renouncing the fullness of his ambition and emotion." Of the paintings that Greenberg considers successes, his favorite is *House at Oisème*, "which, however conventional and indebted to Courbet in its approach to the subject, comes off as a triumph of closely modulated and powerfully felt paint. The color is narrower in range than before but precisely for that reason of a more clarified force; tones are no longer clotted together at too widely separated points of the value register."

It's a deft, insightful commentary on the painting, worth considering at each point. By "conventional and indebted to Courbet," he is clearly contrasting the simple composition of the painting with the composition of earlier and more complicated landscapes like the Céret series. Why he names Courbet is a bit mysterious. Soutine has pressed the house up close to the surface of the canvas by de-emphasizing the perspective that would have dictated that one side of the house or the other would retreat backward on a diagonal. In this, the style is emphatically distinct from Courbet. Aside from the fact that Courbet is among the several painters that Soutine "copied," I do not see that this painting is indebted to him any more than it is to Rembrandt. But it certainly is much more classical in composition, much more legible and familiar to a viewer than the Céret works.

One of the things that scholars mean when they describe the Céret paintings as "challenging" (which they so often do) is that in those paintings Soutine did not conform to the rules that regulate the kinds of paintings we are accustomed to seeing. Between Céret and the late landscapes, he spent decades studying Old Master compositions. As Dunow explains:

The complexity of compositions and multiplicity of forms, which had not been operating since Céret, re-emerge in the landscapes of the late 1930s and 1940s, painted at Civry and Auxerre and then at Champigny and Richelieu.

In some ways, Soutine travels full circle in these landscapes, reinvesting the energies that had animated the

Céret pictures in an image that is now anchored with a more structured and "traditional" armature. The energy is no longer equated with chaos and anarchy and compression but is directed and contained by readable forms in a definable space. There is the same rhythm that animates forms, the same dynamism permeating the whole, but the growing stress on clarity and recognisability, developing throughout his landscape oeuvre, now effects a reorganization and rechanneling of these sensations.[13]

As she puts it, Soutine had acquired a "'traditional' armature" by the time he was in Auxerre and Richelieu. This makes his paintings "easier" for viewers to appreciate and to enter into without ambivalence. Viewers have been trained over time to expect a particular kind of thing from a landscape, the same way we have been trained to expect a movie or a book to function according to certain sets of organizing principles. When we look at a painting that does not obey those laws, and instead obeys a different set of equally complicated regulations, it is difficult to rally, to move past the surprise into a spirit of charitable discernment.

The Céret landscapes are ordered according to strange laws, laws that are complicated variations of those that govern our world. One reason these paintings were more useful to abstract expressionists than his later, simpler compositions is that Soutine was modeling a kind of world-building that they themselves were failing to develop at the time. World-building in painting is not something that every artist wants to attempt. Some painters look at the objects in front of them and aim to repeat them on canvas the way they appear in life. It is sufficient to have a canny grasp of how color behaves in light, and then to repeat those patterns in paint. But if a painter chooses not to do this—if he chooses to develop new rules for regulating spatial and color relations—then he must ensure that those decisions remain consistent throughout the painting. Otherwise the painting will fail by the very terms it sets for itself.

So, for example, in *The Houses* (see inset page 3, *top*), once Soutine had made the decision to distort the objects, he had to render every one in the same rhythmic and tonal language. All the houses are twisted. All the colors fall within the same palette of grayish-yellow and -green. The sky roils the way the land beneath it does. The intensity is equal throughout.

The painting is energetic, but it is not disorderly. If insanity is obedience to an unnatural, unrealistic set of laws, then Soutine's paintings are insane. But they are also startlingly coherent, intelligent—even, or especially, when they are at their most intense. It is not easy to be both ordered and teeming. The more activity and objects a painter attempts to convey, the more opportunity he has to fail, especially if he renders them according to laws that he invented. (Van Eyck encountered his own version of this problem when he sought to convey distant objects with far more detail than was realistic.) Picasso's cubist inventions were shocking for this reason, though for Picasso the decisions were conscious, political (in the sense that he wanted to influence the community of painters in which he worked), and conceptually articulated. He wanted to create a new language for art.

Syntax is a useful metaphor. The grammar of the Céret period is intensely complicated. If Céret deserves special recognition among Soutine's periods, it is because it evinces a startling and uncanny capacity to create an intricate and extensive series of laws that regulate the universe of his canvases. When he succeeds in obeying those laws—and he does not always succeed on his own terms—even if the result is not beautiful, it is memorable.

Let's look closely at a few details in *The Houses* to illustrate a convoluted but essential point. Notice the shadows on the sides of and within the houses. The shock of red in the lower space between the whitish house in the center left and the grayish house to its right fades into a dark black as the houses extend both back and up toward their twisted roofs. This darkness wedged between the houses communicates the fact that the passage between them is devoid of light. There is a distorted stretch of dark black on the alley side of the grayish house, signifying a large shadow formed by the twisted rooftop that looms over it.

The sea of houses stretching behind it sway in rhythm with one another, distinguished by shimmers of yellow and red. Dark patches of blue or green suggest that the roof slants backward. The choices Soutine makes to convey how his world is unlike ours are riffs on familiar laws, in the same way that vertigo is made possible by balance.

As Soutine grows out of Cèret, his composition and his color choices become increasingly classical. His palette does not become "narrower in range," as Greenberg puts it. On the contrary, Soutine's dexterity, the increased skill that Greenberg registers, permits him to incorporate a great range of colors without disrupting the harmony of the picture. In the Céret period his palettes were dominated by a single color, often gray though sometimes red, sometimes blue. *Flayed Rabbit* (1921) and *The Pastry Chef* (1919, see inset, page 2, *top*) are both indisputable examples of Céret-era paintings that suffered from this diffusion of a single color.

Contrast them with the *Pastry Chef* Soutine painted in 1927. It is not a narrower palette that makes this painting much stronger. The cool, dark blues in the background juxtapose pleasingly with the warmth in the subject's hands and cheeks. The two contrasting palettes enliven the painting. It would have required some self-control to keep from diluting the painting's two realms—especially since the chef's white uniform, like all white ensembles, is easy to dirty.

Greenberg's repeated insistence that Soutine's compositions became less interesting and more traditional as he got older doesn't stand up to scrutiny either. While some early works depart from traditional composition, most of the paintings from the first two decades of his career fit neatly into three categories: still life, portrait, and landscape. Only in his final years do scholars run into the challenge of categorizing works that blend the latter two.

It is true that around the time of the beef carcass paintings, Soutine began consistently and skillfully organizing his still lifes and portraits around a single subject. Over time, his canvases became less internally dispersed. Dunow again:

> The coherence and balance between image and field, between subject and pictorial structure, have been achieved partially through Soutine's emulation of traditional masters, particularly Corot (not Corot's *Chartres Cathedral*, 1830, and *View of the Chateau de Rosny*, 1840, both at the Louvre [where Soutine would have seen them]). (Indeed, the same spatial and compositional conception is operating in many of the figure paintings of the mid-late 1930s.)
>
> But Soutine's reliance on a single-object image can also be seen as an out-growth of the Céret and Cagnes

developments. It was the struggle to adjust the parts to the whole, to relate the object or objects to the totality of the surface, both two-dimensionally and three-dimensionally, that had characterized these landscapes. Soutine resolved the struggle by limiting the number of objects he worked with, until he was left with a single object and its relationship to its space.

He learned how (or chose) to reduce the hum of the background so that the energy within the painting directs the viewer's focus toward the subject—typically at its center, or slightly off center. Consider the two chefs: The primary reason that the later painting is more digestible is that Soutine quiets the background. In *The Pastry Chef* (1919), the entire painting is pressed close to the surface. The background and the foreground share not only palette but also hue. Use your hand to cover the upper-right corner that cuts across to the side of the chef. See how the business of that corner pulls the viewer away from the chef so that the eye is confused. If Soutine had painted the whole of that corner in the same deep red as the cloth in the chef's hands, say, it would have been a less demanding painting. The eye would have been directed toward the subject. Many of his later paintings utilize that technique. The most famous of these is the *Madeleine Castaing* (see inset page 5, *top*) that hangs in the Metropolitan Museum of Art.

This painting is *more* conventional than the Céret paintings in that it is organized in a way that is immediately legible. It does not challenge its viewers to the point where complexity or confusion might compel them to turn away. The red of the dress is radiantly conventional in its beauty. If the entire painting vibrated with that same red, it would demand more than conventionally digestible works do. And yet the composition could not have been executed with such harnessed power by any other hand.

The distortions of the subject's body immediately signal that the painting is neither ordinary nor easy. Her entire form twists, flowing downward from her head first to the right, then to the left. Her hands, arms, thighs, and calves all spiral in harmony with the larger swivel. Every motion within the writhing whole remains rhythmically in step, no element out of sync. This is most evident in the subject's face, which decisively refutes the suggestion that Soutine had become conventional.

Here again, the minute, almost delicate twists within the face sustain the rhythm of the whole. If any of the disparate shapes failed to communicate with one another—if they failed to merge into the flow of painterly flesh as seamlessly as the rest of the face and body—the painting would be less successful. There are, in fact, paintings by Soutine in which the twitchings do grow disparate and disjointed. His weakest paintings suffer from this uneven quality. But this portrait is among his most formidable works because of the consistency of his attentions. He upheld all his own laws.

While looking at Madame Castaing's face, recall Greenberg's assertions regarding Soutine's emotionalism. According to Greenberg, Soutine's great mistake was his attempt to use painting as a form of catharsis. For the Soutine viewers who argue that the artist was an expressionist, a similar reasoning is employed, though they draw an opposite qualitative judgment: They agree with Greenberg that painting was, for Soutine, a means of emotional expression, and they admire him for it.

Among the most extreme examples of this assessment was one offered by the celebrated writer and Holocaust survivor Elie Wiesel, who wrote the introductory essay for a 1995 retrospective of Soutine held at Museo d'Arte Moderna in Lugano. The text is singularly representative of how viewers—particularly Jews who wish to claim Soutine as a spokesman for their people's experience—indulge in unfounded stereotypes about Soutine's origins, his Jewishness, his pain, and his psychology:

> Yes, Soutine, Chaim Soutine, the unhappy former pupil of the *héder* of Smilovichi, inspires fear. Is it his wild-eyed stare that betrays the anguish he feels at being displaced and uprooted? Or is it his memory? For he does not seem to live in the present; only the past seems to have meaning, or, indeed, life. Is his art the fruit of violent confrontation between the memory of experiences undergone and the terror of re-living them? On the one hand, he seems to be constantly fleeing the *shtetl*, that small, picturesque Jewish kingdom suspended somewhere between Heaven and Earth, yet on the other hand it would also seem that the *shtetl* is itself constantly pursuing him. . . .
>
> More than anyone in his time or in ours, Soutine translated the blind and brutal passions that have stirred and ravaged our century. . . . I regard Soutine's paintings as survivors. Their murdered universe, laden with menace, continues to torment the memory of hungry and humiliated children. Bringing this memory to life, Soutine must have come to the conclusion that God, even God, has occasion to curse his own creation.[14]

It is a startling text. Is there a more extreme example of a viewer projecting themselves onto a work than Wiesel deeming Soutine's very paintings "survivors"? In other cases it would be difficult to imagine what could possess a serious and scrupulous writer to so thoroughly abandon the realm of reasoned interpretation as Wiesel does here, but of course Wiesel is not an ordinary writer, and it is obvious why he felt licensed to such excess. I am as unqualified to consider the psychological factors that contribute to Wiesel's analysis of Soutine's paintings as Wiesel is unqualified to consider Soutine's artistic ambitions, significance, and worth. But it is correct to consider Wiesel's response to Soutine's works an expression of the traumas that Wiesel endured during World War II—a war that he, unlike Soutine, survived, and the memories of which he was forced to carry to his grave—rather than a serious consideration of the works of art. Imputing to Soutine a fixation on blood and death and fury with God is as reasonable as characterizing artists as nymphomaniacs for painting naked women.

There are artists who used painting to communicate pain and rage, and it does not make them weaker or stronger than artists who did not. Soutine was simply not among them. When Munch painted *The Scream*, he meant to elicit an emotional response in viewers that was commensurate with an emotional impetus in himself. That was the nature of his project. Soutine was not interested in the feelings he inspired, and he did not believe that feelings motivated his own brush. Perhaps they played some role, but to even consider what they were sets one up to misunderstand him, just like insisting that his Jewishness must have in some way shaped his identity is beside the point. Yes, he felt things. Yes, he was born a Jew. But he chose not to treat either his feelings or his patrimony in his work. Soutine never talked about feelings. His regimens, his practice, his relationship with his subjects—all attest to a man who was moved primarily to capture perceived movement.

Nevertheless, it matters that the overwhelming majority of people who stand before a Soutine painting are provoked to feel something. It should figure in an analysis of him and his work that, over the decades, many viewers have looked at a Soutine painting and seen horror. It is telling that Greenberg studied the 1950 retrospective and deduced from what he saw that Soutine was straining to communicate emotion. Greenberg never spoke to Soutine so he could not have asked him, and he never read anything Soutine wrote about his intentions because Soutine did not write about his work (or about anything else). But even if he could have, what Soutine might have consciously articulated about his goals may not have changed Greenberg's analysis. I doubt if it would have changed Wiesel's either.

Viewers see death and horror in Soutine's paintings for a reason, and the reason is *not* because Soutine put them there for viewers to see. Even if he had set out to do so, it would not be *why* they felt fear. The disquiet in the viewer would merely be symptomatic of the painting's power, whether the artist intended that power to have that effect or not. No. What interested Soutine was energy so vivid and overwhelming that people find it disconcerting. People are disturbed by what Soutine *was*, not by what he wanted them to see. Soutine was not trying to shock or scare his viewers. It just happened that other people found his revelations terrifying. This quality, this addiction to something unnaturally powerful, is itself frightening. Most of us find it alarming to see people misshapen. But

Soutine didn't paint people as grotesques because he was interested in grotesques; he painted them distorted because he was interested in their motions, potential and actual, and so he altered their appearance, sometimes grotesquely. But isn't it horrifying in itself that a man would be so engrossed in his own project, so addicted to a strange beauty, that he would intentionally distort faces and bodies in pursuit of that bizarre ideal?

Compare Soutine's grotesques to the work of a different painter who aimed to paint horror. Goya and Soutine have some mysterious affinities, and one of them is this fascination with the uncanny. Goya's black paintings are a genre of horror art, and this horror is precisely what Soutine is mistaken for attempting. Soutine was not attempting it, though sometimes he did realize it. There are many similarities: Goya's elongated faces, his wide eyes and sloping, twisted bodies, the terrible lack of physical ease, the way the figures sway together like a single organism—all these choices rhyme with Soutine's work. And the probing humanity in Goya's monstrous and inhuman subjects is the most perplexing and provocative quality the two painters share. Goya's knife is sharpened by the terrifying decision that he made to keep his monsters almost human. They haunt us because they are almost like us. We see ourselves in them; we see how poverty or war could warp and maim us. The same is true of Soutine. If he had been trying to paint a face distorted by disease or heartbreak, the finished work would have been the same.

The allegiance to veracity in both these artists' works, and its effect on viewers, puts one in mind of a letter from Cézanne to Ambroise Vollard. Writing of Gustave Moreau, Cézanne said, "If everything painted by that distinguished aesthete looks hopelessly old-fashioned, it is because his dreams of art come not from his feelings for nature, but from what he has seen in museums and, even more, from a philosophical attitude based on knowing too much about the masters he admires. I wish I had the fellow under my thumb so as to drum into his head the idea—so sane, so comforting, the only true idea—of an art enriched by contact with nature."[15] This enrichment, this capacity to seal in paint something learned from nature, is essential to both Goya and Soutine. And whereas both men were steeped in classical traditions, their visions did not come from a classroom.

But Goya's allegiance to truth is not the same as Soutine's. He is emphatically interested in human feeling, in how it warps human appearance and relations. He wants to consider how horror works on a person. He is also a political artist. This interest demands departures from what he has seen. It requires conscious invention. When Soutine departed from reality, by contrast, it was not intentional and it was not a protest against reality. Not at all. He felt he was communicating something beyond what could be seen, but that was no less true and present before him. Goya's disfigurements are tempered by virtuosic delicacy. His subject is brutality, and he chose to sharpen that brutality by refined artistry. Somehow the disfigured faces are more horrible because they are so gently conjured. The softness of Goya's brush is a slick blade. Soutine's canvases have no such sophisticated tenderness. His tenderness, when he is tender, is of a different sort, and the distinction is relevant. Softness was only ever a product of what he saw. It is never a conscious manipulation of the viewer.

Often in Soutine's late works he conveys tenderness. His painting *Return from School After the Storm* (1939, see inset page 8, *top*) is a fine example. The roughness of the scene makes the warmth between the two figures more affecting. As Dunow writes, "The introduction of children, often in Paris, immersed in the landscape with overhanging clouds and windswept trees threatening in the distance takes on narrative significance. These children start to symbolize a kind of innocence and cohesion in the face of impending overpowering forces, analogous to Soutine's own feelings of vulnerability as a Jew in occupied France. The figures in these landscapes establish scale and transform the landscape into a metaphorical image of man's relationship to nature."

This work is a fitting model for considering all Greenberg's points together. It is coherent. It is intelligently configured. As Greenberg would have put it, it is decoratively designed. The eye is pulled inward by the path, which moves back toward the upper right corner just as the sky moves down and leftward from that same point. The line of trees cutting across the horizon and separating sky from earth is thick on the right side and thins out as it moves to the other side of the painting. It may be easier to study than a Céret, but this flux of movement is not simple.

The painting defies easy categorization. It is neither a landscape nor a portrait, as the grass, trees, and sky are just as much its subject as the two figures holding hands. The paint is thickly handled. For the trees, gobs of deep green whip over one another. A fleck or two of bright yellow shimmer among the leaves. On each side of the path, the grass consists of a sheet of light blue alongside a stretch of green, dancing with whips of light and dark blue and white. The two figures each wear long-sleeved, short black dresses, which are rendered in thick scrapes of paint. Their legs, faces, and hands are dobbed in pink, red, and yellow. There are no features, only swirls of paint. The roughness of the paint and the tenderness of the two girls accentuate one another. It reads as though the tenderness is as powerful a force as the wind and sky—an elemental force, the only sort Soutine would have noticed and studied and represented.

Greenberg's review of the 1950 MOMA show sealed in ink the legacy that both drew New York artists to Soutine for the next few years and also cast Soutine out of the arc of art history that dictated the syllabi of the students Esti Dunow studied with two decades later. Soutine's fame in New York had an expiration date because it was dependent on how New York artists could use him to advance their own work. He was a tool, not an end in itself. Once they didn't need him anymore, once the advancement had been made, he lost his luster. There were fewer shows dedicated to his work, and he appeared less often in galleries and textbooks. Lecturers coalesced around a historiography that placed Matisse and Picasso at the center of the avant-garde movement (those two artists have appeared in more shows at MOMA than any other), and artists who did not fall into this hallowed trajectory were pushed to the periphery.

Esti Dunow arrived at New York University's Institute of Fine Arts in 1970 after graduating from Brandeis. She was unprepared for the ensuing culture shock: She had left the Brandeis of the sixties, with its marijuana-infused sit-ins, and arrived at a refined establishment populated by women in below-the-knee A-line skirts swaying above black pumps, and men, the few that there were, in coats and ties. She was the only one wearing jeans. She supplemented her formal courses by studying painting and drawing at the Studio School in Greenwich Village for several hours each day.

By taking one day off per week to substitute teach, she managed to pay for both.

The duality became increasingly uncomfortable. When she spoke to people at NYU about her painting, it was clear that her peers considered the act of picking up a paintbrush an unserious activity. And likewise at the Studio School—if people had known she was getting a PhD, she would have been drummed out of the building. She had wonderful teachers who spoke about art history, and they certainly knew the material, but they distrusted academics.

By her second year the dissonance had grown unbearable. She slumped in a chair in her advisor's office, confessed her double life, and told him she didn't think she could suffer through it another year. She would have to choose art over art history if it came to that. Her advisor happened to be Robert Goldwater, the celebrated historian of modernism. He was not convinced that choosing was necessary. Goldwater was married to the artist Louise Bourgeois, and he was editor of *Magazine of Art*, which published essays about downtown abstract expressionists as well as more academic articles written by scholars like his colleagues at the institute. Goldwater knew the abstract expressionists, and he knew that they read what he wrote. (In *New Art City*, critic and historian Jed Perl sometimes pairs Goldwater with Meyer Schapiro as the contemporary scholars who influenced the abstract expressionists.) Goldwater knew there was a connection between painters and the study of art history. And even if the juxtaposition was uncomfortable, it could be fruitful.

"Who do you want to study?" he asked her. She told him Soutine. The choice was natural: Soutine's paintings made Dunow want to paint. She admired his work—a regard that would only grow in fervor and detail as she came to know him better—and resented how he was spoken of, either as a madman or as a footnote in the official version of art history. Dunow wanted to make the case that Soutine deserved recognition purely because he was a great painter. She believed he needed to be considered on his own terms, not because of his contribution to art history and not as an expression of twentieth-century Jewish angst, and especially not as a mad artist who used art for psychological expression. She felt he had been treated unfairly, excluded from the canon because historians and critics couldn't place him neatly on a continuum, as figures like Greenberg insisted they should.

Soutine wasn't part of the twentieth-century painting scene the way Dunow thought he should be. There was a time when he had been. As she would come to know better than anyone else, many Soutine shows had been held in the 1930s, 1940s, and certainly the 1950s. Artists knew him from these individual shows, and they had flocked to the MOMA retrospective. But by the 1960s and 1970s, he had been reduced to a footnote. The Céret paintings had raised his profile slightly because people saw them as contemporary in spirit. The painter and critic Jack Tworkov had written of the MOMA show, "It is precisely [Soutine's] impenetrability to logical analysis as if it had happened rather than as 'made,' which unexpectedly reminds us of the most original section of the new painting in this country."[16] It is ironic that the paintings most radical and most difficult for people to understand were the ones that had legitimized Soutine for a time in New York. But that time had passed.

Goldwater thought selecting Soutine as a dissertation topic was a good idea. He encouraged Dunow to stay at NYU and apply for a Ford Fellowship, which covered tuition at both institutions for three years and included a travel stipend that allowed her to spend ten weeks in France in the summer of 1973. (It was on that trip that she and her parents walked the streets of Montparnasse, visiting her father's cherished Parisian locales.) In a remarkable twist of fate, that same summer the Musée de l'Orangerie held its historic Soutine exhibition. One hundred paintings filled the enormous hall of what was then the Jeu de Paume building. She visited the show every day she was in Paris, and she traveled around the country tracking down Soutines in various small museums. A number were housed at the Musée Calvet in Aix-en-Provence.

Every artist who merits even a footnote in the annals of art history will suffer from simplification. This is acutely true of painters who do not do scholars the favor of defining their projects outright. And so legends grow. By the time of the 1973 retrospective at the Orangerie, one of the legends that remained was the conception of Soutine as a mad genius. Michael Peppiatt's review of that show, which appeared in *The New York Times* begins, "As much as Van Gogh, and in some ways more, Chaim Soutine served the popular imagination as the archetype of the artist with a capital A, a creature whose all-demanding genius drove him unsparingly through life to an early, unhappy death. Certainly, his life was hard and miserable, alleviated only by bouts of utter absorption in his work and the encouragement of a few friends."[17]

Peppiatt's assessment of the paintings are, unsurprisingly, characterized by this trite orientation. He told readers that, in Céret and Cagnes, Soutine painted "dozens of highly distorted, almost hysterically emotional landscapes." He described Soutine's life as an unremitting tragedy culminating in a painful, lonely, and impoverished death. He exclaims, "The essence of Soutine's life story can be found, more intimately and more dramatically, in his paintings. . . . And yet one is disappointed. A handful of superb paintings apart, it remains the tale of a victim, of a man who suffered deeply but who only rarely found the strength to make great art out of the vision that suffering had intensified in him."

Esti Dunow had her work cut out for her.

Her experience was entirely different. In those galleries in 1973, she saw Soutine the way she still sees him today: first and foremost as a painter. She fell in love with his work.

When it came time to write her dissertation, Dunow contacted Maurice Tuchman, a young star in the firmament of American art. He had been a curator at the Guggenheim Museum after obtaining a PhD in art history from Columbia, and then had become the first curator of twentieth-century art at the Los Angeles Museum of Contemporary Art. He had curated the most recent major Soutine retrospective, held at LACMA in 1968, and was beginning work on Soutine's catalogue raisonné.

An artist's catalogue raisonné is intensely consequential because a work's inclusion or exclusion can dramatically affect its status and worth. In the case of catalogues raisonné compiled after the artist's death, the editors of the inventory wield enormous discretionary power and historical authority. Displeased owners of paintings and competitive scholars can become so bitter about a catalogue raisonné and its attributions that they will write or commission others—Modigliani, for example, has five.

It was a stroke of luck that Dunow happened to contact Tuchman just as he was starting to work on Soutine's catalogue raisonné, and that luck was met with two other fortunate breaks. The first was that Tuchman's primary donor for the project was Klaus Perls, the owner of Perls Gallery in Manhattan, a renowned establishment that Dunow had visited with her father since she was a child. The second was that Tuchman needed a partner on the ground in New York to work with Perls, allowing him to remain in California running the LACMA while overseeing such an enormous project. And so the band of connoisseurs was formed, and the work of several decades began.

Work on a catalogue raisonné is singular, obsessive, punishingly difficult, and sometimes impossible. Questions will be posed that cannot be answered. Paintings will be sought that have long been lost. Each catalogue raisonné poses challenges unique to its subject. Some cases are easier than others, though none are easy; even when working on a living artist with a modest body of work, one still has to be assiduous about all aspects of the research. The precedents set will be formative and extremely difficult to overwrite. In Soutine's case, the challenges were plentiful. The three learned that Soutine never titled his paintings; all the titles were given later by owners or by gallerists. Often, the titles were misleading—some of the place names, for example, did not correspond to where the painting was created. They also learned that Soutine did not sign his work; the iconic red "Soutine," so familiar to devotees of the artist, was not written by Soutine himself. Someone else—a collector or curator perhaps—had taken it upon themselves to scribble it onto the canvases to increase their value. And that wasn't the worst of the liberties taken with Soutine's paintings. Soutine was plagued by "fakes" (painted by copycats hoping to make a buck) and by misattributions—paintings that didn't intentionally imitate Soutine but were simply mistaken as his.

Dunow, Tuchman, and Perls decided that no painting could be authenticated for inclusion in the catalogue raisonné unless at least one of them had seen it in person and all three reached a unanimous conclusion of authenticity.[18] This meant that Dunow spent much of her time with Perls. Perls had been born in Germany in 1912 to Jewish parents who worked as art dealers in Berlin. He had studied art history in Munich until the Nazis prohibited Jews from receiving degrees. He moved to Basel, where he completed a dissertation on the fifteenth-century French master Jean Fouquet—the very painter whose poster Soutine had bought at the Louvre some decades earlier.

Perls's parents had fled Germany and then divorced, and his mother had set up shop as an art dealer in Paris, where he joined her in 1935. He lived there for two years before moving to New York and opening Perls Galleries on East 58th Street. Initially, he sold paintings that his mother sent him from Paris—Maurice Utrillo, Maurice de Vlaminck, and Raoul Dufy were early examples. When she was forced to leave France, he began representing contemporary American painters (Alexander Calder was his client beginning in 1954) as well as Mexican and South American artists. Over the decades his gallery worked primarily with modern French painters such as Soutine, Picasso, Braque, and Modigliani. (Upon his death he bequeathed thirteen works by Picasso and two by Soutine to the Metropolitan Museum of Art.)[19]

Together, the three editors were able to track down an extraordinary number of Soutines. Perls's gallery had handled many of his canvases over the years, and through his dealings with other

collectors, members of the School of Paris, and art-world pow-
erhouses, he was able to provide a wealth of contacts and information. Likewise, Tuchman's work on the major LACMA
retrospective had helped him gain his own network of resources.

The bulk of the unglamorous daily labor fell to Dunow. Much
of her work required shuffling from one museum library to another.
She bustled back and forth between the Frick, the Metropolitan
Museum of Art, MOMA, and the Morgan Library, carrying piles
of yellow legal pads, scavenging for and assiduously copying any
information regarding Soutine exhibitions, painting acquisitions, or
provenance that she could find. She took all her notes to Perls's house
and sat for hours on the couch in his office, sorting the information
into coherent and carefully organized lists and folders. At the time,
Perls owned Soutine's enormous rayfish painting, now in the Met's
permanent collection, and it hung right above her head. She came
to feel as if the painting belonged to her in some way, and that sense
of ownership strengthened her personal connection to Soutine. It
seemed that he was in the room while she worked.

Perls became a mentor to Dunow. He was impressed by her
intelligence and diligence. His respect for her grew so strong that
when it came time to decide how to list the authors' names, Perls
suggested that they appear alphabetically so that she would lead
the pack. (He was outvoted on that matter.) Perls's recognition of
her gifts, and his respect for her mind and work, were unusual.
Dunow grew accustomed over the years to being ignored. At first
she told herself that this was the price of being the junior member
of an illustrious team, without the contacts or credentials accrued
over a lifetime of work. But as the decades wore on, the legendary
art-world misogyny became increasingly blatant.

Sexism was a prejudice Dunow would have to face on her own since she was the only female member of the group. But there were other challenges that all three members of the group faced together. They all believed that they had been entrusted with Soutine's legacy. Each had distinct motivating factors for taking up the project. Each had an intense and personal relationship with Soutine's legacy and work, which compelled them to devote so much of their time and risk their reputations on such an enormous work. All were united, though, in the belief that Soutine had been overlooked, that the academy and culture had collaborated in giving him insufficient recognition.

A catalogue raisonné is an honor—not every artist merits one. It serves to solidify an artist's legacy and, at times, to assert and secure his or her rightful place in history. For Soutine, all three felt their purpose was to elevate him from outsider to the status he deserved: as a certified member of the pantheon of modern artists. Over the years, Tuchman and Dunow went on to co-curate many Soutine exhibitions and to advise on the curation of others, often with this goal at the forefront of their minds.

Chaim Soutine (1893–1943): Catalogue raisonné spans 780 pages. Published in 1996, it appeared in two volumes: one dedicated to portraits, the other to landscapes and still lifes. The result of two and a half decades of painstaking work, it remains the definitive record of all authenticated Soutine paintings up to that year. Dunow believes that several hundred more exist; she is currently working on a third volume.

The publisher selected Soutine's *Portrait d'homme (Emile Lejeune)* (circa 1922–1923) for the cover. Dunow explained, "They picked it because of the blue background. They said, 'It's such a bright color—it'll pop in a bookstore window.'"

Even after the catalogue's release, the stewards of Soutine's legacy still had work to do, in part because his star had yet to rise again. His outsider status persisted, though it had begun to wane.

In 2006 Dunow and Tuchman curated *The New Landscape/The New Still Life: Soutine and Modern Art* at Cheim and Read gallery in New York, another effort to affirm Soutine's continued significance. And the show did demonstrate, as definitively as anything can be proven in the realm of art, that Soutine's impact on contemporary art was so enormous, so irrefutable, that his rightful place in the mainstream was beyond dispute. For the exhibition, Dunow and Tuchman compiled a collection of testimonials and impressions of Soutine written by artists, art critics, and art historians over the years, several of them specifically for the show. In the introductory essay, the pair noted, "Repeatedly we have been struck and at times even surprised by the spontaneous outpouring of praise for the work of Chaim Soutine by each and every artist we contacted." It is striking that every commenter saw different and sometimes contradictory powers in Soutine.

Here is a small Soutine lectionary, including texts from the Cheim and Read catalogue.

His landscapes and portraits from the period after the war [World War I] were priceless. One might say he was painting in a state of lyrical panic. The subject (to use the consecrated expression literally) overflowed from the frame. A great fever within him distorted everything. Houses left the ground, trees seemed to fly.

—Maurice Sachs[20]

[Soutine] was one of the rare examples in our day of a painter who could make his pigments breathe light. It is something which cannot be learned or acquired. It is a gift of God. There was a quality in his painting that one has not seen for generations—this power to translate life into paint—paint into life.

—Jacques Chapiro[21]

The mystery of the greatest painting here bursts open, in flesh which is more flesh than flesh, nerves which are more nerves than nerves. . . . It is in the dead meat that he finds his sensual delight.

One thinks Soutine deforms for the sake of deforming, by a perversion that looks to shock and infuriate the viewer. What a mistake! . . . A passion for exact measure and proportion, an architectonic equilibrium torments him and it is just that which compels him to explore the source of these contradictory forces that tear him apart. He desperately seeks an internal order.

Soutine is one of the rare "religious" painters the world has known, because his material is one of the most carnal that painting has ever expressed.

—Élie Faure[22]

Looking at a Céret like the one from the Nan Kivell collection (now in the collection of the Tate Gallery, London) has nothing to do with the experience of gazing at a landscape. Here is a jungle of color, layer upon impenetrable layer, not murky but a luxurious darkness in which light is held as in porphyry or basalt or chalcedony. It is a light that belongs to the forms, not a light thrown upon them. The atmosphere, similarly, has nothing to do with how the weather is behaving in a given area at a certain time. Whether it is noon or dark, whether it is raining or the wind is blowing, is of no concern. Nor is it really a matter of importance what things the shapes stand for, that this is a hill or a house or a tree. We acknowledge that it is, but we get no feeling—such as we do before a Matisse, a Bonnard, a Picasso—that this particular transformation of an object is making us see this kind of object in a new way. We do not read this landscape in terms of objects and relations between objects. Our awareness cuts through objects. It responds to rhythms, to an interplay of forces. To the opposition, for example, on the left-hand side of the picture, between the hectic downward-rushing movement of the torpedo shape (the foliage of a tree) and the slow straining, upward-mounting movement of the two pyramids (the house and the hill) one of which rises out of and above the other. As it reaches the upper apex, goes over the top, this striving motion suddenly explodes into a paroxysm of movement and counter-movement, into abandon and release. And all the experiences the painting evokes are a kind that engage our whole bodies: swinging, diving, staggering, skating, climbing, gliding, riding downhill, teetering on a cliff edge. It evokes them as if they were disassociated from any firm contact with external objects. We enact them as we act in a nightmare, in the void of a nightmare. They arouse panic: only this panic is resolved, for the opposing forces are all somehow contained and held in balance by the overriding rhythm of the picture as a whole—not a frantic but an easy rhythm, like the swinging of a pendulum—which resolves convulsion and conflict into an unexpected serenity.

—David Sylvester[23]

No painter of the years between the wars has had so widespread an effect on post-war painting as Soutine. He has been a major influence on the new American painting. . . . His iconography has been generally exploited and, less generally, his style also has been used and debased by the younger expressionists. And in the last few years a number of the most interesting of the younger English painters (of whom the best known internationally is Peter Lanyon) have either been looking to his example or, without consciously doing this, painting as if they had.

—David Sylvester[24]

[American action painters today employ a style] which the painter could have acquired by putting a square inch of a Soutine or a Bonnard under a microscope.

—Harold Rosenberg[25]

My interest in Soutine has never slackened.

I do not think of him as an expressionist because for me "expressionism" and "truthfulness" are not quite synonymous. "Truthfulness" and "drawing," however, do have something in common; I think of Soutine as an intense draftsman who identifies with his forms, knows them from their core, and follows them all the way round.

I am stimulated by his remark: Chagall and Modigliani never had the courage to destroy their work, as I have sometimes destroyed mine.

—Frank Auerbach[26]

I was also once a student of painting. Soutine was not just my hero, but in our rotten post war period, his images were also a quite perfect replica of a skewed world—our world—perhaps somewhat flat as well, but important precisely because of this. Apart from that, he was a Russian, which was just as important to me, and he was an outsider and no Picasso. There was more of the existential and the broken, as well as the cynical and the hideous, in his images. At that time, he was really very important to me as nourishment, but not anymore. Now he is just another great painter and I believe it is in fact much better to be just a great painter.

—Georg Baselitz[27]

Whether the subject of the painting is a landscape or a portrait or a dead animal, you feel the speed of his brushstroke.

There is something electric and violent and fragile that touches me deeply in all of Soutine's works.

—Louise Bourgeois[28]

[After being asked to identify his key influences:] I think I would choose Soutine—all of his paintings. Maybe its the lushness of the paint. He builds up a surface that looks like a material, like a substance. There's a kind of transfiguration, a certain fleshiness in his work. . . . I remember when I first saw Soutines in the Barnes Collection. . . . The Matisses had a light of their own, but the Soutines had a glow that came from within the paintings—it was another kind of light.

—Willem De Kooning[29]

[I was visiting] the Yale University Museum, and there's a marvelous Soutine there that is a wonderful thing. I mean, here's a room full of Braques and Picassos, and you don't want to look at anything but the Soutine. It's just a house and trees, but it's so mysterious and so inner; so inward, you know. It's as if he ate up the building or squashed the building or. . . . Unnamable emotions about what? I don't know. Not about the building, but it's there forever. It's a thing. There's a powerful emotion in this little thing. And then I saw this big art building, the kind of work they do at Yale, five floors of designing. But which is art? I mean, here's this big modern skyscraper and if that's art then what the hell is the Soutine? If the Soutine

is art, what's this big building about? And the work they
do in it.

—Philip Guston[30]

You know what I am. I'm an expressionist. . . . But I'm
still aware of what reality is. Now who is that wonderful
[artist] that does the Side of Beef and dead ducks? . . . Soutine. . . . Now Soutine, I think he's a better artist than I
am. But he is in the grip of his art. For instance, he does
a landscape, the whole thing is falling downhill. It's mad,
you know. . . . Well, I don't do a completely realistic thing.
It has expressionist moments in it. But at the same time it's
not that pure expressionism like Soutine does. I love what
he does. He can't help himself, you know. He's completely
taken over by his art.

—Alice Neel[31]

"Flesh," the title of a small, potent, and timely Chaim Soutine retrospective, elegantly curated by Stephen Brown
[with assistance from Esti Dunow and Maurice Tuch-
man], at the Jewish Museum, is genteel. "Meat" would
better fit the show's focus on the ferocious paintings of
plucked fowl and bloody animal carcasses that the great
and, I believe, underrated Russian-French artist made in
the mid-nineteen-twenties, in Paris. . . . The centerpiece
of the show, "Carcass of Beef" (circa 1925), on loan from
the Albright-Knox Art Gallery, in Buffalo, activates all
those meanings. Painted in reds and blues as luminous

as those of Gothic stained glass, it communes with Rembrandt's seventeenth-century masterpiece "The Slaughtered Ox," which Soutine contemplated often and intensely at the Louvre, and it crackles with formal improvisations (one swift white line rescues a large blue zone from incoherence) and wild emotion. It's an event—an emergence, an emergency—that transpires ceaselessly while you look. Soutine has long been a marginal figure in modern-art history. . . . But today Soutine feels of the moment, amid quite enough reassurance and decorativeness in recent art. . . .

He painted landscapes that are as vertiginous, to the brink of formlessness, as anything in art to this day: tornadoes of pigment, which are beloved by every painter I've ever talked with about them. . . . If any artist justifies Harold Rosenberg's heady definition of what he called "Action Painting"—a notion of the canvas as an existential "arena in which to act" rather than the ground of an aesthetic pursuit—it would be Soutine, though without the macho pathos that Rosenberg celebrated in de Kooning, Jackson Pollock, and Franz Kline. Meanwhile, being favored by fashion incurred a cost when Pop and Minimalism conquered the art world, in the early sixties. Ever since, Soutine has occupied a blind spot in contemporary tastes. That should end now. Let slide the weary art-historical narratives that lock Soutine into categories of style and sequences of influence. Only look.

—Peter Schjeldahl[32]

The hair on the top of my head trembles in a particular prickle when I catch my first glimpse of Soutine. Every time feels like the first time; every time, I worry I will discover myself insufficient for the experience into which I am throwing myself. Like falling in love or like praying, I worry I lack the machinery for complete immersion. This always happens—no matter which room in which gallery or museum on which continent we find each other. Always, always at the first glance; sometimes a dozen or so paces from the room where he's waiting; sometimes unawares because I'm in an unfamiliar building and I don't know where I'll find him. But the prickle is always the same. In my museum, where I've been able to find him reliably in the same spot for the past several months, the prickle starts about two dozen feet from where he waits; it radiates out from hair to spine to fingertips before he's come into full view. There is a place we've taken to meeting, a room where I often find him, usually alone. I prefer to go alone. It's easier to fall into him, and that is why I come—to rise to his demanding spirit. I am not always up to it, and I like that feeling too. I come to remind myself that there is a way to live that is smarter and quicker than most of us know, certainly than I am equal to. I want to acquaint myself with the weather of that genius—a genius for living.

There are four Soutines in the permanent collection of the Phillips Collection: *The Pheasant* (circa 1926–1927); *Return from School After the Storm* (circa 1939); *Windy Day at Auxerre* (1939); and *Woman in Profile* (circa 1937). The gallery is a ten-minute walk from the apartment I selected for precisely that proximity. Soutine on demand, Soutine a walk away. It has yet to happen that I fail to find one of the four somewhere on a wall, though they rotate often enough that a foreboding at the possibility of his absence never entirely abates. There are too few walls for all the institution's treasures. So I always come afraid that today will be the day he isn't waiting for me.

For a brief period in 2024, three were on view at once: *Return from School After the Storm*, *The Pheasant*, and *Woman in Profile*. *The Pheasant* was put up after the other two, but the curators made the painful decision to hang the gorgeous painting—one of a delicious series from the mid-1920s of pheasants lying dead on a table, and in my view the strongest one—on the staircase, where those inclined to stand and stare would have to block the way. (I did this often, which was the correct, if rude, decision.) But *Woman in Profile*, the portrait Soutine painted of Dr. Tennent's wife as a sort of apology for having dismissed her husband's medical advice, has been hanging in a room on the bottom floor for several months, low to the ground and in gentle light. She has her own small stretch of wall next to a window. I always approach with bated breath. Will today be the day they've taken her away?

I have copied sketches of her face and her cramped, tight body into the pages of a dozen sketchbooks, knowing full well that sketching Soutine in pencil is like kissing a cardboard cutout. What I come away with is my own frustration—notes on the sharp cut of her jaw and the swoop of paint from the bridge of her nose to her nostrils. But the pink shimmer in her cheeks and the rough green scrape that marks her cheekbone, the juxtaposition of delicate flesh over bone . . . one has to visit her to see it. Red pigment glimmers on her lips as if the artist cast a spell to keep the color from fading. But it is the motion in her body and her hair, and the brooding attention in her eye, that fills the room. The Braque and the Blake adjacent and across hardly make a hum.

I look at the woman in the portrait and I feel the man who made her. I feel him, I feel what it is like to be alone with him. This is what living is for—this is what living *is*: forcing oneself as close as possible to the example of racing excellence.

I am met every time with the arresting and exacting awareness that the man before me is granting witness to the spectacle of him wrestling with himself—straining to communicate in all its fullness the rush of the atmosphere he was looking at and living in. There in the painting is the tension that attends all his apparitions: Soutine is throwing himself into and at the same time struggling to constrain the rush of his own vitality. And all he has to constrain that power is his cultivated sense of color and composition. That is the pas de deux: Soutine and Soutine, an eternal dance. It is for that duet that I come back. His inscrutable, intelligent vitality secures my fascination, my addiction. Esti Dunow has told me that her own devotion to Soutine has never blunted, not a bit. *Soutine is endless for me*, she said. The dance is infinite.

I come for the relief of his honesty, for the sweat he leaves on the canvas. Yes—it seems right, it seems inevitable, that truth of this sort should feel like a dare, like a rush toward something we can't grasp, a longing for life.

ACKNOWLEDGMENTS

When Leon Wieseltier was an undergraduate at Columbia University, he wrote a paper for the great art historian Meyer Schapiro on the subject of Chaim Soutine. A few years ago Leon, aware of my fascination with Soutine, which he helped kindle, rummaged through his papers and lent me the essay—on typewriter paper with Schapiro's praise in the margins—to read. I disagreed with it so profoundly that it provoked me to set pen to paper. Endless thanks to Leon for that, and for all his help with and excitement about this project.

This book found a publisher because of Andrew Wylie's commitment and faith. I am very grateful to him, and to Clive Priddle and Anupama Roy-Chaudhury at PublicAffairs, for giving me a shot.

Special thanks to Bill Reichblum and Christopher McCaffery, who tolerated my (and Leon's!) incessant talk about Soutine, which filled the *Liberties Journal* offices for the entire length of time it took me to write this book.

This work would have been impossible without the previous scholarship and true mastery of the subject achieved by Michel

LeBrun-Franzaroli and Esti Dunow. Dog-eared, annotated copies of their books fill my shelves. Without them this one would not exist.

My family's pride and support in this project are magical sustenance. Thank you especially to my mother and father for taking me to the Barnes Foundation for the first time to meet Soutine when I was four years old, and for all the trips back ever since. (Justin, Chelsey, Jake, Lauren, Helen, Michael, Uncle B, I love you!)

Thank you to Morten Høi Jensen, Arash Azizi, Etan Nechin, Christina Cacouris, John Dubrow, Jake McAuley, Jackson Arn, Dexter Filkins, Becca Rothfeld, Agnes Callard, Geoff Paul, Marcia Rockwood, and Steven Ujifusa for your friendship and the gifts of your insights. Sincere gratitude to Greg Jallat at the Philips Collection for his patience and generosity. Thank you to Anne Simmons at the National Gallery Library in Washington for a thousand trips to the stacks, and for converting Esti Dunow's doctoral thesis from microfilm to PDF (that procedure alone saved me incalculable hours of work). Thank you Steven Aftergood for your generous assistance. Thanks to Gilles Kepel and Jérôme Clément for a glorious trip back in time to La Ruche, and to David Assaf for his last-minute expertise.

Leni Kagan, these few are the only sentences in this book that haven't benefited from your oversight. I'm proud of this book because you bettered every element of it, and then because you told me to be. Thank you for the honor of your days. (And thank you to Bob, Tor, and David for sharing her with me.)

NOTES

Chapter 1: Origins

1. Soutine gave the year 1893 to the police prefecture regarding his birth, but he told friends that he was born in 1894. Restellini quotes correspondence between Alfred Barnes and Pierre Loeb in which Barnes asks Loeb to discover Soutine's date of birth. Loeb responds, "Soutine himself is not sure about the real date of his birth. He remembers being born in 1894 but doesn't know the precise details." M. Restellini, ed., *Soutine, Le Fou de Smilovichi* (Pinacotheque de Paris, 2007), 9–10.

2. Hilton Kramer, "Soutine and the Problem of Expressionism," *Artforum*, Summer 1968.

3. David L. Shirey, "Flesh and Blood," *Newsweek*, February 26, 1968, https://archive.org /details/newsweek71jannewy/page/n797/mode/2up?q=%22chaim+soutine%22.

4. Pierre Courthion, *Soutine: Peintre du dechiran* (Edita/Lazarus, 1972), 14; Paulette Jourdain, *Soutine: Musée de Chartres* (Musée de Charters, 1989).

5. Michel Kikoine, "Mes souvenirs sur mon comarade Soutine," unpublished manuscript, n.d.

6. This is the date that is given in the Notice interne du Service des Etrangers du Juillet 1917, Archives de la Prefecture de police de Paris.

7. Hilary Spurling, *Matisse the Master* (Knopf, 2007), 136.

8. No works from Soutine's time in Minsk or Vilna have been authenticated.

9. Rembrandt, Chardin, and Courbet were the only painters whose works inspired Soutine to select subjects for paintings (Rembrandt: *Le Bouef, La Femme au bain*; Chardin: the rabbit paintings, the duck/game paintings, *The Rayfish*; Courbet: *Le Saumon après la truite de Courbet*).

10. Petrovskiĭ-Shtern Ĭokhanan, *The Golden Age Shtetl: A New History of Jewish Life in East Europe* (Princeton University Press, 2014).

11. Benjamin Harshav, *Marc Chagall and His Times* (Stanford University Press, 2004).

12. Andrew Kagan, *Marc Chagall* (Abbeville Press, 1989), 105.

13. Michel LeBrun-Franzaroli, *Soutine: L'homme et le peintre* (self-published, 2015), 9.

14. Eugene M. Avrutin, "The Politics of Jewish Legibility: Documentation Practices and Reform During the Reign of Nicholas I," *Jewish Social Studies* 11, no. 2 (Winter 2005): 136–169, esp. 140; Donna Sutin Queeney, "Who We Are: A Sutin Family History Update," March 2016, https://muhaz.org/who-we-are-a-sutin-family-history-update.html.

15. *ha-Melitz* (המליץ) June 2, 1898, p. 7, National Library of Israel newspaper database, accessed April 9, 2025, https://tinyurl.com/mw2vdc4d.

16. Jolanta Širkaitė, "Where Soutine Started His Journey," *Menotyra* 27, no. 1 (2020), https://doi.org/10.6001/menotyra.v27i1.4242. Remembrances from Faïbich-Schraga Zarfin come from this source.

17. He left before completing preparation for his bar mitzvah, which is unusual for a religious boy, and perhaps contradicts theories of the child Soutine as oppressed by religious relatives for pursuing a career in art.

18. LeBrun-Franzaroli, *Soutine*, 30.

19. Quoted in James Yohe, ed., *Hans Hofmann* (Rizzoli, 2002), 51.

20. Maurice Tuchman, Esti Dunow, and Klaus Perls, *Chaim Soutine (1893–1943): Catalogue raisonné* (Taschen, 1993), 13.

21. LeBrun-Franzaroli, *Soutine*.

22. Jolanta Širkaitė, *Académie de Vilna—Vilnius Drawing School (1866–1915)*, exhibition catalogue (National Gallery of Art, 2017), 304.

23. Širkaitė, *Académie de Vilna*, 52.

24. LeBrun-Franzaroli, *Soutine*, 515.

25. Like all foreign students at the École des Beaux-Arts, Soutine had to secure a certificate of identity, which he did from the Imperial Russian Embassy in Paris. This document, which remains in the archives of the academy, was issued on July 17, 1913, which indicates that Soutine arrived some time in the summer of that year. This same document indicates that Soutine was born in 1893, unlike the document in the "Soutine Dossier," a photo of which was published by Pierre Courthion for the first time in 1972. Courthion took that date for granted, and he also misinterpreted other details in the document. In 1942, another document was added to the police file on Soutine. It relates to a complaint lodged against Soutine, made by a person who was "mentally deranged." There was no follow-up on the complaint. In this document a date is given for Soutine's birth: May 1893. His physical description is recounted as follows: "1.72 m, brown eyes, brown hair, regular nose, shaved beard, medium sized mouth, medium-weight, thick lips." This 1942 document is the best known, but it was publicized by Courthion, who put a photograph of Soutine taken in 1917 on top of the document and included the photo in his book such that it appears as if the photograph was taken in 1942. Courthion, *Soutine*, 16; LeBrun-Franzaroli, *Soutine*, 38; photocopy of the police prefecture file as reproduced in Courthion and LeBrun-Franzaroli.

26. LeBrun-Franzaroli, *Soutine*, 66.

27. Henri Matisse with Pierre Courthion, *Chatting with Henri Matisse: The Lost 1941 Interview*, ed. Serge Guilbaut (Getty Research Institute, 2013), 25–26.

28. Robert Fernier, *17, Quai Malaquis (Atelier Cormon)* (Editions Paris-Publications, 1934), 34.

29. Mané Katz, "Mané Katz-Soutine," *Les Lettres francaise*, 1953.

30. Fernier, *17, Quai Malaquis*, 166.

31. LeBrun-Franzaroli, *Soutine*, 95.

Chapter 2: Immigrants in Wartime

1. Michel LeBrun-Franzaroli, *Soutine: L'homme et le peintre* (self-published, 2015), 77.

2. Miriam Cendrars, *Blaise Cendrars* (Seuil, 1985), 280–281.

3. LeBrun-Franzaroli, *Soutine*, 79; Janine Ponty, *Les polonais en france: De Louis XV à nos jours* (Editions du Rocher, 2008), 110.

4. Kisling, Moïse, Union List of Artists Names Online, Getty Research, accessed April 24, 2025, http://vocab.getty.edu/page/ulan/500027290.

5. Roger Shattuck, *The Banquet Years* (Knopf, 1968).

6. LeBrun-Franzaroli, *Soutine*, 78.

7. Raymond Poincaré, *L'Union Sacrée* (Plon, 1914), 546.

8. Jean-Louis Robert, "Ouvriers et mouvement ouvrier parisien" (thesis, Université Paris, 1989); Thierry Bonzon and Belinda Davis, "Feeding the Cities," in *Capital Cities at War*, ed. Jay Winter and Jean-Louis Robert (Cambridge University Press, 1997); Pierre Darmon, *Vivre à Paris pendant la Grande Guerre* (Fayard, 2002).

9. "Les Incidents de la soirée," *Le Figaro*, August 3, 1914.

10. Hilary Spurling, *Matisse the Master* (Knopf, 2007), 160.

11. Pierre Courthion, *Soutine: Peintre du dechiran* (Edita/Lazarus, 1972). Courthion was a contemporary of Soutine, and his monograph contains many firsthand descriptions of its subject, but like so much of what is published about Soutine, it is not always reliable.

12. Billy Kluver and Julie Martin, *Kiki's Paris: Artists and Lovers, 1900–1930* (Harry N. Abrams, 1989), 71.

13. Margaret MacMillan, *Paris 1919: Six Months That Changed the World* (Penguin Random House, 2007).

14. Ilya Grigoryevich Ehrenburg, *People and Life: Memoirs of 1891–1917*, trans. Anna Bostock and Yvonne Kapp (MacGibbon and Kee, 1961), 146.

15. Quoted in Gabriel Fournier, *Cors de Chasse* (Pierre Cailler Editeur Genève, 1957), 152–153.

16. LeBrun-Franzaroli, *Soutine*, 82.

17. LeBrun-Franzaroli, *Soutine*, 88.

18. Fournier, *Cors de Chasse*, 150.

19. William Fifield, *Modigliani: The Biography* (Morrow Quill Paperbacks, 1976), 158.

20. Meryle Secrest, *Modigliani: A Life* (Knopf, 2011), 162.

21. Emil Szittya, né Adolf Schenk, a bohemian writer born in Budapest in 1886, was a good friend of Blaise Cendrars's, with whom he worked on the anarchist Franco-German publication *Les Hommes nouveaux* in 1911 and 1912. Emil Szittya, *Soutine et son temps* (Bibliothèque des Arts, 1955), 26.

22. Fifield, *Modigliani*, 4.

23. Secrest, *Modigliani*, 16.

24. Jeanne Modigliani, *Modigliani: Man and Myth*, trans. Esther Rowland Clifford (André Deutsch, 1959), 9.

25. Fifield, *Modigliani*, 89; Secrest, *Modigliani*, 185.

26. Fifield, *Modigliani*, 189.

27. John Richardson, *A Life of Picasso*, vol. 2, *1907–1917: The Painter of Modern Life* (Random House, 1996), 358.

28. Secrest, *Modigliani*, 189.

29. Secrest, *Modigliani*, 187.

30. Colette Giraudon, *Paul Guillaume et les peintres du XXe siècle* (La Bibliothèque des Arts, 1993).

31. Giraudon, *Guillaume*.

32. *Homage to Cézanne*, painted by Maurice Denis in 1900, is a testament to Vollard's significance for some of the most important artists of the day. It depicts the group of painters known as Les Nabis (or the Prophets) gathered in Vollard's shop.

33. Giraudon, *Paul Guillaume*.

34. Giraudon, *Paul Guillaume*, 24.

35. Richardson, *Picasso*, vol. 2, 361.

36. Dan Piepenbring, "Painting the Town Blood-Red," *New York Times*, September 14, 2022; LeBrun-Franzaroli, *Soutine*, 514.

37. Élie Faure, *Soutine* (Les Éditions G. Crès et Cie, 1929), 10.

38. Confirmed by Esti Dunow in private correspondence with the author, March 17, 2023.

39. Andrew Forge, *Soutine* (Paul Hamlyn/Spring Books, 1965), 37.

Chapter 3: Fleeing Southward

1. Ilya Grigoryevich Ehrenburg, *People and Life: Memoirs of 1891–1917*, trans. Anna Bostock and Yvonne Kapp (Macgibbon and Kee, 1961), 193–195.

2. "French Locate Gun 76 Miles Away," *New York Times*, March 25, 1918.

3. "French Locate Gun 76 Miles Away."

4. Frederick Holmes, "The Influenza Pandemic and the War," Kansas University Medical Center, accessed April 26, 2025, www.kumc.edu/school-of-medicine/academics /departments/history-and-philosophy-of-medicine/archives/wwi/essays/medicine/influenza .html.

5. Michel LeBrun-Franzaroli, *Soutine: L'homme et le peintre* (self-published, 2015), 121.

6. Miriam Cendrars, *Blaise Cendrars* (Seuil, 1985), 280.

7. Meryle Secrest, *Modigliani: A Life* (Knopf, 2011), 30.

8. Barrey came to Paris from Picardy when she was eleven years old and survived there by becoming a child prostitute. She started modeling for painters, who encouraged her to study painting and art history. She met Foujita at La Rotonde in March of 1917, and they married thirteen days later, commencing a tempestuous relationship that ended when Barrey began living with Foujita's cousin in 1928. Jill Berk Jiminez and Joanna Banham, *Dictionary of Artists' Models* (Taylor and Francis, 2013).

9. This was written in a letter to Pierre Courthion, who quotes it in his book *Soutine: Peintre du dechiran* (Edita/Lazarus, 1972).

10. Jean-Paul Crespelle, *Montparnasse Vivant* (Hachette, 1962), 158.

11. Courthion, *Soutine*, 35.

12. Oliver Philippe, *Zamaron: Un flic ami des peintres de Montparnasse* (Arcadia, 2007), 26, 63; Billy Kluver and Julie Martin, *Kiki's Paris: Artists and Lovers, 1900–1930* (Harry N. Abrams, 1989), 67.

13. Philippe, *Zamaron*, 6, 23; Kluver and Martin, *Kiki's Paris*.

14. Pierre Richard compiled all the discovered letters that Soutine had written: Pierre E. Richard, ed., *Soutine: Lettres et billets* (self-published, 2015). The three earliest were addressed to Commissioner Zamaron from Cagnes in 1918. Before Richard's publication, these letters were entirely unknown. Much can be gleaned from them. What remains of Soutine's correspondence is usually dismissed as useless by scholars. In 1964 much excitement anticipated Harvard University's purchase of the most extensive remaining collection of Soutine's letters, but hopes were dashed when it was reported that the letters contained nothing more than trivial logistical concerns. Harvard's cataloguer lamented that the letters were merely "brief notes chiefly concerned with making or canceling visits. . . . Most contain only a few lines." Noah Pryłucki, Etel Tzukerman, and Nochum Gelfand, "The Yiddish Life of Chaim Soutine (1893–1943): New Materials," trans. Ofer Dynes, *In geveb* (April 2020), https://ingeveb.org/texts-and-translations/life-of-soutine.

Richard concedes that the better part of Soutine's discovered letters appear prima facie to reveal little of worth. They are brief, awkward, and hastily written, and none of them communicate confidences or personal divulgences. But he argues that in fact careful study yields great insight into Soutine's character and frame of mind. He claims, "In their brevity, their variegatedness, their clumsiness, their occasional harshness and even their banalities, these traces nevertheless bear deeply touching witness to the heart of this man and his transcendent and devastating passion."

Of the 1918 letters, Richard explained that he did not have all of the first one, but knew only about the section of its contents that was included in the catalogue for public sale at Paris-Drouot on July 3, 1985. The envelope in which the letter was mailed was sold separately in February 1994, in the Monogramme bookstore in Paris. Written on that envelope was the address "Cagnes rue Sous Barri," which was the address of Pere Curel, where Zborowski, his wife, Foujita, and Fernande Barrey were staying. Evidently Soutine preferred Zamaron to believe that he was included with the general group rather than staying in a different building in a different section of the city, as Fernande Barrey had made clear in her account of the trip. Richard also emphasizes that this letter was not, strictly speaking, written by Soutine—that is, it was not written in his hand, a fact that Soutine reveals in the letter itself. Someone else drafted it. We do not know who that person was.

15. Pierre Richard doubts that this letter was actually written by the artist either, though the catalogue in which it appeared does identify it as his hand. He also notes that the handwriting does not match that of the first letter. Also, in this letter Soutine offers a different address—perhaps the address at which Fernande Barrey discovered him while waiting for Zborowski to return with funds for food.

16. A catalogue raisonné is a compendium that includes every authenticated work of a particular artist either in one medium or in all media. Soutine's was compiled over a

twenty-year period by Esti Dunow, Klaus Perls, and Maurice Tuchman. Dunow and Tuchman are experts on Soutine's paintings.

17. It should be noted that, while the catalogue raisonné is generally chronological, in some instances paintings from a later year appear too early in the book. Since Soutine did not date his paintings, it is very difficult to know precisely when they were completed by simply judging from the catalogue. The editors did their best to place each painting at the proper point in Soutine's life, but perfect chronological clarity is impossible.

18. Clement Greenberg, "Paris Chronicle," *Partisan Review*, January/February 1951.

19. Doris Brian, "U.S. Art at the Fair: Democratic Selection and Standardized Result," *Art News*, March 18, 1939.

20. Greenberg, "Paris Chronicle."

21. Alfred Warner, *Chaim Soutine* (Harry N. Abrams, 1977), 63.

22. David Sylvester, *Chaim Soutine, 1893–1943*, exhibition catalogue (Arts Council, January 1, 1963), 17.

23. *Still Life with Chair* was not included in the original catalogue raisonné because, the editor tells me, it could not be located and so could not be authenticated. It will appear in the third volume of the catalogue, which is forthcoming.

24. Andrew Forge, *Soutine* (Paul Hamlyn/Spring Books, 1965), 33.

25. Léger, in a letter to André Mare, quoted in Jean-Paul Crespelle, *La vie quotidienne* (Hachette, 1978), 121.

Chapter 4: Céret Revolution

1. John Richardson, *A Life of Picasso*, vol. 2, *1907–1917: The Painter of Modern Life* (Random House, 1996), 183; Alex Danchev, *Georges Braque: A Life* (Arcade Publishing, 2005), 117.

2. Kikoine, quoted in R. Cogniat, *Soutine* (Edition du Chene, 1945), 29. According to the scholar and artist Michel LeBrun-Franzaroli, *Soutine: L'homme et le peintre* (self-published, 2015), Soutine's movements between 1918 and 1924 were as follows:

1918 End of March/beginning of April–beginning of October: Cagnes

1918 October–1919 February/March: Paris

1919 April/May: Paris

1919 May/June–1920 January: Cagnes

1920 January/February: Paris

1920 January/February–1920 August/September: Céret

1920 August/September: Paris

1920 September/November–1922 October/November: Céret

1923 January/February–1923 March: Cagnes

1923 April–1923 September/October: Cagnes and La Gaude

1924 April–1924 September/October: Cagnes

3. Léopold Zborowski, quoted in Michel Georges-Michel, *Soutine*, exhibition catalogue (Niveau Gallery, October 9–November 2, 1944), 148.

4. David Sylvester, *Chaim Soutine, 1893–1943*, exhibition catalogue (Arts Council, January 1, 1963), 18. I believe the influence of Van Gogh on Soutine has been overstated.

5. Editors, "From the Archives: Jacques Lipchitz Remembers Amedeo Modigliani, in 1951," *Art News*, December 15, 2017, www.artnews.com/art-news/retrospective/archives-jacques-lipchitz-remembers-amedeo-modigliani-1951-9505/.

6. "Jacques Lipshitiz Remembers."

7. Pierre Courthion, *Soutine: Peintre du dechiran* (Edita/Lazarus, 1972), 48, 56.

8. Marcellin Castaing and Jean Leymare, *Soutine* (Harry N. Abrams, 1964), 32.

Chapter 5: Celebrity

1. *Les heures chaudes de Montparnasse*, directed by Jean-Marie Drot, 1963. Appearances by Pinchus Krémègne, Madeleine Castaing, and Michel Kikoine.

2. "Dr. Albert Barnes Dies in Crash; Art Collector Discovered Argyrol," *New York Times*, July 25, 1951.

3. Sylvie Patry, "Chaïm Soutine and Dr. Albert C. Barnes," *Soutine/De Kooning: Conversations in Paint* (Barnes Foundation, 2021), 35.

4. Albert C. Barnes, letter to Paul Guillaume, January 16, 1923, Albert C. Barnes Correspondence, Barnes Foundation Archives, Philadelphia.

5. René Gimpel, *Journal d'un collectionneur marchand de tableaux* (Calmann-Lévy, 1963).

6. Élie Faure, *Oeuvres complètes*, vol. 3, *Correspondence* (Jean-Jacques Pauvert, 1963), letter 331.

7. Michael Fried, "Manet and His Sources: Aspects of His Art, 1859–1865," *Artforum*, March 1969.

8. Claude Monet, quoted in John Rewald, *History of Impressionism* (Simon and Schuster, 1946), 146.

9. Scott Allan, "Faux Frère: Manet and the Salon, 1879–1882," in *Manet and Modern Beauty* (J. Paul Getty Museum, 2019).

10. Maurice Tuchman and Esti Dunow, *The New Landscape/The New Still Life: Soutine and Modern Art* (Cheim and Read, 2006), 10.

11. Albert C. Barnes, *The Art in Painting*, 3rd rev. and enl. ed. (Harcourt Brace, 1937), 483.

12. Robert Cozzolino, "PAFA and Dr. Barnes: Modernism in Philadelphia," *American Art* 27, no. 3 (Fall 2013); William Schack, *Art and Argyrol* (A. S. Barnes and Company, 1963), 124.

13. James Panero, "Outsmarting Albert Barnes: The Barnes Collection Has Opened Its New Home in Philadelphia, Yet Its Saga Leaves a Cautionary Tale Behind in Merion," *Philanthropy Magazine*, Summer 2011.

14. Stanley Meisler, "Say What They May, the Feisty Collector Had an Artful Eye," *Smithsonian Magazine*, May 1993, 96.

15. Howard Greenfeld, *The Devil and Dr. Barnes: Portrait of an American Art Collector* (Camino Books, 1987), 89.

16. Schack, *Art and Argyrol*, 125.

17. Jean-Paul Crespelle, *Montparnasse Vivant* (Hachette, 1962), 57.

Chapter 6: Soutine and the Masters

1. *"Le Village,"* Musée de l'Orangerie, last modified March 28, 2025, www.musee
-orangerie.fr/en/artworks/le-village-196565.

2. Michel LeBrun-Franzaroli, *Soutine: L'homme et le peintre* (self-published, 2015),
198–200.

3. LeBrun-Franzaroli, *Soutine*, 211. This telling contradicts Michonze's account given in
the documentary of Soutine made by Jean-Marie Drot (an episode titled "Chaim Soutine:
Soutine the Obsessed" in the series *Montparnasse Revisited*, dir. Jean-Marie Drot and Mat-
thew Reinders, 1993), in which he says, "I think I had met Soutine for the first time in 1922
at La Rotonde. He had just returned from Cagnes in a velvet suit covered in paint. He was
already a legend. The people knew Soutine was a painter who started off very well. Some of
the Cagnes landscapes are mind boggling, the landscapes like the bloody beef carcass. The
sight of him is always mind boggling."

4. LeBrun-Franzaroli, *Soutine*, 216.

5. Denis Diderot, *Diderot on Art*, vol. 1, *The Salon of 1765 and Notes on Painting* (Yale
University Press, 1995).

6. Pierre Courthion, *Soutine: Peintre du dechiran* (Edita/Lazarus, 1972), 76–78.

7. Maurice Tuchman, Esti Dunow, and Klaus Perls, *Chaim Soutine (1893–1943): Catalogue Raisonné* (Taschen America, 1996), 425–452.

8. LeBrun-Franzaroli, *Soutine*, 256.

9. Courthion, *Soutine*, 2; LeBrun-Franzaroli, *Soutine*, 280. It is possible that he could
not procure the carcasses in Le Blanc. The paintings themselves indicate that all of them
were painted in the same place, and we know from witnesses that he painted some of them
on the rue du Saint-Gothard, so it follows that he must have painted the rest there too.

10. LeBrun-Franzaroli, *Soutine*, 244.

11. Courthion, *Soutine*, 73.

12. LeBrun-Franzaroli, *Soutine*, 247.

Chapter 7: Companionship

1. Pierre Courthion, *Soutine: Peintre du dechiran* (Edita/Lazarus, 1972), 72.

2. Véronique Dumas, "Faure, Élie," Institut National d'Histoire de l'Art, updated December 3, 2009, www.inha.fr/dictionnaire-critique-des-historiens-de-lart-actifs-en-france-de-la
-revolution-a-la-premiere-guerre-mondiale/faure-elie-inha/.

3. Élie Faure, *Soutine* (Les Éditions G. Crès et Cie, 1929).

4. Pascal Neveux, "Élie Faure and Chaim Soutine: The Story of an Ill-Fated Friendship,"
in *An Expressionist in Paris: The Paintings of Chaim Soutine*, ed. Norman L. Kleeblatt and
Kenneth E. Silver (Jewish Museum of New York, 1998), 150–158.

5. Michel Kikoine, "Mes souvenirs sur mon comarade Soutine," unpublished manuscript, n.d.

6. Maurice Sachs, *Le sabbat* (Éditions livre de poche no. 3201, 1960), 255.

7. Courthion, *Soutine*, 94.

8. Marcellin Castaing and Jean Leymare, *Soutine* (Harry N. Abrams, 1963), 15.

9. Jean-Noël Liaut, *Madeleine Castaing: Mécène à Montparnasse décoratrice à Saint-
Germain-des-Prés* (Payot, 2008), 30.

10. Sachs, *Le sabbat*, 70.

11. René Gimpel, *Journal d'un collectionneur marchand de tableaux* (Calmann-Lévy, 1963); Castaing and Leymare, *Soutine*, 32.

12. Jean-Noël Liaut, *Madeleine Castaing: Mécène à Montparnasse Décoratrice à Saint-Germain-des-Prés* (Petite Bibliotheque Payot, 2008), 89.

13. Charles Baudelaire, "The Painter of Modern Life," 1863, Center for Programs in Contemporary Writing, University of Pennsylvania, accessed April 26, 2025, www.writing.upenn.edu/library/Baudelaire_Painter-of-Modern-Life_1863.pdf.

Chapter 8: Love at Last

1. Adolf Hitler, *Mein Kampf*, trans. Ralph Manheim (Houghton Mifflin Company, 1999), 21.

2. Andree Collie, *Souvenirs sur Soutine* (L'Echoppe, 2002), 14.

3. Brian Moynahan, "Maria Lani Was the Muse of Modernist Masters—then She Vanished Without a Trace," *Vanity Fair*, September 2018.

4. Marcellin Castaing and Jean Leymare, *Soutine* (Harry N. Abrams, 1963), 12.

5. Collie, *Souvenirs*, 14.

6. Noah Pryłucki, Etel Tzukerman, and Nochum Gelfand, "The Yiddish Life of Chaim Soutine (1893–1943): New Materials," trans. Ofer Dynes, *In geveb* (April 2020), https://ingeveb.org/texts-and-translations/life-of-soutine.

7. Henry Miller, *The Books in My Life* (New Directions, 1969).

8. Chana Orloff, "Mon ami Soutine," *Preuves*, November 1951.

9. Garde, *Mes années avec Soutine* (Samuel Tastet Editeur, 2022), trans. by author. All quotes from Gerda Michaelis and memories about her life with Soutine come from this source unless otherwise noted.

10. Orloff, "Mon ami Soutine."

Chapter 9: Storm Clouds

1. Duncan Phillips was an early and avid collector of Soutine. The four in his collection make it one of the most impressive in the world, though the collections at Barnes and Musée de l'Orangerie dwarf it in number four times over.

2. Pierre Courthion, *Soutine: Peintre du déchiran* (Edita/Lazarus, 1972), 128; and Garde, *Mes années avec Soutine* (Samuel Tastet Editeur, 2022), the source for all remembrances from Garde (Gerda Michaelis), unless otherwise noted.

3. Courthion, *Soutine*, 128.

4. Garde, *Mes années avec Soutine*, 16.

5. Robert Paxton, *Vichy France and the Jews*, 2nd ed. (Stanford University Press, 2019), 2.

6. Robert Paxton, *Vichy France and the Jews*, 2nd ed. (Stanford University Press, 2019), 1.

7. Robert Satloff, *Among the Righteous* (PublicAffairs, 2007), 31.

8. Chana Orloff, "Mon ami Soutine," *Preuves*, November 1951.

9. Garde, *Mes années avec Soutine*, 100.

10. Michel LeBrun-Franzaroli, *Soutine: L'homme et le peintre* (self-published, 2015), 499.

11. Courthion, *Soutine*, 142.

12. Garde, *Mes années avec Soutine*, 107.

Chapter 10: Goodbye

1. Remembrances from Garde (Gerda Michaelis) come from *Mes années avec Soutine* (Samuel Tastet Editeur, 2022), unless otherwise noted.

2. Maurice Sachs, *Le sabbat* (Éditions livre de poche no. 3201, 1960), 271.

3. Renée Poznanski, *Jews in France During World War II*, trans. Nathan Bracher (Brandeis University Press, 2001).

Epilogue

1. Pierre Courthion identified his book *Soutine: Peintre du déchiran* as a catalogue raisonné as well as a biography. It remains invaluable to Soutine scholars despite its imperfections. His treatment of Soutine's paintings, however, is utterly unreliable. Many of the paintings appear as thumbnail-sized black and white photos, often misprinted in reverse or upside down, making them difficult to identify, and giving owners of inauthentic Soutines room to argue that their works were included. Sometimes the same picture appears twice in Courthion, listed as two different paintings because it was reversed. But by far the most serious problem with the text is that Courthion included both genuine fakes and misattributions. Paintings that Dunow, Perls, and Tuchman later inspected and determined to be inauthentic were nevertheless accredited by Courthion. Dunow and Tuchman set out to correct the record, as Dunow explained to me. Dunow's recollections come from conversations we had by phone, in person, and through email between January 2024 and September 2024.

2. Arthur Cygielman, "Tomazsow," in *Encyclopedia Judaica*, vol. 20 (Keter, 1972).

3. "Henry Dunow's Oral History," Yiddish Book Center's Wexler Oral History Project, June 5, 2013, www.yiddishbookcenter.org/collections/oral-histories/interviews/woh-fi-0000426/henry-dunow-2013; "Esti Dunow's Oral History," Yiddish Book Center's Wexler Oral History Project, April 17, 2015, www.yiddishbookcenter.org/collections/oral-histories/interviews/woh-fi-0000688/esti-dunow-2015.

4. Norman L. Kleeblatt, "An Expressionist in New York," in *An Expressionist in Paris: The Paintings of Chaim Soutine*, ed. Norman L. Kleeblatt and Kenneth E. Silver (Jewish Museum of New York, 1998), 47.

5. For most of his career he enjoyed more interest in the United States than in Europe, though in recent decades this pattern has flipped.

6. Maurice Tuchman and Esti Dunow, *The New Landscape/The New Still Life: Soutine and Modern Art* (Cheim and Read, 2006), 2–3.

7. Tuchman and Dunow, *The New Landscape/The New Still Life*, 2–3.

8. Florence Rubenfeld, *Clement Greenberg: A Life* (University of Minnesota Press, 1997), 31; Clement Greenberg, "Abstract Art," in *Clement Greenberg: The Collected Essays and Criticism*, vol. 1, ed. John O'Brian (University of Chicago Press, 1986), 199; David Carrier, "Giorgio Morandi: Late Paintings," *Brooklyn Rail*, April 2018, https://brooklynrail.org/2018/04/art_books/Giorgio-Moranidi-Late-Paintings/.

9. Greenberg, "Modernist Painting," in *Collected Essays*, 85.

10. Greenberg, "Abstract Art," 199.

11. Meyer Schapiro, "The Nature of Abstract Art," originally published in 1937, reprinted in *OnCurating*, issue 20, October 2013.

12. Clement Greenberg, "Soutine," in *Art and Culture: Critical Essays* (Beacon Press, 1965), 115.

13. Esti Dunow, "The Late Works: Regression or Resolution," in *An Expressionist in Paris: The Paintings of Chaim Soutine*, ed. Norman L. Kleeblatt and Kenneth E. Silver (Jewish Museum of New York, 1998), 137.

14. Elie Wiesel, "Soutine and the Lost Realm," in *Chaim Soutine* (Museo d'Arte Moderna della Città di Lugano, 1995), 17–20.

15. Hilary Spurling, *The Unknown Matisse: A Life of Henri Matisse: The Early Years* (Knopf, 2005), 198, quoting Ambroise Vollard, *En écoutant Cézanne, Degas, Renoir* (Grasset, 1985 [1938]), 48.

16. Jack Tworkov, "The Wandering Soutine," *Art News*, November 1950.

17. Michael Peppiett, "Soutine as Artist and Victim," *New York Times*, May 27, 1973, www.nytimes.com/1973/05/27/archives/soutine-as-artist-and-victim.html.

18. The chronology of the paintings in the catalogue raisonné is subjective. It is based on the editors' personal analysis, but it is not scientific. Maurice Tuchman's 1968 LACMA catalogue was the first attempt to organize Soutine's oeuvre according to his painterly development.

19. William Grimes, "Klaus Perls, Art Dealer Who Gave Picassos to the Met, Dies at 96," *New York Times*, June 6, 2008.

20. Maurice Sachs, "Contre les peintres d'aujourd'hui," *La nouvelle revue française* 250 (1934): 39.

21. Quote from Chapiro appeared in Alfred Werner, *Chaim Soutine* (Harry N. Abrams, 1977), and in turn was quoted in Tuchman and Dunow, *The New Landscape/The New Still Life*.

22. Élie Faure, *Soutine* (Les Éditions G. Crès et Cie, 1929), quoted in Tuchman and Dunow, *The New Landscape/The New Still Life*, 60.

23. David Sylvester, *Chaim Soutine, 1893–1943* (Arts Council of Great Britain, 1963) (this was the catalogue for an exhibition held at the Tate Gallery, London, and the Edinburgh Arts Festival, August–November 1963), quoted in Tuchman and Dunow, *The New Landscape/The New Still Life*, 61.

24. David Sylvester, "Soutine Reconsidered in Paris Exhibition," *New York Times*, September 6, 1959.

25. Tuchman and Dunow, *The New Landscape/The New Still Life*, 666

26. Tuchman and Dunow, *The New Landscape/The New Still Life*, 63.

27. Tuchman and Dunow, *The New Landscape/The New Still Life*, 65.

28. Tuchman and Dunow, *The New Landscape/The New Still Life*, 67.

29. Willem de Kooning, cited in "The Genetics of Art: Interviews by Margaret Staats and Lucas Matthiessen," *Quest* 77, no. 1 (March-April 1977), 70, quoted in Tuchman and Dunow, *The New Landscape/The New Still Life*, 172.

30. From an unpublished conversation between Guston and composer Morton Feldman, 1968, provided to Dunow and Tuchman by Guston's dealer, David McKee, and poet Clark Coolidge, and quoted in Tuchman and Dunow, *The New Landscape/The New Still Life*.

31. Tuchman and Dunow, *The New Landscape/The New Still Life*, 80.

32. Peter Schjeldahl, "The Vulnerable Ferocity of Chaim Soutine," *New Yorker*, May 7, 2018.

INDEX

Images in the inset gallery are denoted by *ins* following the inset page number.

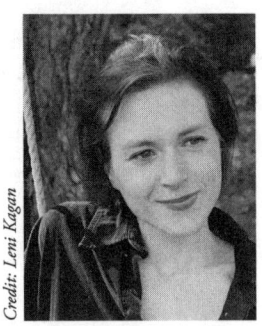

Credit: Leni Kagan

Celeste Marcus is the managing editor of *Liberties: A Journal of Culture and Politics*, which she helped to found. She lives in Washington, DC.